"Pulled by the dialectics of joy and pain, certainties and uncertainties, life and death, first kisses and hookups, this is a tale of forging authenticity in a world that would rather shut it down. Through all his questioning and adventuring, Flanery puts the ending at the beginning, reminding us that it is not about the destination, but about everything we question, discover, and come to believe in the middle. His questions about God, sex, people, and the truth are honest and his heart is bare. For those who feel alone challenging the norms of heterosexist life, this is a must-read."

—Isaac Archuleta, LPC
Founder, Chief Executive Officer of iAmClinic
previous Interim Director of Q Christian Fellowship

"It's a rare privilege to be in someone like Brandon's orbit. He's unashamedly himself in real life and that comes through in the memoir. The layers of thoughtful introspection and struggling with the divine is a fresh perspective on growing up gay in conservative Christian spaces. *Stumbling* will leave readers feeling seen and inspired to do their own self-reflection as they encounter Brandon's own journey regarding spirituality and identity after evangelicalism."

—Adam Evers
CEO and Co-Founder of believr and nuFoundation

"*Stumbling* feels like a love letter to every ex-missionary, to everyone who has to leave their fundamentalist spaces for one reason or another, to every queer person wondering what faithfulness looks like. Brandon's storytelling is raw, communicating emotions on the page like a painter on canvas. If you need a companion as you are leaving hard places, this book is for you."

—Kevin Miguel Garcia
mystic theologian, spiritual coach, author of
Bad Theology Kills and *What Makes You Bloom*

"Brandon Flanery's memoir is riveting, exhausting, and damning. It is the story of the repeated and predictable spiritual torture inflicted on queer young people by most evangelical churches, of the damages inflicted by superficial theology and corrupt church cultures, and of the way refugees from these communities lack a point of reference outside them to process their thoughts about God, world, and self. This book will be an important contribution to the literature now being produced by evangelical exiles."

—David P. Gushee
author of *Changing Our Mind*

"I haven't read a more honest, vulnerable, and therefore a more delightful and disturbing personal account of a queer believer's struggle with their own self, spirituality, family, friends, the church, and their God. I am certain *Stumbling* will help other LGBTQ+ Christians through their own stumbling, but I also hope it will help those who cause them to stumble to change their heart and minds to a posture of love and therefore affirmation."

—David Hayward, NakedPastor
artist and author

"Brandon Flanery's memoir is evocative of a modern-day *On the Road*, with vignettes full of frenetic energy that carry the reader on a journey both around the world and through the writer's heart. With prose and poetry that is simultaneously hilarious and gut wrenching, Flanery navigates his conflicted feelings toward faith and sexuality while trying to find his place in the world. It's a coming-of-age story that is both familiar and original, and one that will resonate with anyone who has discovered the divine as something so much greater than the stories we've been told."

—David and Constantino Khalaf
authors of *Modern Kinship: A Queer Guide to Christian Marriage*

"With wit and raw tenderness, Brandon Flanery's memoir is offered as an invitation into healing for so many other LGBTQ+ Christians who have walked the path of coming out. Flanery offers permission to doubt, rage, and perhaps even find hope in the midst."

—Rachael McClair
author and Co-Pastor of Highlands Church Denver

"Raw, riveting, and healing. Brandon Flanery's *Stumbling* is an intimate and inspiring look into the journey through the rigid and repressive world of evangelical faith toward authenticity and an expansive faith as a queer wanderer. His writing is captivating, his experiences enthralling, and the lessons he shares are truly universal. If you're on a journey through the deconstruction of your religious identity, this book will serve as a much needed companion along the way. Flanery is a wise guide and this book is a true gift."

—Brandan Robertson
author of *Dry Bones and Holy Wars*

"I'm so grateful for Brandon's raw honesty throughout this book. Reading about his spiritual journey has been both encouraging and challenging for me on a number of levels. Brandon's story is powerful and it serves as a helpful guide for those who are wrestling, doubting and growing."

—Dave Runyon
co-author of *The Art of Neighboring*
Executive Director of CityUnite

"Read *Stumbling* as a part of the long-pent-up-release of witness calling the evangelical church to repent of its homophobic cruelty, especially to its gay children. Better yet, read it as the confession of a soul unable to shake their experience of the divine, despite that cruelty, and see if it doesn't unveil your own craving—for love, for belonging, for God."

—Ken Wilson
author of *Letter to My Congregation*
Pastor Emeritus of Blue Ocean Faith Church, Ann Arbor

STUMBLING

STUMBLING

A Sassy Memoir about
Coming Out of Evangelicalism

BRANDON FLANERY

LAKE
DRIVE
lakedrivebooks.com

Lake Drive Books
6757 Cascade Road SE, 162
Grand Rapids, MI 49546

info@lakedrivebooks.com
lakedrivebooks.com
@lakedrivebooks

Publishing books that help you heal, grow, and discover.

Hardcover ISBN: 978-1-957687-27-8
Paperback ISBN: 978-1-957687-12-4
eBook ISBN: 978-1-957687-15-5

Library of Congress Control Number: 2023937507

This book is memoir. It reflects the author's present recollections and information gathering of experiences over time. Some of the names of individuals or institutions and their characteristics have been changed, some events have been compressed, and some dialogue has been recreated.

Cover design by Jarrad Hogg
Photo by Dave Reed, Unsplash

For Jay,
You left the door ajar, giving me courage to come out.

Contents

Before Reading

I didn't write this book for everyday Christians, or maybe any kind of Christian, for that matter.

So if you're happily sitting in pews on Sundays and contently studying Max Lucado on Wednesdays, you'll likely hate this book. I talk about sex, I curse, and I ask questions that make me look like a heretic (and come up with some answers that definitely do). Not to mention I'm gay.

Instead, I wrote *Stumbling* for the ones whose prayers went unanswered. For those who doubt, for those who got tired of jumping through intellectual hoops to make the Bible make sense, complete with its endorsements of genocide, the subjugation of women, slavery, and the murder of queer people.

It's for the scared, for those who want to have some semblance of faith but are terrified to look anything like the people who sided with Trump, those that chose nationalism over kindness, chose all lives over Black.

It's for the angry, for those who left the church because the people in the pews look nothing like the man on the cross, and they can no longer stand the hypocrisy.

It's for the hurting, for the queer people who gave everything to the church they loved but were cast out the second they came out.

It's for the tired, for those who wake up with a hangover on Sunday because they didn't want to feel anything on Saturday because Monday through Friday were simply too much, or rather, not enough.

It's for the "faggots." It's for the "faithless." It's for the "backsliders" and "Jezebels."

It's for you.

It's for me.

I don't claim to have the answers. Anyone that does is selling you something.

Rather, my hope is to, as Henri Nouwen writes, "cry with those who cry, laugh with those who laugh, and to make [my] own painful and joyful experiences available as sources of clarification and understanding" because while all our stories are unique, "all people are one at the well-spring of pain and joy."[1]

That's why I wrote *Stumbling*—to leave some breadcrumbs for my fellow wanderers, to tie red string where briars and cliffs may lie, to carve markings on trees where one might find a quiet stream. But above all else, I wrote *Stumbling* to tell those anxiously afraid, desperately trying to keep themselves warm in the shadow of the night, alone by the fire of their soul, that there's a glade just on the other side if they but raise their eyes.

And maybe, by beholding my stumbling, you'll find your own path worth treading.

Some warning signs before your journey:

Pretty language not utilized: Yes, I say fuck. Because sometimes life fucks you up. And there's no better word to explain it than fuck. Fuck.

Sex abounds: I talk about sex. Gay sex. Because people have sex. Including gay people. Because sex is a part of life.

Identities unknown: I have changed some of the names that appear in this book. But if a name wasn't changed, I checked with the person, and they gave me their permission. However, in some instances, I kept the name because the meaning of the story would be lost. With that in mind, nothing was written to slander another human. My only goal is to simply share my story in hopes that it might help someone else, not ruin anyone else's life.

Memory is a flawed and creative thing: if something was remembered incorrectly, I apologize. Lying was not my intention.

Happy stumbling.

Part One

Finishing

In my beginning is my end.[1]
T. S. Eliot

How It Ends

My best friend dies. That's how the book ends.

But if you want to find out how or why that matters or why I'd tell you at the beginning of the book instead of the end, you'll have to turn the page...

And the next page...

And the next...

Till you get to the end...

The end you now know.

Part Two

Falling

Unmaking, decreating, is the only task man may take upon himself, if he aspires, as everything suggests, to distinguish himself from the Creator.[1]

E. M. Cioran

Journey of Faith

"Dresden."

That's what our sign reads as Josh and I stand on the curb of the autobahn, thumbs out, pretending like we know what we're doing.

We have *no* idea what we're doing.

I anxiously smile at every car, trying to convince them we're not psychopaths. I must be doing a horrible job because every one of them keeps driving by. But in spite of my pathetic attempts at not looking like a murderer, I'm excited.

We're doing it. We're finally doing it, I think to myself.

This trip had been in the making for quite some time. But rather than calling it a hitchhiking trip, like a normal person, I was branding it on my blog and social media as my "Journey of Faith" like a crazy person.

But that's what you do as a good Christian missionary—you brand things.

Rather than calling a church sleepover a church sleepover, it has to be called "Caged"; rather than a weekend retreat simply being a weekend retreat, it's "Rescued"; a building fundraiser: "The Nehemiah Project"; a mission trip: "The Commissioning."

Branding. It's all about branding.

So when I decided to travel Europe, I didn't say, "Hi! I'm hitchhiking Europe. Please give me money." I needed to brand it; I needed to make it look spiritual; I needed to give it that Christian spice, and all the better if there's some Old Testament namesake, a scripture reference, or a sprinkling of biblical Hebrew and ancient Greek.

(Evangelicalism didn't raise no chump.)

Over the past nine months, I had been working with an organization called YWAM—Youth With A Mission—and that mission was "saving souls."

Saving them from what, you may ask? Hell. We were saving them from hell. You know, simple stuff, light stuff, stuff that everyone can get on board with, especially the unsuspecting strangers we'd accost every Tuesday.

During that time, I had "proclaimed the good news" on the streets of Berlin, ran an after-school theater program for underprivileged kids, led a youth group, volunteered for a Mother Teresa Home for the Sick and Dying, created a musical, toured through Europe with said musical, and saw "many come to a saving knowledge of Jesus Christ." Hallelujah!

(And that's just the good stuff you include in your missionary newsletters to get money so you don't starve. "Look at all the cool, shiny things I'm doing on behalf of Jesus with the money you gave me!" Remember, it's all about branding, and donors want to know you're spending their money well. It's an "eternal investment," one might say, "a jewel in their crown." So you better be wise with that investment. You better be faithful with what's been given. "Dance, monkey, dance! Go save souls and tell me about it so I can feel good!")

My time with YWAM was horrible and beautiful and difficult and lovely, full of moments that I cherish to this day…

…Telling strangers how beautiful they are.

…Telling a manipulative preacher how terrible *he* was.

…Crying when miracles happened.

…Crying when they didn't.

…Proclaiming, "Jesus can save you from homosexuality," even though I nearly joined a group of men having sex in the woods just a day prior.

…Oh! And starting to doubt that everything I believed in was a lie.

(You know, the kind of stuff you *don't* put in your newsletter. The kind of stuff you hide and pray no one finds out. *Look at all the chaos and trauma you're purchasing for the low price of twenty dollars a month! Thank you for your donation!*)

But now that my time as a missionary had come to an end, I'm off to the next adventure: my Journey of Faith.

The idea came from a desire to travel Europe and not wanting to return home.

Problem: I had no money. I was *paying* to be a missionary. Thus, the carefully curated newsletter. I was literally broke. (Guess I should have branded better.)

But a thought came: *What if I did it anyway? What if I traveled without any money and dared to believe that God might take care of me? Like the stories in the Bible! Like Jesus's disciples!*

Terrified to hitchhike alone, I texted my friend Josh, justifying my fear with the fact that even Jesus sent out his broke disciples in pairs.

Josh is the type of guy who chooses to sleep in his trashed Subaru over a nice suburban house owned by his well-to-do parents, smelling of essential oils rather than cologne. If anyone was going to say "yes" to bumming around Europe, it would be him. And if he said "no," which most normal people would, I'd take it as some cosmic sign that I should just go home. But to my surprise, he didn't just say "yes," he was truly ecstatic.

"This is exactly what I need!" he said. "I went ahead and bought a ticket to Berlin for June 1. Does that work?"

And thus was born my "Journey of Faith."

This wasn't just about some kids traveling Europe, this was about God showing up; this was about seeing miracles; this was about moving past my fears; this was about faith! Glory to God in the highest!

(Or so I wrote in my newsletter.)

So here Josh and I stand, traveling as far as our empty pockets can take us, sticking out our thumbs and holding a cardboard sign like they do in the movies.

I take another deep breath as more and more cars pass by, my cheesy smile convincing no one.

I push down my anxiety, down the belief that no one would pick us up, down the fear that we'd starve to death on the side of the highway with no one to care or cry over our emaciated bodies buzzing with flies, burrowed by maggots.

This is gonna be good. Journey of Faith! God is going to come through for us!
...Right?

"It is illegal to hitchhike," the stranger with a thick German accent says after he picks us up. "You are lucky I saw you before the police did."

"Why did you stop, then?" I ask.

"Back in the '70s I also hitchhike. I figure I would give back for all the times strangers pick me up."

Huzzah! Journey of Faith, baby. God is coming through!

"But you can get arrested and fined, so I would not do this again. Try the trains. Much safer and not too expensive."

Any money is too expensive for two guys traveling Europe, trying to trust God with nothing but youthful zeal. We couldn't just buy a train ticket. That wouldn't be faith! It's okay. He doesn't get it. God is going to take care of us. He'll see. Maybe I should send him my carefully crafted newsletter. He'd be so blessed!

We're a few weeks into our travels, and it's been breathtaking.

Hikes in real-life Narnia. Homemade wine with cheese boards. Singing "Country Roads" by cozy fires. Castles upon castles. Intimate rooftop conversations with shit beer and kind strangers as the city around us danced and sang in revelry.

Now, we're in Nuremberg, staying at a friend-of-a-friend-of-a-friend's-cousin's house.

After a long day of exploring the city and eating great food and having picnics in castle gardens, we collapse on the bed, drunk on more than wine.

Journey of Faith!

I look over at Josh in the dark, smiling.

I've come to love these nights right before bed. Josh and I stay up late, talking about everything and nothing, feeling close and safe with each other. Eventually, at some point in the conversation, we'd pass out from exhaustion. The good kind. The kind that comes when your day is full.

"This may sound weird," Josh says from the shadows, "but I feel like I should pray for your eyes."

There are different flavors of Christianity: there's the flavor with potlucks after church where everyone gossips—I mean prays—about who is backsliding; there's the flavor that has a soup kitchen, preschool, and counseling department; and there's the flavor that marches outside vet funerals with signs that read, "Thank God for dead soldiers" and "God hates faggots."

The flavor of Christianity that *I* was raised in was somewhere after speaking in tongues (gibberish) and before flaggers (people who whip around a flag during the music part of church).

So the idea of praying for weird miracles, like the healing of my eyes, even though I had glasses, was not *that* out of the ordinary. Besides, I'm legally blind without my glasses—I can't even tell if someone is holding *up* fingers, let alone how many. If God wanted to heal me, my life would be a whole lot easier.

"Okay. Let's try." I scoot over to Josh, so he can touch me (an important Christian ingredient for miracle-making).

I close my eyes.

He prays.

I open them.

Nothing.

I'm still blind.

"Sorry, Brandon. I truly thought I felt something."

"No worries, Josh. At least I have glasses. Thanks for trying. Night!"

"Night."

"So you are taking holiday in Germany, yeah? How do you like our beer?" asks the German Chad (or whatever the German equivalent to Chad is) who picked Josh and me up.

The question is valid. We'd noticed the same thing. Every time we bump into other Americans during our travels, they've come for one thing: to get *impressively* drunk on the famed German beer.

"It's alright I guess," too-honest Josh replies.

The car becomes deathly silent.

Want to quickly offend a German? Talk shit about their beer. Well, that or talk too loudly in the U-Bahn.

The tension is palpable.

We're going to get kicked out. We're going to get kicked out. We're gonna get kicked out because Josh is too honest!

Normally, whenever conflict arises, I run. But I can't run while a car is doing ninety miles an hour down the autobahn. I'm trapped. So I do the next best thing—I stick my head out the window like a golden retriever and let the wind drown out the impending argument.

Look at that lovely tree! Look at that tall tower! Look at anything *and* everything *as long as it keeps you distracted from this awkward tension. Look at that church! Look at that castle! Look at that—*

My glasses fly off my face.

I jolt my head back and anxiously stare forward, pretending nothing happened.

"Did you just lose your glasses?" the assumedly annoyed, German-beer-loving, Chad-equivalent driver says.

I just nod my head. Words refusing to come out. I'm far too embarrassed.

He starts laughing.

But not me.

I'm not laughing.

I'm the opposite of laughing.

I'm freaking out.

How the hell am I going to hitchhike through Europe if I can't see? Is this gonna be my Journey of Faith? Wandering cobblestone streets blind? *Listen, God, it's hard enough trusting that you'll provide when we don't have any money, but now I have to trust you to travel while blind? I get it, that takes faith, but if you weren't listening earlier, that was more about branding and not actually about needing to trust you. Didn't you read the newsletter?*

But Josh's prayer from the night before comes to mind.

Please, dear God, come through on that prayer.

"Here," the driver says as he hands me a pair of glasses. "Someone left these in my car the other day. I doubt they will work, but you can try."

I put them on.

"Are you kidding me? I can see! That's crazy! My prescription is super strong! But these are pretty dang close! Thanks, man! I really appreciate it."

"No worries! It is not like I will be using them."

The near-disaster changed the mood of the car—we all returned to casual conversation, avoiding heavy topics (like beer), and I thought to myself: *Maybe Josh's prayer worked! Maybe God does answer prayers. I can see! Well … sort of … I can sorta see. God is* actually *coming through for us! This is amazing! Journey of Faith!*

A headache starts, and I rub my head.

But a headache would quickly become the least of my worries…

〜

…"Brandon, I need to tell you what's going on before you hear about it on social media." It's my mom. Her voice is shaking. "Nathan had a seizure while driving. He crashed into a flatbed truck. It's pretty bad, but he's gonna be okay. We're praying, so he's gonna be fine. After all, don't we serve the God of miracles? You really don't need to worry. Don't stress about trying to get back. Enjoy Europe."

But I wouldn't enjoy Europe. I would stress. Stress about what was going to happen to my brother.

〜

…"Did you hear the news?" my friend Taylor writes me.

"What news?"

"One of our YWAM leaders had an affair with one of the student leaders!"

"WHAT?!?"

"Yup. Glad I got outta there when I did. The whole place is a fucking shit show right now. No one knows what to do. I'll be surprised if the ministry lasts a year."

But it did last a year … and the leader left his wife … even though he had three kids … to be with this girl who was his secretary … while leading a missions organization … while telling us every Wednesday to stand up on our chairs and roar in the spirit to see God move in our lives, roar like the mighty Lion of Judah!

(Guess he didn't roar loud enough.)

⤳

…"Hey Brandon." It's another leader from YWAM. Not the one who had the affair. A different leader who now had to clean up his mess. "I just wanted to reach out and send a friendly reminder that you still owe YWAM €354.12. Please send it as soon as you can. You're past due."

Twelve dollars. That's how much is in my bank account.

"P.S. Please stay connected with YWAM Berlin! We'd love it if you would consider giving a charitable donation for our next school with all God is doing. Hope this finds you well!"

I am not being found well. I am being found the *opposite* of well. I am being found *un*well. My brother is in the ER, and the man who has been taking all my money and bossing me around for the past year has been having an affair with one of the girls he was responsible for. On top of that, now I'm broke. Very broke.

Journey. Of. Faith.

⤳

"I'm tired of the fakers," I say to Josh as I stare at some stone wall in Geneva that I'm apparently very fascinated by.

(The masonry must be riveting.)

"I'm not a faker, Brandon."

I break my gaze from the wall and glare at Josh.

"I never said you were, Josh! This isn't about you!"

And in one moment, while yelling at my friend, the friend that flew from the States to hitchhike with me through Europe, I realize that this isn't just about having a brother with a broken body or a bank account with a balance of twelve dollars or a leader who betrayed all of us while we served him faithfully. In truth, this had been building for a while, and it's about so much more...

...It's about my childhood pastor preaching against homosexuality, then having an affair with a man.

...It's my Bible school founder expelling students for hiding secrets, then lying about millions of dollars of debt.

...It's my old pastor, who also happened to be my boss, firing my mom, then telling the congregation that she was "called to better things."

...It's that missionary back in India who tried to knock me over while praying for me, to make it look like God was "slaying me in the spirit," a.k.a. falling backward when a preacher touched you because of the power of God. (Side note: Why do we use a word that represents someone getting aggressively murdered for some manifestation of God?)

...It's about all the Christian leaders who have manipulated me and lied to me over the years so they could advance their own fame and glory at my expense.

...And now, it's about this YWAM leader, telling me to have more faith, telling me to give more money, to surrender more to God, to be holy as God is holy, to think about others before myself, all while having an affair (and using drugs), not giving a damn about anyone *but* himself.

It's too much, and all the pain of the past came rushing in with the crack of his betrayal.

But I don't tell Josh that.

I don't tell Josh anything.

I let it billow and rage inside, torrent upon torrent.

And on the outside, I turn my eyes back to the very old wall, in a very old city, for a very long time, writhing in silent pain because all of this was too much, and I didn't have the words.

"Wanna get drunk?" Josh asks.

I turn my head to see he has an open bottle of Jägermeister because, as mentioned earlier, he hates German beer. Apparently medicinal-grade incense wine is better libation.

Poor Josh, I think. *He came out here to have an adventure, to explore the world, to live like there's no tomorrow like any other normal twenty-something, and here I am having an existential crisis like a forty-year-old.*

So much for pillow talk after getting drunk on life. Now we're just getting day drunk to cope with life.

"Yes. Yes, I fucking do!" I grab the bottle from his hand and pound it back.

The liquid rushes into my throat, tasting of acrid mint and licorice. It burns.

Why do people like this?

I wince in pain and, a glare that says, *how could you betray me like everyone else?*

He only shrugs his shoulders, a shrug that says, "Hey, it gets you drunk."

Then I pound back more.

The day has worn on, and Josh and I stumble through Geneva, fuming about how much of a shit show life is, fuming about how terrible Christians are, fuming about how stupid all these stupid hills are that we have to climb with stupid forty-pound backpacks while the sun begins to set and we don't have a place to stay.

Geneva was the *one* place I didn't plan our housing ahead of time. All throughout our travels, I would message everyone I knew, looking for a place to stay. But Geneva was the one spot Josh and I wanted to go to but knew no one. Now, it's become some personal test of faith.

Will God come through when I didn't take care of us? Or will he fuck us over like everyone else had?

"Let's go to that church!" I slur through a drunken sneer. "Christians are supposed to let in the stranger and take in the foreigner, right? It's in the Bible. If they actually *love* God, they should let us stay there, right? After all, it's in their precious book!"

Josh scurries after me, really unsure and intimidated by my uncommon rage.

I march up to the door, emboldened by booze and cynicism.

I pound on the door.

Ohhhhh! This is why people drink Jäger!

A middle-aged woman answers.

"Oh, hi you two! Can I help you with something?" She speaks perfect English upon seeing us because, apparently, we don't look Swiss (might be the forty-pound backpacks).

That said, it's not uncommon for a Swiss to speak English. In fact, it's not uncommon for any European to speak English because many Europeans speak many languages, especially English. Come to find out, it's really just Americans that speak only one language. As the phrase goes, "If you speak three languages, you're trilingual. If you speak two languages, you're bilingual. If you speak one language, you're American."

"Yes, you can!" I slur while holding my nearly empty bottle of Jäger. "My friend and I do not have a place to stay, and we were wondering if we could sleep on the floor of your church."

"Oh ... oh, I see..." She gets a bit nervous. "Well, I don't have permission to do that."

"Figures." I turn to go, but she calls after me.

"But I'll call our pastor and see what we can do." She takes out her phone and looks at us as she speaks in French to the pastor.

I glare at her, mad that she didn't turn us away immediately like I thought that she would.

How dare she not disappoint me like all other Christians?

Her voice is a bit frantic. Although I can't understand, I can sense that she actually *wants* to help, and it makes me feel a bit guilty for my tirade.

But after a few moments, her eyes dart, refusing to meet mine, and the anticipated betrayal left me satisfied.

She turns back to Josh and me after forcing a smile. "I'm afraid we can't do that. If we were to help you, we'd have to help everyone. I'm so sorry boys! Do you want me to take you somewhere?"

"Nope! We're fine! Thanks for nothing!"

"Are you su-"

I turn and stomp away.

"See! I told you, Josh! All Christians are fucking fakers! They don't even believe in what they preach. Just a bunch of hypocritical assholes!"

Josh and I drunkenly wander the streets of Geneva as I continue my fuming rampage, now fueled by further evidence that all Christians suck, that all of them are hypocrites, that all of them just want your money and obedience while never actually helping you when it matters.

I'm such a schmuck for ever believing any of this crap.

And yet...

Disguised by anger, there's a deep sadness. Sadness, because, underneath it all, I truly want to trust ... I truly want to believe ... But I am tired of getting let down ... I'm tired of getting my hopes up ... so tired ... tired of getting hurt ... tired of being betrayed ... by God ... by man...

Journey of Faith...

As the saying goes, "Life's a bitch, and then you die."

Death and hardship, pain and broken promises, stupid nine-to-five jobs that only give you two weeks of vacation, so you can escape that annoying guy named Carl who still hasn't figured out how to *not* use the "Reply All" button, only for you to return to the life you're trying to survive.

It sucks. It all sucks.

As my mind wallows in nihilism, Josh and I find ourselves on the edge of Lake Lemon, where hundreds of college students laugh to spite my pain, guzzling life, oblivious to its bitter aftertaste, while I sneer at the golden sun disappearing behind the Alps, its glow dancing on the water.

We need to find a place to stay. God didn't come through. So we stumble toward a willow tree, thinking those drooping branches might offer some semblance of privacy.

When we pull back the leaves, we happen upon a convenient rug laid out as if it knew we were coming.

I look around, trying to see if there's someone close it might belong to.

No one.

(But what exactly should I be looking for? A guy with a large Ikea bag who brings his carpet to the lakeshore on hot summer evenings?)

Huh ... odd...

Josh and I stretch out our sleeping bags on the misplaced rug and crawl in.

No cute pillow talk tonight. No cute prayers for miracles. We're too exhausted. And not the good kind of exhaustion. The bad kind. The kind that comes from carrying *more* than forty-pound backpacks all over Geneva.

"Josh," I say weakly.

"Yeah?" His voice is tired and annoyed.

"Can I put my arm around you?"

"Yeah." His voice softens when he hears the desperation in my voice.

I pull myself close.

Normally, I'm insanely anxious when holding a man like this. I never want to look too gay, so I overcompensate and show no male affection. It's safer that way.

But tonight, I don't care. Tonight, I am too tired and too scared and too hurt. Tonight, I can't add loneliness to the list of heavy things I'm carrying. That's just too much. Far too much. And wondering where God is in this mess makes me feel a deep loneliness I had never experienced before.

Journey ... of ... Faith...

My eyes close, and I push out the thoughts and questions and accusations. They'll be there in the morning, greeting me with the day, that spiteful day.

I begin to drift as the Jäger carries me off, when…

Wake up!

The voice is in my head, and it comes with a tightening in my gut.

I gasp awake and sit up.

There, at the edge of the tree, is a shadow staring at me. It's frozen in motion, knowing it's been caught.

"Hey!"

The shadow runs away, becoming a person as it emerges from the curtain-like branches, streetlight illuminating his silhouette.

I lie back down, adding "fear for safety" to the list of things overwhelming me.

I'm never gonna get any sleep.

The voice in my head comes back.

If I could wake you once, could I not wake you again?

God? Jäger? Exhaustion?

Journey of Faith?

Is this God protecting me from a stranger? If it is, why didn't he get us a place to stay? Or convince that pastor to let us stay in the church? Or get me glasses that have the correct prescription? Or heal my eyes? Or heal my brother's leg? Does he deal in half-miracles? Does he only deliver kinda-sorta-but-not-really miracles?

If this is a Journey of Faith, it's fucking rocky.

I fall back asleep, comforted and yet annoyed by the voice in my head, when a few minutes later, I hear the voice again.

Wake up!

I immediately sit up and look behind me.

The shadow is back.

"Get lost!"

It runs away again, and I lay back down for the third time.

I slowly drift, till the thought hits me: "Fuck. We're totally sleeping on this guy's carpet."

English Ales at the Fête

"I don't understand how you can still believe that shit, Brandon." Rachel, an old friend from Bible school who has since deconverted from Christianity, stands across from me.

We're outside an English pub on the streets of Lyon, while Josh and Rachel's boyfriend drink inside.

The irony of being at an English pub while in France is only magnified by the fact that Bastille Day (or the *Fête Nationale* as the French call their independence day) is tomorrow. Apparently, Rachel's boyfriend thought the most French thing we could do to celebrate was drink English beer, which, for some weird reason, actually feels quite French.

While the pub may not be the best setting for a French revolution, it's perfect for how I'm feeling—out of place, confused, introspective.

I once heard a Northern Ireland theologian say, "Your sports bars are crammed with loud noises, bright televisions, and drunk bodies. British pubs are dark and quiet. You Americans go to bars to forget life; we go to pubs to talk about it."[1]

And Rachel wouldn't let me forget.

"The whole thing is just one big scam to control people and take their money," she continues. "I mean, look at this past year, Brandon. You just paid thousands of dollars to work your ass off for some guy's ego, all while he was sleeping with one of his staff. Does he have kids?"

"They just had their third."

"Fuck that guy! Are you fucking kidding me? Seriously, fuck him! He's just like so many other Christian leaders: they act so high and mighty when all the while they're frauds. The story of Christian leaders having moral failings has become all too commonplace."

My mind wanders to Geneva and Jäger.

"I just think it's all shit, Brandon. Remember at the Honor Academy where everyone was trying to fix me?"

Rachel and I had met at a crazy-cult-Bible-school thing started by Ron Luce called the Honor Academy. We paid ten grand to work forty hour weeks, take classes on how to defend our faith against liberal scientists, and scream, "Sir, yes sir," while rolling through mud and vomit. Think "I'm in the LORD's army," but not cute. (Then again, having kids march in place while singing about shooting down their enemies for Jesus isn't really cute either.)

The whole thing was quite intense, but that's why I picked it—it seemed like something I would hate and that means it was something that God probably wanted me to do. After all, isn't "the heart deceitful above all things?"[2] Or so I was told from the pulpit thousands of times.

It was this mentality of self-denial (likely informed by denying my sexuality) that dictated most of the major decisions in my life.

So when I heard that there was a ministry in East Texas that would take my money and make me feel miserable, all in the name of Jesus and to make me a better Christian, I signed up with a zealous smile.

And not only did my shame-informed masochism love every second of it, but I was also planning on staying another year. I had found purpose that was bigger than me and a community that was richer than anything I had experienced in the world, in spite of all the pain we were forced to endure. (I guess that's trauma bonding for you.)

Rachel continues. "Everyone would be 'experiencing God' during worship while I would be crying in the corner, wondering what was wrong with me. 'Why wasn't God talking to *me* and why was he talking to everyone *else*?' It was horrible, and everyone had an opinion as to how to fix me. 'Try harder!' 'Try less.' 'He comes when you least expect it.' 'How about fasting?' 'How about staying up all night praying?'

"I thought I was crazy or didn't have enough faith or that God hated me, till I found out there's a specific part of the brain that is associated with praying and hearing 'God's voice.' It's also the same part of the brain that allows people to be susceptible to groupthink and schizophrenia. Some people just don't have that part of their brain developed as much as others, and I'm one of those people.

"What people *think* is God really is just synapses and chemicals firing off in the brain. Religion is just a bunch of people manipulating those chemicals to get other people to surrender their money, power, and will."

She takes a swig of beer as if to say, like Jesus, "It is finished. Brandon doesn't know what he's doing." And she's right—I don't know what I'm doing. I'm scared and afraid and lost and overwhelmed.

Chemicals? Control? How have I never heard this before? Does this mean I've been believing a lie, so people could just take advantage of me? If everything Rachel is saying is true, then everything I've been investing my entire life in has been a waste. What am I supposed to do now? Where am I supposed to go?

Rachel feels my panic and reaches over to touch my arm.

"Brandon, I'm sorry if I'm being intense. I'm not normally like this with people. Normally, I ask more questions and keep my opinions to myself. But seeing you stay in Christianity as a gay man feels a lot like watching someone stay in an abusive relationship. I just want you to be free and not hurt anymore. This isn't fair to you, and I hate it."

She looks into my eyes with this deep compassion, a compassion I've rarely witnessed from Christians after they find out I'm gay. Typically, they pull away. But here's a friend fighting for me, wanting me to not hurt anymore.

Maybe she's right. Maybe this has all been my imagination. It would explain so much…

∽

When I was in Berlin, I'd go on these walks.

There was this one time, while reading my Bible, that I felt like I heard, *Put down the Bible.*

Like any good "God-fearing" Christian, I immediately thought it was the devil, trying to "lead me astray." But I couldn't shake the feeling. So I got quiet with myself and listened to the voice.

The Bible is simply a tool. It can be used for evil, justifying things like the Crusades and the Inquisitions. Or it can be used for good, inspiring people to stand for justice, like Martin Luther King Jr. Most importantly, it can be used to see me. It's like a window. But it's not me. Brandon, it's time to see me, to engage with me. Not just a book.

Terrified, I put my Bible down and started walking, talking to this voice in my head like someone with schizophrenia, and as I talked to the voice in my head about my frustrations, dreams, and desires, I'd feel peace and get clarity about my life.

I'd know what to say to the leader I was mad at. I'd realize I was being petty with the friend I was annoyed with. I'd think about going back to college, becoming a journalist, and writing things that mattered.

Then, sometimes, after I stilled myself, I'd let my hand dangle by my side and clench it, pretending I was holding the hand of God. We'd meander like lovers through those cobblestone streets, walking in rhythm with each other. Then, carrying that peace, I'd hear that head/heart/God whisper: *Turn right. Now left. Straight* (or as the gays say, *forward*).

Together, we'd happen upon these gorgeous, hidden cafés. One was even built into the wall of a drained-canal-turned-rose-garden with a fountain splashing joyfully within.

I was wowed and wooed, enjoying the divine outside of the Bible like some delusional heretic.

Maybe it was God who told me to put down my Bible after all. Maybe it wasn't the devil.

But then, one day I went out and got terribly lost.

I started my routine of calming myself, asking God where to go, and I ended up in the middle of nowhere. A massive thoroughfare ran next to me where cars screeched by. There was no café in sight, let alone a cute one, and to top it off, my phone was dying, and I had to use the bathroom.

I kept holding out, hoping that maybe there would be a café just around the next corner, a cute spot to journal and read, but my colon was screaming— if I went another block, I was gonna shit myself.

I dipped into the next open business: a dive bar. It's ten o'clock in the morning, but my body can't wait, so I set down my stuff and scuttle past two angry, middle-aged German men glaring at me, as if to say, "You better be buying something."

Once in the bathroom, I threw myself on the toilet, releasing a holy explosion, emerging as a new human, screaming, "Hallelujah!"

It was going to be okay. I am going to be okay. I didn't shit myself. I'm not crazy lost. I'll just hang out here in this … dive bar … charge my phone, get directions, and head back home. We're gonna be okay. I'm going to be okay. I'm not lost. This is good. We're good.

Problem: there wasn't an outlet. Plus, there really wasn't anything to order at a dive bar at ten in the morning, especially for a good little missionary boy.

So I grabbed my things and left, the two German men yelling after me.

I felt defeated. And as I walked home, a small voice whispered, *Maybe all of this* is *made up. Maybe I'm just super imaginative.* (I mean, it would make sense. I was that dork of a kid on the soccer field who never played the game. Instead, I'd stare into oblivion, chasing after butterflies. I was far more entertained with a colorful, imaginative world playing out in my head than a boring game with a black and white ball.)

∾

"Do you know where the Fête Nationale comes from?" Rachel's boyfriend emerges from the dark pub, calling me back from dark nostalgia.

"No idea."

He angrily mutters something in French that I assume roughly translates to "Stupid Americans! Don't know anything about the world!"

"The fête is about the storming of the Bastille. You see, with French history, we have a lot of revolutions. We would get angry at whoever was in charge and then kill them. Then, we would start something new, get angry again, and kill the new people in charge. Lots of blood. Lots of wars. But *vive la révolution*, eh?

"Anyway, we needed to pick a national holiday to celebrate our independence, so we picked the day Parisians stormed the Bastille, which is not even *that* dramatic of a moment: the Bastille surrendered after only one casualty. There were many events leading up to the Bastille, and there were many events after that were just as significant, if not more, like when we chopped off the king's head. But we picked July 14th, the day the Bastille was stormed, and in doing so, something so small became so significant."

When I reflect over all the moments that led to the downfall of my faith, there were plenty of them that *should* have been when it all came crashing down: failed leaders, broken ministries, emotional manipulation. But for me, my fête was that day I nearly shat myself in a Berlin dive bar—so small, but significant.

Satisfied and bored, Rachel's boyfriend goes back inside since I had nothing else to add to his talks of history and revolutions. (Stupid Americans don't know anything about the world.)

I swirl my beer like the confusion in my head, trying to make sense of it all when a thought comes. "What about miracles?"

"Isn't it interesting that those stories are always one or two people away?" Rachel coyly smiles at me, taking another sip. "Growing up, we'd always have those missionaries or traveling preachers come into town, talking about how God did such-and-such miracle in Mexico or such-and-such miracle at that revival years ago. It always happens somewhere else, with someone else, at some different point in time. I've never seen a miracle. I've only heard of them. It's like they're always *just* conveniently out of reach. Think about it: have you ever seen a miracle or had a close friend or family member experience a miracle?"

"Well, yeah! While working with YWAM, I saw miracles. One time, I prayed for these girls, and their back pain went away."

"Placebo. The mind is crazy powerful, Brandon. Doesn't count. There are so many studies that prove that if we believe our pain is gone, it'll go away."

"Well, one time I was talking to this stranger on the street. He was super angry at the church and was shouting at me. Then I felt like I heard God tell me to tell this man that his dog was a guardian angel. He immediately started crying. He felt so loved by God because I said something that I thought was crazy."

"Intuition. Our bodies can hear each other. There's an interconnection to the universe. We all have frequencies and energies. You could have seen one micro emotion or one glance he made at his dog and formed a story in your head that would help him. That's it. It wasn't God."

Rachel has an answer for everything. She's been thinking about this for a long time and has worked it all out. Now, she's coming after me like some evangelist in a "heathen" nation, except she's the "heathen," an atheist evangelist.

The night is thick with ironies.

"I know it's a lot, but the more I've researched, the more it just doesn't make sense. But I get it; lots of people *need* to believe. It makes them feel safe. It adds meaning to life and makes death bearable. If my pain has a reason, then I don't need to panic. If there's some happy heavenly bliss beyond, I don't have to fear death. But I don't *need* some lie to make me feel safe anymore. Life is what I make it, and oblivion isn't as bad as everyone thinks because we won't be there to feel it."

Maybe that's why I am so resistant to everything she's saying—I'm too scared; I need to believe in something; I need life to have meaning and to believe there's some-thing beyond; otherwise, I'm too scared, and what I believe helps me cope.

She throws me a bone. "I do agree with you about miracles. If they *were* real, it would be the only thing that wouldn't make sense and prove Christians right. But think about it, have you *ever actually seen* a miracle?"

But here's the problem: I had.

∽

"Dear God, come into my heart and make me powerful."

Me. Age five. Sounding like some creeper out of a horror film.

After getting spanked with a belt for what felt like the hundredth time (young minds have a way of exaggerating; it was likely the twentieth), I ran outside and laid down on the cool lawn, staring up at the few stars I could see with California's light pollution.

I was angry and yet in awe—angry because my ass hurt; in awe, because my little brain couldn't comprehend the cosmos.

(Shit, my adult brain still can't comprehend the cosmos.)

My mind was racing, contemplating the stars, the power of them, the distance of them.

In my heart, it felt like they were put there for a reason—like they were hung for me and the world, just to make us feel small, to make us gape, to make us wonder, not only of their majesty but also of the power of the one who may have made them.

And in that moment, I wanted to feel powerful.

I couldn't run from being spanked. I tried once. I made it to the street corner with my Toy Story suitcase, got scared, came right back, and sulked.

And I couldn't fight being spanked. My dad's too big and strong. (He still brags about how many more pushups he can do than me.)

So I allied myself with someone who might be able to protect me, someone who could do more pushups than my dad, someone who could hang the stars.

No one led me through a prayer, like one of those tent revivals. No one specified what specific words to say, as if it were some magic incantation: repeat after me to cleanse your soul. It was just me and God with a pretty improper prayer, from a pretty selfish kid, who really just cared about his ass hurting.

"Dear God, come into my heart and make me powerful."

It felt like a barter, like, as Donald Miller puts it, "a magical proposition."[3] Look here God, I'll let you reside in my body, but you have to give me limitless power. Deal? Deal. (I was most definitely a five-year-old in the '90s who loved the Power Rangers, thinking God was some bald, white guy trapped in a tube. Give me magic robots!)

Barter complete, I prayed for a little brother to "annoy my parents." It was the first thing that came to mind to get even with them for spanking me. Little annoying miracle baby would distract them and take all their energy, so I could go on living my life in peace.

(In retrospect, I could have maybe just prayed for my ass to not hurt so much or my dad to be more patient with me, but I was five years old and apparently pretty petty and spiteful.)

With confidence, I marched inside and told my mom she was going to have a baby, and it was going to be a boy.

At this point, I had no concept of where babies came from or sex or that there's some level of choice in the matter. (In fact, I wouldn't learn girls had pleasure during sex till I was nineteen years old at Bible school of all places. Ten points to parents for sex ed.)

But with or without my mom's permission, she was going to have a kid. Why? Because I prayed, and God was now living in my heart, and now *I* was powerful, and people said that if you asked God for things, he *had* to give them to you.

That's how it worked. It's in the Bible. Look it up.

Little did I know that my parents weren't "planning on having any more kids" anytime soon. (That's code for they were using condoms.)

But nine months later, here comes miracle-baby-brother Jay, which is fitting since he got through the wall of that condom; that 99 percent effective will get ya.

How could this have happened? Maybe the Bible was true? Maybe God meant what he said? Wonder of wonders!

Shortly after that, my mom asked me to pray for her friend to have a kid.

"She can't have babies, Brandon. They've been trying for a long time, and nothing has happened. But if *you* prayed for her like you prayed for me, maybe she'll have one."

Nine months later, she had a baby, and then another. Miracle of miracles!

Later, one of my teachers couldn't have kids. My mom asked me to pray for her. She also had a beautiful baby, providing for her like he provided manna in the wilderness.

I was on a roll.

Like some aphrodisiac, I was being passed around from infertile woman to infertile woman, and they all got pregnant. *L'chaim!*

But my barter went beyond babies.

A few years later, after the fertility escapade, my mom became a preschool teacher, and one of her kids was diagnosed with leukemia.

Like any good Christian family, we went to the hospital, offered encouraging verses and prayer.

The little girl was not allowed to see guests, due to her immunocompromised condition, but that didn't stop us from praying with the dad in the waiting area.

Prayers sent up to heaven, we were about to leave when I stopped my parents and asked if I could say something.

I opened up a Bible I found in the waiting room and quoted a verse like some minister.

(In my creative memory, I imagine clearing my throat and raising my chin to add to the effect.)

"Trust in the LORD with all thine heart; and lean not unto thine own understanding. In all thy ways acknowledge him, and he shall direct thy paths. Be not wise in thine own eyes: fear the LORD, and depart from evil. It shall be health to thy navel, and marrow to thy bones."[4]

I then prayed and thought nothing of it.

I was ten.

I had no idea leukemia was a bone thing, let alone a marrow thing. Truthfully, I likely didn't even know what marrow was. In fact, no one had told me what was going on with her. All I knew was that this little girl was sick, and we needed to pray because that's just what you do if you believe in Jesus. And since I had seen my parents and pastors read verses before praying, I thought it was a good idea, like it's what you're supposed to do whenever you pray for someone who's sick. So I picked up my Bible, turned to the first verse I saw and spoke it out like some oracle.

The next day the girl's parents asked the doctor if they could run more tests, just in case, before starting treatment. The doctors were annoyed, but they complied. When the tests came back, she was cancer free. To this day, she is healthy, living a happy life.

From a very early age, I've experienced some crazy things in the name of God.

One time, I thought I saw a vision of people jumping into water during a prayer meeting. So some friends and I jumped into the pool. Why not? We saw it in my imagination; seemed like a good enough reason.

When I came out of the water, it felt like electricity was coursing through my body. It was intoxicating, pure ecstasy. I was so overwhelmed that I started uncontrollably muttering and speaking a language I didn't know, "tongues" for the church folks.

At a church service, I somehow knew someone's heart was hurting. I scanned the room, trying to find the person. I approached this guy and asked if it was him. He said he'd been having heart murmurs for years. I prayed, and then walked away like it was nothing.

But it was more than just miracles, as if God were some genie; God was also my friend.

As a child, when I would get spanked (and my mom was already pregnant, so I couldn't pray for another baby brother to annoy them), I would turn myself into the corner, where my bed met the wall, and I would pray to God, and I would feel like he would hear, and I would feel seen and safe.

It felt nice, and I didn't feel so alone, and for some reason, I *always* felt alone, regardless of who was in the room. Maybe it's because deep down, I felt different, and instinctively I knew, even at an early age, that my family wouldn't be okay with that difference.

What I did know was that this God person was a friend, and I wanted everyone to know my friend.

As a third grader, when kids were talking about Santa, I squashed their hopes and dreams of a fat, friendly, red guy when I announced to everyone that "Christmas isn't about Santa; it's about baby Jesus. Santa isn't even real." I then went on to pray with kids who would like to meet Jesus in my classroom, leading an altar call like I was a traveling preacher.

(I would later find out that Christmas was originally a pagan holiday, and that Christians stole it. So any time someone says, "Jesus is the reason for the season," I burn with indignation and lash out in response to the Facebook post from my unsuspecting grandparents. It's weird how I haven't heard from them in a while.)

God was this friend when I had none, family when I felt like mine would never understand me, and lover when I felt like no one would pick me.

It was intimate and powerful and euphoric.

But here I am, sipping on a beer, wondering if it was all made up, if I simply had a vivid imagination, if I suffer from schizophrenia, if those third graders needed counseling after I told them Santa wasn't real.

Maybe it's all just placebo. Maybe it's just the power of belief. Maybe it's the connection of the universe or whatever my astrology friends would say. But how could I not believe after experiencing so much?

Sure, I had experienced some lovely things, but life and faith are more complicated than some precious moments and childhood prayers. Far more complicated…

…Christian schools kicking out kids for being gay.

…Rich missionaries who make six figures, flaunting pictures of orphans to make more money.

…Preachers standing on pulpits, telling congregants to repent of their wicked ways, all the while having affairs.

…The Bible talking of love and acceptance, while the church is the most bigoted, hateful, proud entity on the planet.

I can hear my Christian friends interrupt my depressive soliloquy, "But all those stories are about people. Not God. Don't hold God accountable for broken humans. They're not him."

Sure. Let's not hold God accountable for people who tote him around and carry his name and the weapon of his death around their necks. Sure. For argument's sake, let's separate them. Let's just hold *him* accountable for *his* actions, or lack thereof…

…A parent begs God to spare their child, but the child dies just the same.

…A girl at Bible school tries everything to make God speak to her, to give her a sign, but he ignores her, and she loses her faith after desperately trying.

…A boy prays for God to make him straight every single night, cries every single night, because the Bible says he'll go to hell if he likes boys, and he doesn't want to go to hell because he likes boys; but he still likes boys, can't stop liking boys, no matter how hard he prays, no matter how hard he cries, no matter how hard he wants to just be straight, he still likes boys, those stupid cute boys.

And let's not forget genocide and child soldiers and pandemics and famines and diseases and all the other, everyday, run-of-the-mill atrocities that plague our world: slavery, war, murder, rape, global warming, people who take off their shoes in planes and then put their feet on your armrest and then get upset with you for asking them to stop as if *you're* the one committing a heinous crime.

It's all too murky.

It doesn't make sense.

There's too much brokenness in the world for there to be an all-powerful God orchestrating everything.

If he's real, why are his people so fake?

If he's real, why is the world such a mess?

If he's real, why does my friend Rachel make sense?

If he's real, why did he hear a selfish little boy when he wanted a brother to annoy his parents but ignored him when he begged to be straight?

⌒

"You ready to head back?" Rachel says as I stare off into the distance, a raucous crowd of French folks stumbling over the cobblestone nearby.

I'm apparently too drunk because when Rachel asks, "You ready to head back?" I imagine "back" being far more existential, like, "Are you ready to head back to Christianity? To return to it all? To give it another chance?"

But to say the word "back" insinuates that you've moved away, that there's now distance, that what was once near and dear has become a stranger.

And at that moment, I realize I am on my way *out* of Christianity and toward the door Rachel has opened for me...

But then I realize Rachel was talking about heading back to her flat, and my existential epiphany dissipates.

"Sure," I say honestly, eager for a bed and to not talk about big and heavy things I didn't have answers for, big and heavy things I wasn't sure I *wanted* to have answers for.

We snag Josh and Rachel's boyfriend and start our long walk back through the streets simmering with excitement over the fête.

The introspective English pub was in the old city of Lyon, located across the river. To get to our sweet beds and sweet oblivion, we had to cross the Saône.

Once on the other side, Rachel's boyfriend turns back to where we came. We follow his gaze, curious.

A cathedral, the Basilique Notre Dame de Fourvière, towers above us on the other side of the river. Blue, white, and red are projected on its façade and dance on the water. The image is simple but alluring, making it hard to look away.

We breathe in the night as sounds of raucous liberty echo in the distance.

"Vive la révolution!" Rachel's boyfriend yells.

Vive la révolution…

On a Plane Over the Atlantic

I'm staring out the window, as resiliently moonlit clouds float in an inky night, high above a raging Atlantic.

I can't sleep. There's too much in my head, too much in my heart, all spinning and knocking about.

I'm headed home, back to Colorado, after living a year in Berlin, after nine months of stopping strangers on the streets to "talk to them about Jesus," after two months of nursing the dying in Mumbai, after four weeks of traveling Europe to "share the good news," after six weeks of hitchhiking through Europe on nothing but faith and reckless youth…

After being a part of a ministry that actively lied to everyone around them to save face, after finding out my mission's director was having an affair with one of the young staff girls, after learning my brother had a life-threatening car accident and was now likely going to lose his leg, after hard conversations with atheistic friends I didn't have answers for, after my faith came crashing down when I nearly shit myself in a dive bar…

And that's just what was behind me. Little did I know the future was just as heavy, just as messy, just as hard. Little did I know that my brother's leg would never heal, that I would continue to try and change my sexuality only to fail miserably, that my girlfriend and I would try to make it work in spite of my attractions but fail in spite of honesty and love, that my life would come crashing down after coming out, that I'd sleep with more men than I can remember, that I'd become homeless, that I'd have to start life over at the age of twenty-four.

But for now, I stare out the window, as resiliently lit clouds float in an inky night, high above a raging Atlantic, unsure of what is to come.

Legs

"Nathan, do you believe God loves you?"

My brother lies in a hospital bed.

Rods protrude from his skin, connecting to two metal rings, forming a cage-like contraption. It's an external fixator, and it makes me think of Frankenstein's monster.

My mom whimpers silently through a weak smile as she rubs my brother's arm. Her eyes dart between the elders and Nathan, scared.

My father stands behind her, rubbing *her* back. He doesn't know what to do. He just knows to rub his wife's back. That should help, right? What else do you do? None of us know. This is all new and horrible. So we look to the church elders. Look to them for answers, while they ask their questions.

"Yes," Nathan answers with airy breath.

"Do you believe that God would withhold any good and perfect gift from his son?"

"No."

"Do you believe God is able to heal you?"

"Yes."

"Do you believe he *will* heal you?"

He chokes back tears.

Silence.

I get the strategy. You ask questions that are obvious and intrinsically connected to someone's faith: Do you believe there is a God? Of course I do! Do you believe that he's all-powerful? Oh, but of course I do! Do you believe he loves you? Oh, absolutely! Well, if God is all-powerful and he loves you, why wouldn't he heal you!

Great fucking question. Why wouldn't he heal you?

So what do we do when he doesn't heal? Does that mean God isn't real? Does that mean he isn't powerful enough? Does it mean he doesn't love you?

No, that can't be the case. And we can't ever blame God. That's against the rules.

So instead, we find a solution to absolve him of all guilt: we put it on the person who didn't get healed because they didn't have enough faith. That must be the reason they didn't get healed. It's a faith problem. Not a God problem. Because God is perfect. Or so we're told.

So in addition to my brother having a broken femur, tibia, and fibula, he now gets to carry the guilt of lacking faith, the faith that would have healed him. It's *his* fault. *He's* to blame.

This theology is not only problematic, it's torture.

As my brother continues answering questions, trying to muster up his faith as the elders pull out their oil, I leave the room.

I don't want to ruin this. Because it's not just about the lack of faith from the sick person, it's also about the lack of faith from everyone else nearby. The ritual requires all faith, no doubt, and oh, how I doubt. In a weird juxtaposition, I leave because I believe my lack of belief will affect the healing because I know how I would have answered the elder's questions…

Do you believe God exists?

Not sure.

Do you believe he loves you?

I'm gay, so no.

Do you believe he's all-powerful?

Maybe. But the world is kinda fucked up, so if he is all-powerful, what the fuck is going on?

Do you think a good father would withhold something good from you?

He already did. And not just from me … from her…

⤫

"Isn't it lovely outside, Angeline?"

"Oh yes! So lovely! It is so nice to get outside and smell the flowers and feel the sun. This is the first time I've been outside in three years."

My mouth dropped, and my heart sank.

Three years?

We were walking through the garden at the Mother Teresa home I volunteered at in Mumbai, India. Correction. I walked through the garden. Angeline sat in a wheelchair while I pushed.

"Why don't you come outside more often?"

"Too much hassle. There's only one wheelchair, and the nuns are too busy with other people who need help more than me."

Classic Angeline: the "good Catholic." She puts others first, denies herself, and carries all the guilt, including the guilt for her missing leg.

A few years back, Angeline slipped into the street. It was an accident. No one was at fault. It just happened, as most shitty things do. But because she slipped, a bus hit her. And because a bus hit her, her right leg got destroyed. And because her right leg got destroyed, they had to amputate it.

One misstep and her entire life changed—a fact she liked to remind herself of often.

From walking around town on her own two feet to sitting on a rotting piece of wood with one useless leg. From enjoying the sun and flowers in her garden to being trapped in a cold cement building. From having friends and family caring for her to being alone in a Mother Teresa Home for the Sick and Dying.

But Angeline wasn't dying. She wasn't even sick. She was a beautiful woman no one could afford to take care of. So they gave her to those who could—the nuns.

From that day on, Angeline spent the rest of her life two inches off the floor, paddling around with her hands, on her tiny piece of wood with tiny wheels, living with women who were clinically insane, sick, and dying. This would be her company till her final days. Well, them and a bunch of curmudgeonly nuns who were overworked and undertrained. Oh! And on rare occasion, a bunch of punk white kids from Europe and the States, full of far too much zeal, a zeal that would cause far too much pain.

I was born into the raging, charismatic '90s. For those of you who didn't go to church during this time, consider yourself blessed (far too many shoulder pads). On a typical Sunday morning, one could see hundreds of people dancing, their permed hair rhythmically bouncing, electric guitars squealing to "Shout to the Lord all the Earth let us sing," as a terrible montage of planets and stars rolled behind the lyrics.

When the final song fades, the worship pastor would share the most recent atrocity happening in Israel. After which, we'd all stretch out our hands to the flag of "God's chosen people," because "God blesses those who bless Israel."

After the prayer, some guy in a bright blazer would come on stage to give a mini-sermon-guilt-trip, proclaiming, "God will give back to you tenfold if you would just believe and give till it hurt." A metal plate would pass before you as the worship team came back in with a moving song about God's faithfulness.

The preacher would then come, and he'd talk about how "You were born for such a time as this," and how "Millennials are going to hell in a handbasket," and how "If you will not tell your friends about Jesus, who will? Their blood will be on your hands!"

You would go to the front of the stage, crying (if you were feeling extra guilty that Sunday), asking God to forgive you for masturbating again (because you're a horny teenager), and promising to never masturbate again (or at least to Thursday) and convert every student at your high school while preaching about celibacy (because Jesus can't love a "used flower").

I remember one time when we had to write life mission statements at the age of sixteen … Six. Teen. At sixteen I barely knew what I wanted with my body let alone the rest of my life. (I still don't know what I want with the rest of my life … and sometimes my body.) But we had to declare, for all to see, what our lives were going to be about.

"I will be a missionary to Africa!" (Classic.) "I will evangelize to everyone I meet!" (Lies.) "I will be on fire for Jesus!" (What exactly does that mean?)

In short, if you were not evangelizing, praying, or fasting, you were wasting your life, a life Jesus bought with his precious blood, you selfish piece of shit!

So week after week, I'd come to that little cold concrete compound and sit with the mentally ill, doped up on too many psychotics; week after week, I'd wash the sheets of the most recent terminally ill woman who died in the middle of the night; and week after week, I'd see sweet Angeline, pushing herself around on her makeshift pedalboard, like this was some shitty gym class, attempting to keep a smile on her face because she didn't want to be a nuisance to anyone else.

But her plight was a nuisance to *me*.

Every time I'd see her, I'd feel her pain. Every time I'd see her, I'd feel guilty for not doing enough. Every time I'd see her, I was confronted with the fact that there was unfairness in the world even though I believed in a fair and just God.

Why wasn't he being fair and just to Angeline?

With my charismatic upbringing blaring in the background, I knew I had to do something.

My time was short. If not me, who? I was made for such a time as this! God called us to do scary things. Stupid scary things! For glory and honor and God! Carpe diem! You only live once! (And all those other inspirational quotes people say before doing something irreversibly stupid.)

"Angeline, you've read the Bible, right?"

"Of course. I'm Catholic."

"Have you read the part where Jesus heals a lame person?"

She got quiet. She knew where I was going with this.

My heart knocked hard against my chest, begging to get out. It was terrified. *I* was terrified.

"Well, you see, Jesus spoke to the lame man and said, 'Get up and walk,' and his legs were healed. The man had to believe something would happen. So he showed his belief by standing up. Maybe God will heal your leg if you try to get up and walk. Can you get up and walk for me, Angeline? Can you try?"

Her tear-filled eyes looked up at me. She was in *so* much pain.

"Why won't God give me back my leg? Why won't he heal me?"

"Well, maybe if you try and stand up he will."

I reached out for her hands, but she pulled back. She shook her head and began to sob.

"What did I do wrong? Why is he punishing me?"

"Angeline, he's not punishing you." I crouched down in front of her.

"Then why won't he give me my leg back?" She looked at me with eyes that pleaded for an answer.

I didn't have one.

"I ... I don't know." Our eyes held for a moment, but then the pain was too much, and she looked away.

"I would like to go back inside now."

"Okay ... We can do that." I stood up, wiped the tears from my eyes, and pushed her back inside.

I took the long route. I told myself it was for Angeline, so she could get a little more time in the sun. But I knew it was for me—I didn't want to go inside looking so defeated.

❧

"Father, we *praaay* by the *power* of your *Hoooly* Spirit that you would *heal* Nathan's leg."

"Yes, LOOOOORD."

"We *knoooow* that you *are our healer*, that *you* are *mighty* to save."

"Yes, Gaaaaaawd."

"We come to you *now*, *humbled* by your power."

(Prayer apparently only works if you emphasize certain words and extend the vowels.)

I hear the voices through the wall as I lean against it, crying and praying, yet again, for legs, even though I wasn't even sure if this prayer thing worked, even though I wasn't sure there was a God to pray to. But could it hurt?

It hurt Angeline...

Please dear God, heal my brother. Pleeeeease. If you're there, please, heal him.

I dare not say the words aloud. I only think them. Think them with every fiber of my being. Begging God to heal my brother's leg. Begging God to care. Begging God to be there. Begging God to be real.

Pleeeease God. Please...

❧

The accident happened a few weeks prior. Nathan was driving his Jeep Wrangler to work after working a double the day before. Nathan has epilepsy. And when he doesn't get a lot of sleep, he seizes. But the blessing and curse of my brother Nathan is that he doesn't know how to say, "No."

The sun was barely up when it happened.

Brain fired. Muscles contracted. Legs flexed. Pedal came down. Engine roared. Wheels squealed. Jeep smashed into flatbed. Flatbed carved into Jeep. Jeep engine rammed into Nathan's leg. Femur cracked. Tibia shattered. Fibula piece tore through muscle and skin, flying into the air, crashing onto the street.

All while every neuron in my brother's body fired to life. All while every muscle tightened to iron. Eyes vacant. Foam gurgling from his mouth.

He didn't feel a thing.

But he would.

It would all come racing at him till shock swallowed him back, burying him in sweet oblivion. When he finally came to, in a hospital bed with my parents, he'd discover that his life was forever changed, as a police officer cited him for reckless driving since he had a history of seizures.

"You're lucky no one else was hurt."

Lucky? This is lucky?

For two years, he would attempt to recover…

…But he got a massive blood clot.

…But he needed to keep his leg elevated above his heart rather than walk and heal.

…But the fibula didn't grow back. (You know, the one in the street.)

…But he had another seizure.

…But his nerves were permanently damaged.

…But he would have to wear a compression sock for the rest of his life.

…But he was denied Medicaid.

…But he was denied disability.

…But but but…

("But" is the best word for this whole nightmare.)

As I write this, it's been eight years since his accident, eight years since his brain decided life was too much and needed to reboot, eight years of bumping into repercussions from that accident. From that one moment. All because of a stupid seizure he had no control over. All because his brain said life was too much. Life was far too much.

⤳

"Amen. Stay strong, Nathan. Don't stop believing."

"I won't."

"Good. We're gonna see a miracle. I believe it."

The elderly elders are wrapping up their prayers. I wipe my face with my sleeve. Have to remove any signs of weakness. (Ever since I was little, I've had this need to look strong. Maybe it's because I'm the oldest. Maybe it's because I knew I had a secret that would be too heavy for everyone, so I needed to be as light as possible.)

There's an irony that, of all the people who came to pray for my brother, it's this elderly couple from Ted Haggard's church. There's an irony that the Jeep that nearly killed him sits smashed and rotting on Ted Haggard's lawn, after he offered to keep it until my brother could try and fix it. In fact, it seems poetic. Because this accident, the accident that would change my brother's life, happened because of stupid seizures, stupid seizures that started the night Ted Haggard confessed a horrifying truth seven years prior.

∽

November 1, 2006, early afternoon.

"Man claims three-year sexual relationship with pastor,"[1] the Channel 9 News headline read.

"I did not have a homosexual relationship with a man in Denver,"[2] Haggard told the reporters.

"I have no question in my mind that everything this man says is false. I know Ted to be a man of the utmost integrity and the highest moral character."[3] Rob Brendle, associate pastor at New Life Church responded.

"Everyone come to the house tonight. We need to pray," the text read. It was from Craig, the leader of this Bible study my brother Nathan and I had been attending. We were all members at New Life, Ted Haggard's old church, but Sundays weren't enough. We needed more. So every Thursday we'd get together, worshiping and praying and confessing all our sins to our leaders, so they in turn could tell us how to live our lives and who to date and what sins were causing us to be ill. (They'd later blame Nathan's seizures on him looking at women's lingerie pictures in old Macy's magazines.)

"We'll stay up all night if we have to, praying and fasting for our pastor. The enemy and his lies will be crushed. Truth will triumph!"

Indeed, the truth did triumph…

November 1, 2006, late into the night.

"It is important for you to know that he confessed to the overseers that some of the accusations against him are true," reads the email from Ross Parsley, acting interim pastor.

It was true. Not some of it. *All* of it.

We had stayed up late into the night, praying continuously. When the email came, we were defeated. The air and energy left the room. Everyone silently disappeared to different corners of the house, finding whatever furniture they could to pass out into confused sleep.

Nathan ended up on an air mattress that had a hole in it, and I ended up on something called a "love sack" (maybe that's why I'm gay) that wreaked of dog. Apparently, it was the Great Dane's bed.

As I began to stir, early in the morning, stiff and cold, Nathan was already up, staring up at me. His mattress had deflated, and he ended up on a cold tile floor. He'd been up for hours.

"Wanna play pool?"

Growing up, Nathan would get these random obsessions where he'd fixate on something. He'd need to buy all the gear, research all the data, practice all the time. Then the fixation would suddenly end, and his closet would be filled with yet another abandoned hobby. Hockey. Bass guitar. Woodworking. They're all still there, collecting dust.

At this current moment in time, his fixation was billiards.

To be honest, the last thing I wanted to do was play pool. But what else was I gonna do? It was like seven o'clock in the morning, everyone else was fast asleep, and if I wanted to sleep, it meant rolling over to the other side of the smelly love sack, freezing from the open window. (I guess playing pool wasn't the last thing I wanted to do—sleeping on that god-awful sack was.)

"Sure."

We went upstairs and chalked up our sticks. Nathan broke the set, and I went in for a shot. Nothing. Of course. I suck at pool.

I looked up to Nathan, expecting him to move. But he didn't. He was staring up at the wall behind him.

"Nathan it's your turn. Nathan? Nathan!"

His head moved, as if following a fly.

But there was no fly.

His face turned towards me. His eyes rolled back. His body straightened tight. Foam gurgled from his mouth. He was gagging. Choking on his own phlegm. And then he fell.

I raced toward his convulsing body, screaming for help. I had absolutely no clue what was happening or what to do, and his body was too heavy for me to move or restrain.

After what felt like an eternity, the parents who owned the house frantically entered the living room.

"Ivan, grab a spoon and call 9-1-1. Brandon, help me push him to his side."

Kimberly and I strained to move Nathan's rigid body, so he wouldn't drown on his own phlegm.

Ivan came back with a spoon in his hand and a phone to his ear.

"Brandon, has this happened before?"

"No."

"What were you guys doing prior?"

"We were just playing pool, and then he fell!"

"Do you know if he's allergic to anything?"

"I don't think so."

Ivan kept pestering me with question after question, as I continued to hold my brother on his side, Kimberly shoving a spoon down his throat.

"It's so he doesn't swallow his tongue."

He can swallow his tongue!?

I don't remember what happened next. It's blank. What I *do* remember is that at some point after the paramedics arrived, I ran to the toilet, dry heaving into the bowl as I cried.

I kept replaying the scene. His turning head. His tight body. His vacant eyes. The gurgling sound from his mouth.

I hid there in the locked bathroom, feeling stupid and powerless, till I heard my brother screaming from behind the door.

"AHHH! Bandon? Where's Bandon? Don't touch me. Don't touch me! Bandon? Bandon!" The "r" was nowhere to be found, like he was a kindergartener with a speech impediment.

Someone pounded on the door. "Brandon, Nathan needs you. He's acting weird."

I rushed out of the bathroom and searched for my brother. His eyes were wide, pupils narrow, scanning the room while he pushed everyone away, screaming.

"Bandon!" He ran to me, his large muscles clenching me fiercely as if he couldn't get enough of me, as if I'd disappear if he let me go. He tore at my clothes; he hung onto my neck. His drool-covered face pressed against my chest.

"Bandon! Bandon. Bandon…" He slowly began to calm down as I held him close.

"It's gonna be okay, Nathan. You're gonna be okay." I said it, not sure if I was lying or telling the truth. But that's what you do after someone has a seizure, right? You make sure they feel safe. That's what you do. That's something *I* can do. That's where *I* can help. No longer powerless, I can tell him lies to calm him down. To calm myself down. Because people who are hurt need everyone else to be calm. Right? And the truth wouldn't make him calm. In fact, the truth is what got us into this mess. A truth confessed by our pastor. A truth that kept us up late into the night. Late on a cold tile floor. I couldn't trust truth. Truth hurts people. It disappoints. It sends churches spiraling into chaos and prayerful teenagers into defeated sleep. Or lack of sleep. So I lied. I lied because making sure my brother felt safe was more important than telling the truth. I lied because when you have no clue what to do and you think your brother may be dying, you can at least lie. You can at least tell him it was going to be okay. You can at least tell him he was safe, even though you had no fucking clue if he was safe. So I lied to him. I lied and told him he was safe. I told him he was going to be okay.

∽

"Don't give up. He's gonna be okay. He's a fighter." The elders from Ted Haggard's new church emerge from the hospital room, my parents following behind.

"Anoint him with this every day," they say to my parents like spiritual pharmacists. (Apply twice daily until missing bone is restored. Side effects may include bone still missing, an unshakable feeling of guilt, an inability to carry on with life, and acne.) "Don't give up. We're gonna see a miracle."

But we wouldn't see a miracle. He would get a half-miracle. Like my glasses on the autobahn. Like that willow tree with a rug. Like Nathan's still-broken-but-not-*too*-broken leg he'd have to limp on for the rest of his life.

We'd get half miracles. Because, "we serve a wonder-working (kinda) God." That's what they said at least, right? That's what they told us? But maybe they were lying, too.

Plastic Brains

"So what are you going to do to make sure it doesn't happen again?"

My parents had invited Ted Haggard and his wife Gayle over for dinner so that we could get to know them better considering we started attending his new church.

But I didn't want to simply "get to know them better," I wanted to bring up the glaring past.

The room goes petrifyingly silent as I ask the question burning on everyone's heart.

I have a habit of doing this—of giving voice to what everyone else is feeling but refuses to say. People sometimes say, "Thanks so much! You're so brave." I just get annoyed. "Why didn't you speak up? If we all did, something might happen." Instead, I'm normally reprimanded or "set straight."

But Ted doesn't set me straight. (Mainly because he and I are both attracted to men.) Instead, he casually pats his mouth, taking his time, and takes a sip of water to wash down his salad while everyone waits in awkward anticipation.

"What a question, Brandon. You certainly don't hold back. Just to make sure I'm understanding you correctly, Brandon, what you're asking me is, 'How do you know I'm not going to build up a church and have another affair, ruining the lives of everyone around me again?'"

I don't break eye contact. "Exactly."

Gayle looks at him with these eyes that are full of tenderness, longing, and pride.

I honestly don't get it. He hurt her the most. Why the hell is she still with him? How could she look at him that way?

"Well, Brandon, I think the reason I met up with Mike all those years ago was because I wasn't honest or vulnerable about what was going on inside of me. I felt like I couldn't be, especially as a pastor. I hid my life from everyone. I don't do that anymore. Gayle knows everything about me. But beyond that, I have done extensive counseling, exploring why I chose to meet Mike, and I have people in my life that I'm accountable to who love me."

My gaze refuses to break, arms crossed over chest.

"But at the end of the day, Brandon," he puts his napkin back in his lap and interlocks his fingers, placing them on the table, "no matter what I say, you *shouldn't* fully trust me. I'm human, and I'm going to make mistakes. But at St. James Church, we're trying to do that—to see people as fully human, mistakes and all, instead of pretending we're all perfect. We're just a bunch of broken people trying to love each other. To be honest, getting caught was the best thing that ever happened to Gayle and me because I fell into grace."

He looks at his wife, lovingly, with gratitude. He grabs her hand and rubs it gently.

What are they hiding?

To answer the question, I start attending their church. Not because I believe. But because I'm skeptical and curious. Like the old imperial anthropologists, I attend every service, taking notes, observing, wondering when the masks would break.

Week after week I attend. Holding my breath. Guarded. Because I'm curious. Well ... that, and because of Ted.

Every week he finds me and fiercely hugs me, picking me off the ground like I'm a sack of corn. He then puts me down, and with the biggest smile says, "I am so glad you're here, Brandon. I'm glad you're home." He then looks at me with these eyes, proud eyes, eyes that look like you're his kid and you just received some lame participation ribbon at a dumb high school science fair event. But to him, to him you won the whole damn thing and solved world hunger at the same time. It's a look that sees you. All of you. And likes you.

But I'm guarded. Regardless of the hugs. Regardless of smiles. Regardless of the proud eyes.

Growing up as a closeted boy, I am hit differently by Ted's debacle. It told me, "See! That's what happens to gay people when they go into ministry. They get married. They have a family. Build a church. Then, they can't restrain themselves. It's too much. They fail. And when the world finds out, they crucify them and throw their bodies to the birds. You should *never* go into ministry. You will *never* be safe as a gay man in ministry."

His story will haunt me forever.

But I keep going. Because I'm curious. And if I'm honest, it's also because of the smiles ... and the hugs ... and because he owns his shit from the stage, not pretending like the affair didn't happen or his life fell apart. He owns it all, and that somehow makes me feel a bit safer. So I come for that, because I feel a little bit safe and definitely wanted ... and also because of the conversations...

"Sexuality is composed of three things: origin, history, identity. Origin: what was your first sexual experience, history: what has your story been concerning sex, and identity: how you choose to identify."

I'm sitting in Ted's office. We've been chatting weekly about being gay. It feels nice talking about a piece of my life that's been hidden for decades with someone who gets it.

Well, sort of gets it.

"You don't have any control over origin. Your first sexual encounter was with a man. But you *do* have control over history and identity. Identity, you can affect right now. You can choose how you want to identify. History is different. That's the one that takes time. But you have control over history and how it affects your life. Your brain is plastic. It changes and moves and remakes itself every day. If you masturbate to bridges, you get aroused by bridges. If you masturbate to men, you get aroused by men. It's a partnership with God. He uses our actions to accomplish his will. Take your brother Nathan for example. He should have lost his leg. But he didn't. Why?"

"Because he's stubborn and didn't want to chop off his leg when he probably should have."

"Okay, fair, but it was also because of doctors. God gave his doctors and surgeons the tools to heal your brother. God has given you tools as well. Where Nathan needed assistance from medical professionals to heal his physical body, you need help with healing your sexuality. And that comes with neuroplasticity. But the real question is do you want that?"

I look at him confused.

Being raised in the church, what *I* wanted was of little importance. In fact, it was considered selfish. And you can't be a good Christian and selfish. Screw your heart. Instead, as a Christian, it's your job to figure out what *God* wants. (And no one explains why God doesn't just tell you. You're just somehow supposed to figure it out, and if you don't, you're fucked. You'll make it to heaven. Sure. Fine. But you'll be living in a shitty shack of a cloud house. A cloud shack. That's your eternal reward. You pathetic, untrusting, faithless bum. Should have figured out your super-secret calling.)

To hell with what I want.

But here is this pastor, the pastor of my childhood, the pastor who chose what *he* wanted, blowing up *everything* around him, asking me what *I* want.

"What do *I* want?"

"Yes, Brandon. What do *you* want? Because at the end of the day, this is *your* life. *You* have to make a choice. God loves you regardless, but what do *you* want?"

Choice is a powerful wind that blows away the fog of uncertainty, bringing clarity.

I had two friends that hated their marriage and felt stuck with each other because they had to be "good Christians," and good Christians don't get divorced. But when they gave themselves permission, when they began to plan the divorce, they realized something: they wanted each other.

Choice revealed what they *actually* wanted.

The pressure to stay married, to make sure their marriage looked good and right, was all they could see. It consumed them. But when divorce was truly an option, they realized they didn't want divorce. Life was hard, but they wanted each other and couldn't imagine doing life with anyone else.

A good Christian can't be gay, either. I don't have a choice. *I* have to change. *I* have to somehow become straight.

But here was this man, a pastor who understood what it was like to want a man, telling me *I* had a choice.

The winds of choice blew the pressure to be a good Christian man away, and my vision focused as the sky cleared.

"I want to be with a woman."

"Great. Then let's get to work."

For the next few months, Ted would give me books on brain plasticity (and not like casual books you read before bed, like textbooks, like books people read when they're in college for therapy or psychology).[1,2] They would talk about how the brain changes minute-by-minute, day-by-day, how things that fire together wire together, and I was gonna wire my brain to women, goddammit!

I would gobble it up, determined that if I learned enough and tried hard enough, I could change. At the time, I was working at Starbucks. On my breaks—those ten-minute breaks that feel like barely five—I would pull out my I-should-be-in-college-not-pleasure-reading books and inhale the content: stroke patients remapping their brain; kinks changing and forming through life experiences; perpetual anxiety converting into hope.

Maybe this was it. Maybe this was the answer. The brain changes itself. Maybe I can change myself.

I would masturbate to straight porn. I would imagine life with a woman. I would text my old girlfriend from YWAM. She would move to Colorado. We would give this another try. We had already tried twice, but third time's the charm, right? Right?

Maybe this would work. After all, wonder of wonders, right? Maybe God could turn me around? Maybe he could do something. Just like my brother—God saved his leg by using doctors. Sure, he hobbles around, and his life is forever different, but at least he's walking, at least he didn't lose his leg. Maybe I can at least marry a woman. Maybe I could use brain plasticity like God used doctors. Maybe I could do this!

I was reminded of Abraham in the Bible, how he was old and incapable of having children. But he had a child nonetheless.[3]

Here I am, gay. Unable to be sexually aroused by a woman. But maybe God could do something despite my gayness. Maybe what God did for Abraham he could do for me. Maybe a gay man could be aroused by a woman. This woman. Anna. She would be my miracle. She would be my Isaac ... (Wait. Is that gay?)

But no matter how many times I "trained my brain" (a.k.a. masturbated to straight porn), I would still find my coworker—my very straight male coworker, the one with the really cute butt, the really really cute male butt—super attractive!

Jesus! Take me now! Wait! Not like that! Save me from temptation and have your way with me! Wait! Not like that! Why does everything sound so sexual? Why is that butt so attractive! Ahhhhh!

Maybe it just takes time. It doesn't happen overnight. After all, Abraham was over one hundred before he had a kid. Please, dear God, don't make me wait one hundred years.

Perky Smiles

"You should try this place called 'Praise Horde,'" my mom says while peeling cucumbers at the sink.

It seems like she's always cooking. My dad has cooked maybe three meals throughout their marriage, while my mom has cooked for *literally* everyone in my life at least once, all while working at least one full-time job. She's like that mom in *My Big Fat Greek Wedding* who asks, "Are you hungry?" and the other character says, "No." but she replies, "Okay. I'll make you something." Except my mom isn't Greek; she's not even Italian. She's just a very host-y American with some British heritage.

"So many people your age are going to it now, especially those who are tired of the church." (The more accurate statement would be, "Most people your age are tired of the church.")

My mom does this a lot: she puts me in the position she believes I'm in, in this case, disillusioned, and then offers a solution that other people have. It's her way of getting around the fact that I hate getting advice from my parents. She does it in this roundabout way that allows her to speak her mind. And when you confront her about it, she says, "I'm just telling you what I heard from *other* people." That Pam Flanery's a smart one.

"All they do is worship. No agenda. Just a bunch of people getting together to worship as long as the Spirit leads" (a term used by Christians any time a church service goes abhorrently long or does something off-script). "Sometimes that's an hour. Sometimes it's six. They've gone till the next day before. It's so beautiful! I wish more churches would function like that. Just let the spirit lead, you know?"

"Mmhmm…" I say, staring down at my cereal, refusing to give her the satisfaction of feigning interest.

"You should go. Taylor goes. I'll talk to her for you. She works with me now."

"No, Mom. I'm good."

These are the moments that I wish lived in Jersey. I hear myself saying "Ma" with how pushy my mother is. And it would fit her Greek/Italian-mom vibe better. Instead, I live in Colorado, where we say weird things like, "Colo-RAdo" and "14ers" and "hydrate." No "Ma." Just "Mom."

"If I want to check it out, I'll just go. A few of my friends have already talked about it."

"You sure? It's really not a problem. I'm sure Taylor would love to take you."

"Moooom!" ("Maaaaaaa!" See? Better.)

"Okay, okay. I'll mind my own business." (Till she brings it up again the next day or next hour; till she gets her way because she always gets her way, and everyone's business is my mom's business. How Mediterranean.)

So, I go. After much reluctance, I go. But not with Taylor. By myself. In my own car. Because if it gets weird (church stuff *always* gets weird), I don't want to be trapped, dependent on someone else. I don't even know if I believe in God, and now I'm off to sing songs to a being I'm not sure even exists, for potentially hours on end? Yeah, no. I'm taking my own car, so I can escape whenever I want.

Jesus Christ … Why am I doing this??

As I enter, I'm greeted by a ton of smiling faces. Like, super smiley faces. Like, no-one-should-be-this-happy smiley faces. And people I don't know are hugging me super long. Like, *suuuuuper* long. Like, please-let-me-go-I-can-feel-your-clammy-hands long.

"Good to see you! Have you been to Horde before?"

They realize the word "horde" doesn't really have a positive connotation, right?

"Nope. First time."

"Oooooh! So exciiiitinggggggg!" they say, eyes barely visible, cheekbones frozen in place with their perpetually perky smiles.

Where the fuck am I? Why does everyone look like they're high?

"Do you play any instruments?"

"Just sing."

"Hey! The voice is an instrument! Don't sell yourself short! We can always use another vocalist. Let me introduce you to Greg. You'll love Greg. He's the best."

Use another vocalist? I didn't volunteer for anything. I thought I was just sup-posed to sing "Hallelujah" till the sun came up or something.

They take me downstairs, giving me a tour of the basement-turned-studio where there's black felt and curtains hanging everywhere. You would think it was some emo-child sheet fort. But instead, it was a quasi-recording studio, full of professional musicians, all with those weird perky smiles.

"Greg, this is Brandon. It's his first time. He's a vocalist."

A man with a scruffy, perky face looks down from the ceiling where he's jimmy-rigging some chords behind more black felt.

"Hey! First time? Oh man, you're in for a treat!"

What is this treat everyone keeps talking about? If they bring out Kool-Aid, I'm out.

"You wanna sing tonight?"

"Uhhhh … You just met me. I'm not sure if you want to throw me on a mic just yet. Plus, I'm not really up to it. I'm just here to feel things out."

"Totally get it. Feeling it out. Gotcha. Let me snag your email, though, and I'll keep you in the loop."

Email can't be too risky, right? What's the worst they can do with an email? Spam me?

"Okay."

I give Greg my email and ascend from the dark, felt-covered basement to join more perky smiles.

There's a television on the screen with multiple frames of all the musicians downstairs. It reminds me of that terrible Hulk movie from like 2003 or *The Brady Bunch.*

Across from the screen, a scruffy man with a guitar begins to talk. "Alright, everyone. For those that are new, we'll sing up here with a more acoustic feel while the musicians downstairs play. Some cameras will be recording for our next YouTube video."

YouTube video? No one told me about YouTube. Oh, hell no!

Panicked, I look around for an escape, but instead find someone I know: Rachel. Not atheist-evangelist Rachel. Girl-I-used-to-be-a-youth-pastor-for Rachel. She's working one of the cameras.

I convince her to let me run the camera so she could be a part of the night (completely selfless act on my part).

After a few minutes, everyone starts up, the room swelling with sounds and melodies that have no coherent pattern, yet all mesh together perfectly some-how. It works, but there's no actual song.

The band on the Hulk/Brady-Bunch-movie screen begins to join in—cymbals growing, synth swelling, guitar echoing—it's all one overwhelming and euphonious cacophony, and, regardless of my resistance, I'm getting caught up in it, swallowed by it like a wave of unbridled harmony.

Music, especially communal music, has a way of doing this, of pulling me in. After all, what person refuses to sing when a guitar is brought out around a campfire? It takes a true psychopath to resist "Kumbaya."

I'm even tempted to don one of those perky smiles, but the wave isn't quite *that* powerful. My cynical heart digs its feet in, refusing to let my cheekbones rise.

Bunch of hogwash. Bunch of groupthink. Just like atheist-evangelist Rachel said. They don't even know what they're singing.

Just then, everyone starts into a song, like they all knew what they were singing, and like I was on the outside of a joke.

"Hosanna. Hosanna. Hosanna in the highest." The voices grow and dance and take off into the song I'm familiar with, birthed from a soothing melodic chaos.

The communal movement is hypnotic, enticing me to once again surrender to the wave. The undertow sucks at my feet, and yet still I refuse—I don't want to lose control.

I miss this. I miss how this feels. I miss just surrendering to this feeling. Maybe it is groupthink. But it feels good to let go. To get taken away. To get sucked in the current. To be carried by the waves.

"You wanna switch out?" Rachel is standing next to me.

I look at the crowd one last time, the current of rushing voices.

What's the harm of trying?

"Sure."

I hand over the camera, stepping out from the shore and into the throng of worshipers. And in their midst, the waves crash over me, eroding my resolve, and that stupid perky smile swells on my face.

I love it.

I hate it.

I'm confused by it.

I'm scared by it.

The voice of a siren breaks out, louder than the rest, singing a new song I haven't heard before.

His eyes are shut, and he's smiling, like he's reading something on the inside of his eyelids.

"You pull me close ... You tell me how much you love me..."

Everyone is quiet and listening. Some open their eyes and look in the singer's direction.

"Come on, A.J.! You got it, man!"

His voice grows louder.

Oh! This is something spontaneous!

For those who have no clue what this means, "spontaneous" is a word used in charismatic Christian circles that means he's making up the words right here and now. It's always connected to some "move of the Spirit," meaning, God is the one giving this man a new song. It was something that was more of a "spice" in the flavor of Christianity I came from—not something that happened all the time, like when someone from the Midwest accidentally stumbles into a Thai restaurant—sure it happens, but we're always surprised and impressed when it does.

After some verses about God and faithfulness and all those other Christian things, he lands on a chorus, and the group joins in.

But not me. I'm still cynical. I don't trust this. A rock in the bay.

Can't people just come up with a song in their head, and it has nothing to do with God? People do this all the time. It isn't something special or holy.

But then I hear words. Not out loud. Out loud I only hear the voices singing. No ... this is different. This is in my chest. It's inside me. Like that stupid voice I heard under the willow tree in Geneva.

Let go of fear. Fall into me. Let go of fear. Fall into love. Fall into love.

I push it back down like vomit and focus on the people around me.

It will go away eventually, I think. *Just give it time. Ride it out.*

But instead, it bubbles back up, building pressure in my chest. I can't keep it in. So I whisper-sing it, hoping that a whisper-sing would somehow make the vomit feeling go away, somehow releasing the pressure.

"Let go of fear. Fall into me. Let go of fear. Fall into love. Fall into love."

"Shhh Shhh! Brandon is singing. Brandon is singing!"

"Who's Brandon?"

"The new guy!"

Fucking shit. How the hell did they hear me?

"Sing louder, Brandon."

Fuck. Welp. Here it goes.

"Let go of fear. Fall into me. Let go of fear. Fall into love. Fall into love."

"Yeaaaaah!"

"Sooooo gooooooood."

"Keep it coming, Brandon."

"Sing it louderrrrr."

I get a little louder, scared to let down the perky people.

"Let go of fear." Someone joins in. "Fall into me." More join in. "Let go of fear." Everyone sings. "Fall into love. Fall into love."

Then it's gone from me. It's no longer mine. It's everyone's. Like rain into the sea. They all start singing the chorus with force, carrying it away, carrying *me* away, sweeping me up with a rhythmic current, riding the wave.

I begin to smile and cry like some high, happy, hippy perky person.

I *did* miss this.

Maybe I can trust this. Maybe this time it'll work out.

But just like a wave must one day crash into the shore...

Two of the Praise Horde leaders, Timothy and his wife Lacy, start talking about radical grace and how fear is the only real enemy of love, how love must win over fear.

"If we're scared of something, we should move towards it, conquering the enemy of love. Don't give it power. Conquer it. Move towards it. We're stronger than that fear."

They start meeting with local church leaders, telling them we need to broaden our understanding of love since love is the ultimate definition of God.

Out of the "goodness of their hearts," they open up their home to a bunch of young adults, seventeen to twenty years old.

"They just need a safe place to process and heal, and we're honored that our home can be that safe place as they work through so much."

When I meet any of these seventeen-to-twenty-year-olds, they talk about how "God is bringing up a lot of pain and wounds. But it's good, you know? God brings up the pain for you to step through it. Like poison coming to the surface. It's all good. Just really hard, but so is healing."

Sure. It sounds good. But all of them are saying the exact same thing, with the exact same tired look, all while trying to keep up those perky smiles.

One by one, everyone staying with Timothy and Lacy begins to fade away, never showing up at Praise Horde or even out in public for that matter. Instead, they spend all their time at the house.

And then the rumors start...

"Timothy and Lacy are turning my girls against us."

"They have an open marriage."

"They're swingers."

"Timothy has been soliciting the girls for sex."

"I heard Lacy is going after the boys."

Then the ultimatums from churches...

"You can't volunteer with the youth anymore. There's weird stuff happening at that group called Praise Horde that you go to. Enough is enough!"

"You're either excommunicated from the church or you leave Praise Horde. Like the Bible says, 'You can't serve two masters.' Decide!"

"We won't stand for this. Satan is deceiving you. You either trust God and his leadership, or you leave the church. We will not tolerate this!"

In the end, hundreds of excited, passionate, young people were severely hurt, without a home, without a family. The place they felt seen and loved (seen and loved in a way the church was never able to provide) was now evil and wrong and twisted. And the churches that could have helped them, helped them navigate what was really going on, turned their backs on them because "They were a part of that creepy horde place." The majority of them never set foot into another church again. Because of the pain. Because they were abandoned. Because they got it wrong and were punished for it.

And here I am, yet again, in the rubble of another blunder. But unlike my newly disillusioned friends, I've been disillusioned for a while. (Huzzah! Cynicism for the win!)

Of course, this failed. Of course, there was something funky going on. Of course. This is just how it goes.

And the perky smiles faded.

Gay Glass Ceiling

I'm at a new church. Not Ted's. He talked about hell, and I got scared and left.

My parents, in their perpetual musical-chair-church-hopping way, found a new church that serves beer and plays rock music during worship. They thought that was cool and hip and not religious, so they went. (They eventually would leave because they serve beer and play rock music.)

After a lot of "You wouldn't believe what he talked about today," and "It's not like any other church I've been to," and "Just come with us to *one* service. I promise you'll love it. Call it my birthday present," I decided to go, in part out of curiosity (it will be the death of me) and in part to stop the begging.

Laser lights flash. Subwoofers shake the building. Old people put in earplugs. And as promised, the classic Christian worship songs give way to "Carry on Wayward Son."

After we "laid our weary heads to rest," a man comes on stage and says, "You probably weren't expecting Kansas at church this morning, were you? Hahaha!"

So different! So edgy! Look at them go! (This literally looks exactly like every other megachurch in Dallas.)

The associate pastor continues about how if you wanna give, there are boxes on the wall or you can give online. That's it. No guilt-tripping mini sermon.

So different! So edgy! Look at them go! (Because apparently not manipulating people into giving is a novel concept.)

Richard, the pastor, comes on stage. He talks about how his affair ruined his life years ago and how if his story is safe here, every story is safe here, regardless of where you come from. *All*. Stories. Are. Safe. Here.

So different! So edgy! Look at them go! (The fact that safety in church can be toted around as something "special" should truly be concerning.)

After talking about his moral failure, he moves on to Ezekiel 36,[1] a prophetic passage in the Old Testament where skeletons transform into a zombie army and hearts of stone turn to flesh with the word of God carved into them.

"You're a new creation in Christ Jesus. God has transformed your heart, and now it is good! The desires of your heart aren't evil! *You're* not evil! It's time to trust your heart! It's on your side!"

Everyone around me claps and says amen, while I rage. I've heard this message before, and it pisses me off.

Christians like *the idea* of this verse. It's fun and cute when painted on restored wood, safe in bathrooms and foyers. But then you bring up the things your heart wants—things like loving a man—and all of a sudden, they start backpedaling, making excuses:

"Well, are you *actually* a Christian if you like men? I'm not sure this verse *actually* applies to you if you're not *actually* a Christian. An *actual* Christian looks like *me*. They look like *us*. They look like the things that *we're* comfortable with. And *we're* not comfortable with *you*. *You* make us uncomfortable."

In practice, they hate this verse. They hate the idea of true freedom, of true autonomy. It's terrifying to them. After all, what would people do if they could do whatever they want? There would be madness! There would be chaos! There would be homosexuals everywhere!

So they add a "but." They apply an asterisk. Because without the asterisk, there'd be no control. And humans *need* control. Because *actually* we *don't* believe this verse. We *don't* believe our hearts are good. They're *bad*. *We're* bad. So lock us up. Bar us in. Keep us safe from ourselves. Because unlocked cages are dangerous…

Dangerous to the institutions that hold the keys.

"The devil dwells in the urge to control rather than liberate the human soul,"[2] Eugene Kennedy writes. "We stand by a dark forest through which fearful religious and political leaders would force us to pass in single file through their exclusive pathway of righteousness. They want to intimidate us, make us afraid and hand over our souls to them once more."[3]

And with our souls in hand, they demand adoration for their unquenchable egos, they wring us dry of free labor for their institutions of power and bankrupt us of money for their next million-dollar house.

In the words of Anton Szandor LaVey, founder of the Church of Satan, "Satan has certainly been the best friend the Church has ever had, as He has kept it in business all these years!"[4]

So, maxed out on the inconsistencies and pissed with the power trips, I storm out of the sanctuary.

Lucky for me, Richard makes himself readily available to guests in the lobby after service. (Because apparently a pastor being available to the congregants he leads is another new church-growing strategy.)

Unlucky for Richard, he makes himself readily available to guests after service, specifically me, the guest who's raging.

"Hi, Richard. My name is Brandon." (I refuse to call pastors "pastor.")

"Hi there, Brandon! How's it going?"

"It's fine. I have a question about your sermon. The whole thing was about how your heart is new and good and right. Well, I'm gay, and the church and the Bible say I'm not good and right and that I shouldn't trust my heart. So if you're telling me that my heart is good and that I *should* trust it, what am I supposed to do as a gay man?"

Richard gets quiet.

Checkmate, bitch.

"I don't have the answers for you, Brandon."

Of course you don't. No one does. No one wants to touch this with a ten-foot pole. Because unlike secular music and pressure-free giving and straight *moral failures, supporting gay people isn't a church-growing gimmick currently in vogue.* (As I said, it's all about branding.)

"But I can tell you that you're safe here as you figure this out. Regardless of where you land, I promise that this church is a safe place for you, and you are always welcome."

What?

I'm taken aback, and I let out a breath, feeling a little bit lighter.

"Really?"

"Absolutely! Like I said on stage, your story is safe here, and I mean that. I mean that for everyone."

He hugs me. It's not as good as a Ted hug, but it's nice, and I walk away feeling like I might be okay, breathing a little lighter.

But it's a lie. My story is not safe here...

Over the next year and a half, I get more involved. I attend the legendary men's retreats—the ones with beer—and I volunteer for the worship team—the one that plays rock music. During that time, the worship leader and I become friends. We go out for drinks. We talk about life. But I never lead during worship. That's fine. I'm not volunteering because I need to headline "Hotel California." But at my previous church, I was good enough to lead. In fact, I led all the time. Maybe this church just has higher standards.

I would later find out that I was not *allowed* to lead a song because I was gay. Because apparently my gayness wouldn't get on the congregants if I did background vocals. But my gayness would *definitely* get on the congregation if I was the front man.

I would also later find out that I wasn't allowed to be a leader in the children's ministry. Because apparently all gay people are also child molesters. Because if I like dudes, who knows what other dark and twisted desires I had slithering beneath the surface. As they say, "If we give those homos marriage, it's a slippery slope. Next thing you know they'll be wanting to marry dogs!"

My being-in-a-chair-every-week was okay. My consistent tithing was okay. My background vocals were okay. But there were invisible ceilings that I was never told about, that I was never made aware of. While everyone else's story was safe here, *mine* wasn't. It had to be put in an invisible box to make sure my story wouldn't get on anyone else.

Churches may have good intentions with this kind of rhetoric, a rhetoric that says, "Well, *everyone* is welcome! Come on in! The water's fine!" As if they're doing *us gay people* a favor by *at least* opening up their doors. Look at them go! They're so amazing!

But regardless of "good intentions," this ploy is common and damaging and ultimately not loving. It's a surprise attack that preys upon the hearts of queer people who hope against hope that *maybe* this church is different, that *maybe* this time they'll be safe, only to realize they were lied to in hopes to be converted and transformed into the church's image, rather than their own.

The most loving thing a church can do is just. be. honest. Honest that you actually *don't* accept LGBTQ+ people; honest that queer people are more than welcome to attend and give, but they will always be a second-class citizen; honest that I can serve in the church but never in the children's ministry because "We actually think you're a pedophile"; honest that our story is actually *not* safe here. It's not. It's not safe here. In fact, we don't want you to share your story. Keep it locked up. Keep it hidden. But keep attending and giving us your money.

The most loving thing a church can do is frankly say, "These are our beliefs." It empowers people, like myself, to make informed choices that protect our well-being. It's called informed consent, and let's be honest, consent isn't something that has been taught or esteemed within the church.

Instead, the vast majority of churches jump us, promising to love us unconditionally when their love is anything but, hiding behind rhetoric that says, "*You're* welcome here unconditionally, but that *behavior* is not," "Love the sinner; hate the sin," "Is it love if I let you drive your soul off a cliff?"

It's called a bait-and-switch. That's the kind word. The more honest word is gaslighting, and gaslighting is an abusive tactic employed by narcissists to control those they "love," just like the church "loves those homosexuals."

It's harmful. It's damaging. And churches ultimately do it, not for the LGBTQ+ people in their church, but for themselves, for their ego and pride. They do it so they can say, "Well, I tried; it's not *my* fault that gay people don't wanna be here," relieving their conscience all while making a few more bucks off those poor saps.

That's not love. That's not Christ. It's selfish.

Honesty is Christ, for he is "the way, the *truth*, and the life,"[5] as the Bible says. Instead, churches are masquerading as Christ followers, but in reality, are emulating their sworn enemy: the Deceiver, the one they call the Devil, lying about their true intentions, dancing his dance, letting him take the lead.

In the words of Christ, "You belong to your father, the devil, and you want to carry out your father's desires. He was a murderer from the beginning, not holding to the truth, for there is no truth in him. When he lies, he speaks his native language, for he is a liar and the father of lies."[6]

So when the masks finally fell, when their father was exposed, I saw the fear; I saw the disgust; I saw that my story was in fact *not* safe here, and I walked out the door.

Lies

A divorce lawyer flier sits on the counter.

My mom is looking at me with tear-filled eyes pleading.

"Brandon, you're the only one who can save this family."

My stomach falls out.

I've told myself this a thousand times—*It's all up to me; I must carry this alone.* For years, I'd curb the voice, telling myself that I was just imagining it, that it wasn't all up to me, that I was just a child, not the grownup. *Take it easy on yourself.*

But here was my mom, the grownup, echoing the voice in my head.

No more imagining. No pretending. It's real. It's all real. The voice in my head wasn't lying. It was right all along.

Nathan's the one who breaks bones, costing my parents lots of money. My other brother, Jay, is the one who sneaks off with his boyfriend, costing my parents nights of sleep as they lie outside of his bedroom door. Dad's the one who's emotionally unavailable, forcing my mom to come and cry to me because I've learned how to listen. My mom's the one who pulls away when conflict arises, forcing my dad to come to me and say nothing because he has no clue how to say something when he's scared or emotional, so we just sit over coffee and talk about everything, everything except what's *actually* going on, so nothing, because somehow talking about nothing helps him.

I was supposed to be the easy one, the one who was there for everyone else, the one who always comes through, the one carrying but never being carried.

I muster a smile.

"It's gonna be fine, Mom. We're gonna be okay. We're gonna make it through."

So as the divorce flier lies on the kitchen counter, and Nathan lies in his hospital bed, and my parents spend their nights lying outside Jay's door, I lie to my mother, like I lied to Nathan; I lie that everything is gonna be alright, that everything is going to be okay, promising we'll somehow make it through.

Through to where?

I hug her. I kiss her. I rub her back.

She smiles and turns away.

Then I lie to myself.

No, I'm not *having an existential crisis.*

No, I'm not *trying to "fix" my sexuality and nothing's working.*

No, I'm not *having to start my life over at the age of twenty-four because I've spent the last two decades of my personal and professional life* attending *churches,* volunteering *for churches, giving* money *to churches, going to* school *for churches,* working *at churches, to now doubting everything the church has ever taught me, doubting everything I've ever done, not to mention I can't work there because I'm a homosexual, and churches hate homosexuals.*

But no, I'm fine. We're fine. Everything is fine. We're gonna be okay. We're gonna make it through.

Because I need to lie to myself. Because if I don't lie to myself, how can I help everyone else? How can I be strong? How can I be the easy one? How can I be the light one?

But there's a problem with lying, especially when you lie to yourself—the truth always finds a way to catch up to you because it's always been the faster runner.

Part Three

Stopping

A man traveling across a field encountered a tiger. He fled, the tiger after him. Coming to a precipice, he caught hold of the root of a wild vine and swung himself down over the edge. The tiger sniffed at him from above. Trembling, the man looked down to where, far below, another tiger was waiting to eat him. Only the vine sustained him.

Two mice, one white and one black, little by little started to gnaw away the vine. The man saw a luscious strawberry near him. Grasping the vine with one hand, he plucked the strawberry with the other. How sweet it tasted![1]

The Buddha

Root

I'm sitting in my friend's car. I don't own one. Mine blew up in the care of my family while I was away being a missionary and "saving the world."

So, I'm sitting in my friend's car...

In a townhome parking lot...

Staring into nothing...

Panicking...

Because I just hooked up with a guy for the first time.

⌁

Ever since I was a little kid, I've been drawn to the male body.

Starting at the age of five, a boy and I would sneak away to a storage area every Sunday after church. My mom and dad were too busy. Too busy at worship practice. Too busy running the children's ministry. Too busy talking with their friends about all the amazing things God was doing in their lives.

They were heavily involved. They loved this church. It was their sanctuary. Their safe place. The place where their three little boys could run wild and free, laughing and playing hide-and-go-seek.

Then I sought George...

A boy six years older than me...

And we kept hiding...

Hiding together...

While seeking each other...

Week after week...

Dropping our clothes...

Gazing at each other's body...

Anxious…

Adrenaline and endorphins pumping through our veins…

Because of the naked body before us…

Because of the naked *male* body before us…

Because of the secrecy…

Because of the burning urge…

The urge we couldn't put out.

We knew we were playing with fire, but you don't stop playing with fire because it's dangerous. You *keep* playing with it because it's dangerous, especially if it could burn you and the whole world down.

So no one would find out. No one *could* find out. Especially since he was six years older than me. Especially since we were both boys.

They'd freak out! It would be the end! And we couldn't let it end! Even though it should end. Even though it needed to end…

But we couldn't stop…

We *couldn't*…

Because we loved how it felt…

How *we* felt…

Even though we knew we were playing with fire…

Because fire is always hungry.

So we kept hiding from the world and seeking each other. Every Sunday. As our parents talked of worship and ministry and all that God was doing in their lives, in their boys' lives.

But then I moved away…

Moved away from George…

And the burning raged…

To feel again…

To touch again…

To burn it all down…

But George wasn't here…

And I was all alone…

Alone with my burning…

But here's the thing about the glorious internet…

You're never *truly* alone.

A girl screamed, and my world changed forever.

"What's wrong?" I ran into the computer lab.

"A naked man popped up on the screen. I can't get it out of my head!"

"That's horrible! I'm so sorry that happened! What was the exact website and exact search you ran, so I don't *accidentally* see it too? I'd hate to see a naked man! That would be terrible!"

"I searched 'Billy Boyd' on AltaVista. I was trying to show Kyle one of the actors from *Lord of the Rings*."

I will forever remember Billy Boyd and AltaVista. (And *Lord of the Rings*, but that's just because it's one of the most amazing cinematic series of all time.)

For those of you who are too young to remember, AltaVista was a search engine like Yahoo and AskJeeves. They all existed at the beginnings of the internet before Google monopolized it all. Now we just use Google like it's a verb, like it's the only way to search anything, like all other search engines never existed. But to me, AltaVista would *always* exist.

I was attending a private Christian school at the time, and I was a horny twelve-year-old in the early 2000s without a George. We didn't have the internet conveniently dangling in our pockets, ready at our beck and call (or any time our hormones called). We had to *dial* the internet on massive computers that could barely fit on our desks, let alone in our pockets.

So after school, since my mom was a teacher (at my private Christian school) and I was left alone for hours after my final class, I would go to the library (at my *private Christian* school) to look up naked images of men (*at my private! Christian! School!*).

Jesus Christ, save me.

Nervously, I darted my eyes everywhere, like I did with George, scared to get caught but burning with desire. While hiding at church, desperate to satisfy the fire burning within me.

This could destroy me. Burn the whole world down.

My sweaty hands typed "AltaVista"...

Then they nervously moved the mouse...

Clicked the search bar...

Typed "Billy Boyd"...

Deep breath.

Enter.

And my repressed, gay heart leaped for joy and terror!

Naked...

Men.

And thus began the long history of horny, closeted Brandon, looking up gay images at my private Christian school.

Yet secretly devouring image after image wasn't enough. I needed more.

So I convinced my 70-year-old grandma, the one who sometimes forgot my name, that she needed a computer. After all, Grandma, how else are you going to keep in touch with all your other 70-year-old friends? On the phone? So 1970. You need a massive computer that can barely fit on your 70-year-old desk.

But she never used that massive computer.

I did.

All the time.

All.

The.

Time.

But then my youngest nosy brother kept coming in, nearly ruining it all. So I convinced my family that the *one* computer my *whole* family shared should be in *my* bedroom because, after all, *I* use the computer the most. To do homework. To do *so* much homework. Like, *so so* much homework. Because I was a *good* student. A *really* good student. And I attended one of those private Christian schools. And you know how *they* can be. *Sooooo much homework.* And I *care* about my grades, mom and dad. I care a *lot* about my grades. Like a *whole whole* lot. Because I'm *such* a good student. A *really really really* good student.

And on and on it went…

Because fire is never not hungry…

It always wants more…

And it raged…

In the small confines of my closeted soul.

My sexuality was always something I dealt with in secret. I knew that if *anyone* knew, I would be labeled a pervert, an abomination, a reprobate.

I had heard the sermons. I had learned the jokes. I had seen the look of disgust on my dad's face every time a gay character came on the screen.

So I had to keep it under wraps…

Even though I so desperately wanted to explode…

Even though I was furiously burning inside…

Slowly suffocating from the lack of oxygen.

Here's the thing about fires: they are desperate and living. And like any living thing, it refuses to die. It scrapes and claws to survive, scrapes and claws to eat again. And when it's deprived of that precious oxygen, when it's shut and locked away for years upon years, that desperation grows and grows and grows, till a door or window or crack finally opens, finally gives way. And when it does, that inferno leaps forth in ravenous rage, ravenous hunger, gasping for breath, destroying everything in its path, exploding with vicious retribution.

It's called a backdraft. And for me, that tiny little crack, that sip of oxygen, was my doubt in God.

For decades, I had not acted on my attractions because I wanted to please God. (And I didn't want to go to hell, you know, light stuff.)

Every Sunday I went down to the altar, crying and praying, asking God to change my attractions, promising him I wouldn't look at porn again.

The commitment would last till *maybe* Thursday (if it was a good week), and the process would start all over again.

Porn. Guilt. Altar. Promise.

Porn. Guilt. Altar. Promise.

I would rise and fall, rise and fall, trapped on some horrible roller coaster that I couldn't escape, my stomach and heart leaping and lurching in my chest.

But I couldn't tell anyone. I couldn't let anyone hear my screams. So I'd muffle them. Shoving words like "lust" and "porn" into my mouth because any time a squeal would escape my lips, any time the words "gay" or "men" or "same-sex" would whisper with breath, people would panic.

They'd call for the elders.

They'd lay hands upon me.

They'd exorcise me.

They'd alert the staff.

They'd call specialists.

So it must stay hidden…

It must remain a secret…

My own *horrifying* secret…

No one could know…

But I knew.

And I knew God knew.

And that kept me from acting out my sexuality in any meaningful way.

But now I wasn't sure if there even *was* a God, let alone if he cared about my attractions. And if he *did* exist, he was an asshole. So fuck that asshole and fuck abstinence. I'm going to do what I've wanted to do since I was five. I'm going to finally open up the door…

Backdraft.

Like the beginning of a horror film, I posted a Craigslist ad.

"Slim dude looking for playmate."

(The language is reminiscent of hide-and-go-seek and George.)

But that's *actually* what the title of my Craigslist ad read. As if getting naked with someone was some "play date," some cute and childish thing rather than some serious grown-up thing.

Ready or not, here he comes.

Next thing I know, I'm in a random guy's house.

And yes, the small talk is awkward, in case you were wondering.

"So … you've done this before?"

"Sorta. You?"

"Nope. First time."

"Cool."

"Cool."

"What do you do for wor—"

"Wanna get naked?"

∽

When all is said and done (with barely *anything* said and honestly barely *anything* done), I sit in my friend's car, staring at nothing, tears streaming down my face.

What did I just do? What just happened? Who am I, and is this who I want to be?

My stomach lurches with shame. My mind races with panic. It's all too much. I can't handle this alone.

I call a guy named Frank, an ex-pastor I know. We've been having fairly open conversations about doubt and fear and anger towards God and also about me being gay. But I would never say *gay*. It's always "same-sex attracted." It makes it less personal. It puts it at a safe distance. "*I'm* not gay. I just *have* same-sex attraction. What I *have* is this problem. *I* am not the problem."

Never once did Frank freak out or try to "pray the gay away" or try to exorcise me. He just held space and heard my story.

It made me feel safe. Safe enough to call him immediately after fooling around with some random guy from Craigslist.

"Hey, Brandon. What's up?"

I immediately start crying, words stammering and stalling, bottlenecked while trying to escape my mouth. I'm not exactly sure what I say, but I think the words "man" and "hookup" and "I don't know what to do" eventually get out because Frank is just quiet. Horrifyingly quiet.

Is he thinking? Praying? Whatever he's doing, can it stop because the silence is deafening?

"Brandon, I think this is a *kairos* moment. Do you know what 'kairos' means?"

No clue.

"A kairos moment is a divine moment where God is near and there's some destiny in the air. I think right now might be one of those moments, and I don't think I'm the best person to talk to. I think God is." (I'd later learn that "kairos" is just the Greek word for timing. Christians love taking Greek words and assigning mystical language to them. It's like a formula: dead language plus mystical meaning equals Christian hand job.)

Problem, Frank—God and I aren't on speaking terms. We haven't spoken since he decided to be an asshole and I nearly shat myself in a dive bar!

But I don't say that. I say, "K, thanks, Frank. Bye."

I stare at the trees while a familiar pressure builds in my chest, the same pressure I had while trying to push down the lyrics at that horde-cult place, that same familiar pressure that woke me up underneath the willow tree in Geneva.

Fine. I'll talk to God, Frank. But I need help. I need to be somewhere pretty. Because pretty things help me believe there may be a pretty God. Like that one time under the stars, asking God for a brother.

I turn the keys.

The car doesn't start.

I turn it again.

Nothing.

"Fuck!"

I pull the lever to pop the hood.

I unclick my seatbelt.

Nothing.

"Come on!"

I press the button again.

It doesn't release.

"What the fuck?"

I pull at the belt.

It refuses to budge.

Nothing is working!

Frustrated, I slam my hands down on the steering wheel and scream, "Why the fuck do you keep trapping meeeeee!"

That head/heart/gut voice talks, the one that atheist-evangelist Rachel says is just the part of my brain associated with schizophrenia.

Because I'm not willing to let you go.

I begin to sob. It's been a long time since I've heard that God/schizophrenic voice speak, and as much as I hate to admit it, I missed it. I missed the voice.

My hand reaches over the console to the passenger seat. I form a fist like I did on those walks in Berlin, and it feels like a tether, like I'm grounded. I'm no longer adrift. My anchor has struck something, and now waves of emotion beat against me.

I begin pouring out my heart, telling the God voice how I feel, and asking him what the hell I should do.

I feel like the God/imaginary/I-don't-fucking-know voice in my head/heart/gut says, "Root."

And then I ask him/they/it/whatever what that means. I feel like I hear that I should stay in Colorado Springs, that I shouldn't move to Greeley, Colorado for school, and that I should cancel the show I had written and cast.

The plan, up till that point, was to move on with my life, to enroll in school, and chase my dreams of writing and acting. Greeley seemed like the best option, and I was on my own anyway. There wasn't a God out there who cared. So I needed to figure this out my way, figure out how to live by myself.

But here was this voice saying I needed to simplify, to focus, to not race off and try and survive.

But like any interaction I have with God, I have to be a little shit and make it into a deal, like that time I would only let God into my heart if he made me powerful, the time I prayed for a baby brother.

But it wasn't just then. I had done it a lot over the years.

During my time as a missionary, there was a girl having panic attacks, scared she was going to get sick from the water in Nepal. As she panicked and cried, I felt like God was asking me to give her the water purifier I had bought from REI specifically for my time in India.

I too was terrified of getting sick from the water. That's why *I* bought the water purifier. *I* had planned for my crippling anxiety about getting dysentery. *I* was prepared.

But I couldn't shake the feeling that maybe she should have it. I said I'd give her my water purifier *only* if God promised to keep me from getting sick while in India.

Deal dealt, I gave it to her, headed to India on nothing but a literal prayer to curb my dysentery panic. So when I started to throw up, I screamed at my body. "No! We made a deal with God! Body, you get to throw up *one* more time, and then you're done. Get with the fucking program!"

I vomited one more time, and I never got sick again ... in India.

As soon as my plane landed in *another* country, I began to violently hurl for hours on end, as if my body was making up for lost time. And while huddled over the toilet, I thought of the deal I had made:

I said I couldn't get sick while in India ... *I guess God* technically *came through. What was that about the devil's in the details?*

Learning nothing from my time abroad, I barter with God *again.*

"Fine," I say to imaginary voice/God while sitting in my friend's borrowed car like a crazy person. "I'll stay. But I want a better job and to move out of my parents' house."

I had been living with them for a year after coming back from Germany, helping take care of my brother. But he was now stable, and I needed to get out, or I was going to lose my mind.

That day, I would email my school and withdraw my registration; that night, I would text my cast and cancel the show; and the next week I would get a better job.

But weeks would pass and the living situation would not come through.

We had a deal, God! I've set up a living situation with four different people, and all of them have fallen apart! I gave up school and moving to Greeley for you! I did this for you! You need to hold up your end of the deal! You need to come through! I need a place to live!

Like everything else, I was set up for a joke, giving up college and a show, just so I could live in my parents' house and rub ultrasound gel on people's butts. (My new job was at a physical therapy clinic.)

What the hell, God! Where are you?

A Not-Christian-
Frat-House Thing

I'm at an angry-at-church party. Ted Haggard's church had started a not-church college-group thing where they meet every week to get drunk and judge all the other Christians for being so judgmental. (Yes, the irony is palpable.)

My brother is attending this not-church college-group thing, but he needs a chauffeur, because, you know, the whole leg-is-still-broken thing. So, being the responsible older brother that I am, I go to the party and stick around. It didn't make sense for me to drive all the way downtown just to turn around and pick him up in a few hours. Begrudgingly, I stay at the party. (When in actuality, my self-sacrificing ego feels great. It loves hurting so I can look like a martyr.)

In classic, introverted-emo-Brandon fashion, I sit on the couch and don't engage. I mean-mug the entire room, judging all the judgmental ex-church people for their judgment of judgmental church people. (The irony continues.)

Then, a Brazilian with his master's degree in sociology decides to sit down next to me.

We chat for a bit, till a guy named Matthew sits down next to him.

I would later find out that Matt joined the conversation to hopefully flirt with said Brazilian sociologist. But Matt is let down when the man departs. Now Matt is stuck with a boring, judgy, introverted, emo white guy who doesn't even have a bachelor's degree, let alone a master's.

However, despite his disappointment, Matt and I hit it off, deciding to snag coffee the following day.

Here's the deal with Colorado Springs—there's a lot of evangelicals. Like, a *loooot* of evangelicals. And then there are those who aren't evangelicals: the anti-evangelicals. You really only get two flavors. (Well, that, and tired military families. But they never get out because, well, they're tired.)

So Matt and I go to a bar/coffee shop/meeting house run by "cool" Christians who just want to create a "safe space" for people to "meet and build community," hoping to "be a light" for the anti-Christians. Problem: the place is full of Karens and Richards from the megachurch down the street who "couldn't help but notice" (a.k.a. eavesdropping) "you talking about the church" (a.k.a. they're feeling threatened by people's pain), "and I wanted to come over" (a.k.a. lack of consent) "and share how *my* church is different" (a.k.a. no true Scotsman fallacy).

So much for creating a "safe space."

I finish my coffee and head up to the bar, when I notice a cross tattoo on the barista.

Again, in douchey-judgey-introverted-emo-Brandon fashion, I say, "Nice cross tattoo. You a Christian or something?" (That sentence could *actually* be read as nice. Don't think nice. Think sarcastic and flat.)

"I mean, sort of. But I consider myself more spiritual than religious."

I throw up in my mouth a little, knowing I would have said that exact same thing a year ago. "I'm more spiritual than religious" roughly translates to "I don't really like being associated with Christians because Christians are assholes, and I don't like looking like an asshole, so I say 'spiritual' instead of 'religious' because that makes me look better, and, after all, isn't it all about looking bett— I mean having a relationship with God—not religion?"

Cross guy introduces himself as Chris, and he goes on to talk about how he recently moved from St. Louis because he "felt like God brought him here." (He would later feel that God told him to marry a woman he just met and move to Michigan with her. I hear they're doing well.)

"I honestly don't know why. I don't know what's in Colorado Springs for me (apparently a wife), but I do know I'm supposed to be in this community house."

I've literally been disengaged the entire time till he says the words "community house."

"Community house? What's that?"

Chris does a terrible job describing this place. It sounds like a halfway house/Christian fraternity/cult thing. But I have an affinity towards cults. And I also hate living with my parents. So I go off to investigate.

"What's the address of this place?"

A bit later, Matt and I finish up our second cup of coffee, and I invite him to come check out this halfway-house/frat/cult thing with me so that I don't die alone. Remarkably, he agrees, and we walk together.

When we finally arrive at the address Chris gave us, we're greeted with a gorgeous Victorian home, complete with iron fencing, white pillars, a red door, and a majestic oak tree nestled in a budding garden.

The iron letters on the pillar read 1211.

For a cult, this place looks pretty nice. (Said everyone who ever died in a cult ever.)

We stare in awe, moving around the fence, trying to get a better look.

"It doesn't seem culty." Matt says. "Maybe it's associated with the college right down the street? Like some Christian-frat-house thing?"

"Maybe. I honestly have no clue."

"Can we help you?" A stern, bald man exits the house, hands on his hips.

Matt and I continue to gawk like creepers.

"Yeah, my friend is interested in your Christian-frat-house thing!" Matt shouts over the fence.

"Excuse me what? This is *not* a frat house. You guys need to leave!"

"Sorry! Forgive my friend." I jump in, nervous how the conversation is going. "We talked with your roommate Chris. He said you guys are doing some community-house thing and that you're looking for roommates. Again, so sorry. We didn't mean to offend. I was just curious. Seems pretty cool. But we'll let you go. Thanks!"

Stern bald man visibly relaxes.

"Sorry! Just got a little nervous." He approaches me and reaches out his hand over the fence. "My name is Aaron."

His shake is firm, like his voice and eyes.

"Aaron! Where did you—Oh … Oh, hi!" A whimsical redhead with an airy voice exits the house. "My name is Ela! So nice to meet you! Do you guys know Aaron?"

"No. We just met."

"Chris invited them to come check out the house."

"Oh, lovely! Come on in! I just finished cleaning."

They open the wrought-iron gate and lead us into the house.

"Do you happen to know your Meyers-Briggs?" Ela says as we enter.

"Meyers-Briggs?"

"No worries. We'll have you take a test before you leave."

Three weeks later, I move in…

To a place I didn't fight for…

To a place I never saw coming…

While I was too busy trying and trying…

Hoping to get into a house…

Any house…

All of them failing…

Every door shut…

But maybe it's because something or someone was shutting door after door…

Refusing to let me simply get a house…

Because a simple house wasn't enough…

It had to be more…

So every door shut…

Shut in my face…

And I got angry…

But maybe there was a reason…

Maybe *this* was my reason…

So that I could find my way to a not-Christian-frat-house thing…

A not-Christian-frat-house thing…

That somehow…

Became a home.

1211

This chapter is hard for me. It's hard because 1211 was so special, and I know I will never be able to adequately explain and describe all that it was for me, especially in prose.

Prose works under the assumption that, with enough words, or rather, with enough *right* words, you can adequately render a proper description. It seeks to make things clear and concise. It doesn't thrive in mystery.

Poetry is different. Poetry dances, gently hinting and wafting its essence, never letting us quite bite into it. A nearness without touch. An afterglow without image. And yet somehow, its essence is all the richer. The lack of clarity somehow creating a deeper impression.

A poem. That's what 1211 was...

A kernel went flying,
Tossed to the wind and swept by the storm.
Dancing without purpose,
Angry, forlorn.
Hardened on the stock
And broken by the gale,
The kernel unstopped;
It would not beguile.
But as fate would allow,
Winds thrust it down,
To a gentle soil,
Tilled and plowed.
Fate would further bless,
A glasshouse be built

'Round this harden'd kernel
Warm soil and silt.
Protected from the storms,
Ever cast a beaming light,
Till that harden'd kernel
Found a home of deep delight.
With safety formed,
And comfort felt,
That kernel broke;
Its shell did melt.
Tendrils crawled;
Leaves emerged;
That kernel grew,
Stretched encour'ged.
It had found a place,
Hidden from the storm,
Full of love,
Full of warmth.
Yet no one quite knows,
What might have happ'ed
If the kernel kept flying,
Lost, untrapped.
But as fate would allow,
Nay enforce,
That kernel came home,
Yes, but of course.
For fate would have its way;
It would not be denied,
'Specially when
It loved a kernel, hard and tried.

In Colorado Springs's Old North end, sits a gorgeous Victorian home with white trim, gray walls, and an inviting red door. And on August 1, 2014, a hardened, angry kernel of a human would literally wander in off the streets to a place that would forever change his life.

Of course, it wasn't the gorgeous home with blushing gardens that changed the kernel. Of course, it wasn't the French doors and the cozy fire and the hammock hidden amongst the trees that softened its shell. It wasn't the cheap rent or freezing cold room. It most certainly wasn't the haphazard furniture that was hand-built or found.

No, it wasn't any of those things.

And yet, defining what it *was* is quite elusive as well, for it was no singular part, but its sum and all the connections in between, those magical forces holding it all together.

It was the six of us cuddling up on the couch, feeling safe and warm, crocheting by the fire.

It was laughing after family meals because the cheese made me gassy, and we all knew the smell was me despite my atrocious lying.

It was arguing over who was trying to kill Abi with gluten because they didn't clean the dishes well enough.

It was falling in love with Christmas for the first time, as we sang carols, roasted chestnuts, and bought cheap-but-meaningful gifts, because being known is more important than being lavished upon.

It was all of us curling up in the same bed to read books as the snow gently fell.

It was the weeping as I told everyone I looked at gay porn and thought I was going to be kicked out because this would be the moment when I would normally be kicked out. But instead, I was loved and held and protected.

It was Aaron and I walking under autumn leaves, talking about my anxieties of being gay and Christian, or if I even was Christian.

It was Dallas holding me after sharing I was terrified of being physically close to men because I didn't want to look *too* gay or *too* clingy or *too* much, but how underneath the fear, I desperately wanted to be physically close.

It was Ela contagiously laughing, Aaron gently smirking, Janell high-pitched squealing, Abi raucously dancing, and Dallas playing spontaneous songs.

It was the coming home to friends who were truly happy to see me and truly *saw* me—*all* of me.

It was safety and warmth, truth and vulnerability.

It was adventure and pain, loss and love.

It was fighting and disagreeing yet still being there for each other after the dust settled and the tension laxed.

It was the picnic by the river.

It was crying with smiles.

It was saying goodbye, goodbyes that hurt, because we gained something we weren't sure we'd ever get back.

1211 was the place where God, or whoever or whatever they were, began to whisper to my heart that maybe I could trust them, even though I didn't have the answers.

Why do horrible things happen in the world when there's an all-powerful God?

Why has the church caused so much pain when the Bible says the church is his bride?

Why is my brother still awaiting a miracle, recovering two years after the accident?

To be honest, I don't know. I didn't get answers that year. I didn't spend it reading books or seeking scholars or studying theology, ironing out my beliefs with tact and poise. I didn't lock myself in a cloister until the divine spoke the mysteries of the universe to my heart in the shadows.

I stumbled into a house because I made fun of a barista with a cross tattoo. I was cynical and mean and messy. But I stumbled in nonetheless, and it made me believe that maybe there was someone or something looking out for me, and maybe I was okay.

In a word, 1211 was a greenhouse. For a year, I was protected from the storms of life, and it softened my heart and warmed my soul as I was showered with his kindness, and in the end, hope sprouted from the surface.

God, if he or she or they was there, was good to me, and no matter how my faith would change and move and bend, no matter how many times I would have more questions and more concerns about God, the Bible, the church, then I would always come back to the fact that this beautiful place was a gift. And it was a gift that I did not fight for—it was given to me, by something or someone that is good, by something or someone I could maybe trust. Just maybe.

In the end, I will be forever grateful for that greenhouse, for that home.

But just as every oak tree can't stay in a greenhouse forever, I too couldn't stay within those glass walls. It was time to throw me back in the storm, and oh, how it raged.

Part Four

Stalling

She waited for the material pictures which she thought would gather and blaze before her imagination. She waited in vain. She saw no pictures of solitude, of hope, of longing, or of despair. But the very passions themselves were aroused within her soul, swaying it, lashing it, as the waves daily beat upon her splendid body. She trembled, she was choking, and the tears blinded her.[1]

Kate Chopin

Bodies

I'm sitting in a car ... again ... except now this one is mine, though the house I'm parked outside of is not. Not even close. It belongs to some stranger I just had sex with, whose name I can't remember. Scratch that. It belongs to the twenty-second stranger I've had sex with, whose name I can't remember.

The last few months have been rough...

❧

My relationship with my girlfriend, Anna, took off. We were doing it. Well ... not *it*. Because we were good quasi-Christians with a backlog of purity culture playing on loop in our shame-informed brains. Thanks, Joshua Harris.

What I mean by "doing it" is "dating."

I had called Anna, the ex-girlfriend from YWAM, and we started talking again. And then she moved out to Colorado. And now we were officially dating, believing God for this whole "straight" thing. And I'd be brutally honest with her (i.e., I would tell her I just looked at gay porn). And she'd be brutally honest with me (i.e., she would tell me she slept with her previous boyfriend right before moving out here). And then I'd get a semi-boner because I'm a dork, and emotional vulnerability apparently gets me hard. And then I'd race home to tell my roommate, Dallas, about my semi-boner, like I was some crazy twelve-year-old because apparently trusting God looks like getting semi-boners.

"I got a boner!"

"You did?"

"Well ... not exactly. Like a semi-boner. Like I could feel my pants expanding a bit."

"That's a good thing, right? Normally when I get a boner with a girl, I view it as a bad thing because I'm trying to be a good Christian. But in your case, I guess it's a good thing. Is it a good thing?"

"Yeah! Well … I think it's a good thing! It means this might work!"

"Alright, man!" He'd give me a high five, and I'd skip down the hall to take a shower while belting Adele as loud as I could in celebration of getting a half-boner with a girl.

My friends would cheer me on, believing God was doing something special.

My parents would house Anna, talking about how cute we were.

It's happening. It's really happening. I can live a normal life! I can be with a woman! Screw my attraction to men! I just needed to find the right *girl! And Anna is the* right *girl! I'm doing it! We're doing it! It's finally happening. God is finally coming through! And I'm getting everything I ever wanted…*

This is everything I ever wanted … right?

Wanting to prove to myself and others that I didn't need a community house to succeed, I moved out of 1211 and into some friends' basement. Plus, I really wanted to stay in 1211, and I have this weird relationship with desires where I do the exact opposite of what I want, believing that God wants me to do the thing I hate (probably has something to do with the fact that my natural desire to be with men was labeled evil and perverted, but what do I know), and I hated being alone. Perfect!

I needed to stand on my own two feet. I needed to do this alone. Right? That's important, right? To do this alone. That's what all those straight, Christian twenty-somethings do that take dating far too seriously. They stand on their own two feet, or rather four feet, to become a couple. It's called interdependence or some other psychobabble that they say in those straight Christian complementarian marriage books that everyone reads.

Well, apparently, our four feet weren't very strong, because after a month of living in my friends' basement, Anna and I broke up.

And a few weeks later, I downloaded a hookup app…

And a few days later, I slept with a stranger…

And a few weeks after that, I slept with another…

And then another…

And then another…

Till my conscience forced me to tell the friends whose house I was in…

And then they asked me to move out because they were uncomfortable…

So I moved into another basement…
The perky-smile basement…
With all the black felt…
And people singing to a God I wasn't sure I believed in…
While I was thinking of the last man I was with…
The last *stranger* I was with…
Buried under shame…
And then life became too much…
And I had no clue how to move forward…
I was lost…
I was overwhelmed…
I was confused.

Did I make a mistake leaving 1211? Should I have stayed with Anna? Should I have tried harder? But I like guys! But do I like this? I don't know if I like this. *And what will everyone think? What do* I *think? What does life look like from here? Where do I go? What's next? Is there any going back?*

The panic rose. And as it did, so did the body count. One stranger. Two strangers. Five strangers. Ten strangers. In two months, I went from zero to twenty-two bodies, shame ravishing me over and over again, causing me to oscillate between feeling like shit, deleting the app, then downloading the app again because I still felt like shit. Compounded shame as Alan Downs calls it.[1]

Download. Delete.
Download. Delete.
Download.
"Hey."
"Hey."
"Looking?"

That's all it takes. Three messages. And it's always there. So close. In my pocket. Not my grandma's computer. My pocket. At my beck and call.

We send pictures. We set the terms. We chart our course.

There would be no risk. No question. No uncertainty. (Except that maybe he looks nothing like his photo or that maybe he wants to take advantage of me or that maybe he has an STD or that maybe he's actually a homophobic serial murderer or that maybe he's a crazy person that falls in love immediately after sex and won't stop texting me and now I have to block him and the other three accounts he's made to try and get in touch with me. You know, the usual risks. The run-of-the-mill risks. *Those* seem light in comparison to the heavier things,

things like rejection, commitment, broken hearts, shattered denial, and accepting my reality as a gay man. Yep. Hooking up. That seems better.)

The deck is set and counted. The bets are made.

My friends text, asking me where I am.

Ignore.

My mom is curious if I'm coming over for dinner.

Ignore.

I race through the streets in my car, checking my phone to make sure we're still on, always talking to at least three other guys at once.

(Men are all flakes, including me. So you have to be ready. You have to anticipate them bailing. You have a first choice, second choice, a third … all the way down to the man you don't even find attractive, but you know he's desperate, and you're desperate, and you can't find anyone else, and it's now 2 a.m., and you need this because you can't think about anything else.)

All there is is the desire…

All there is is the need to have sex…

All there is is this moment…

No more panic…

No more shame…

Just *this* moment…

This tunnel…

Where *all* else disappears.

I pull up.

My heart is racing.

Terror used to riddle me with questions.

What will he look like? Will he be into me? Will I be into him? Will he be too closeted? Will he like it? Will I like it? Will it hurt? Am I ready? Do we talk? Or get right to it?

Now I just go in, have my way, he has his, and we move on. Like nothing ever happened. Because I would like to pretend that nothing ever happened. It was all just my imagination. A fever-dream wet dream.

After it's said (or not said) and done, we both get what we want.

We shake hands. We say, "Thanks, dude." And I move on with life as if the other person is a neighbor who just helped me move a couch, as if he just did me a favor, as if this isn't at all abnormal or uncommon, and now it's back to business as usual.

Mutual gratification.

You scratch my … back, and I'll scratch … yours.

I leave. Sometimes shaken. Often numb. Mind *always* clear as I emerge from the tunnel and shame greets me on the other side.

This isn't who I thought I would be.

That thought is always haunting, contrasting my now-person with the hypothetical-person I've made up in my head that somehow always makes the right decision and lives the perfect life, shoving it in my face, reminding me that it *could* be mine if I would just make better choices, if I would just stop, if I would just get my shit together.

I think of the first time I hooked up. The night the word "Root" came to mind. The night I heard that God/divine voice.

It came through. Clear.

I gave up things. It felt right.

God delivered.

I experienced community and love and hope and beauty and all those wonderful things people write songs about.

So what happened? Am I too far gone? Does God only come through once? Did I use my one-and-only get-out-of-jail-free card? After that, do you have to figure things out on your own? What do I do? Where do I go? How do I stop?

The voices are too much…

So I drown them out…

With the tunnel…

With more bodies…

Then drive home…

As if it's a Tuesday…

Because it often *is* a Tuesday…

Or any other day…

Just give me sex.

Because I *love* sex…

I consume it, and it consumes me.

But I *hate* sex…

It dominates me and screams in my face, raging, disgusted.

Yet I *need* sex.

It lets me hide and makes me feel good, when all of life is anything but good.

But I *need* to *not* need it.

Because when I *need* it, I can't think of anything else…

It's all-consuming…
Nothing else matters…
Nothing else exists…
Just me and my tunnel.
I'm propelled forward by an uncontrollable urge, by a racing current. There's too much momentum, too much force. If I try to stop myself, if I try to climb ashore, I'll be dashed on the rocks; I'll be smashed to bits.
Instead, I'm taken…
Swallowed whole…
All that exists is the light at the end of the tunnel…
The light on the other side…
I must go there…
I must see this through…
Till I exit that safe and secret tunnel…
Till I emerge…
And the euphoria fades…
And my eyes focus…
And I can clearly see…
See I'm defeated…
See I'm ashamed…
Don't talk to me.
Don't touch me.
Don't look at me.
I need to get out.
I can't stay here a minute more.

Till the tunnel calls me again…
Till I'm lured to its wretched womb…
Birthed…
For perpetuity…
Through desire…
Through pain…
Through filth.

That is…
Till I meet *him*.

Flags

Outside is the prayer house, enthroned with hundreds of American flags, violently thrashing about...

Just like my stomach.

It's as though I've swallowed a thousand bees, and they refuse to still, questions whipping and whirling about in my chest.

Who pays?

Should I be wearing something less nice?

Were skinny jeans too much?

Do gay men like it when you dress up for a date?

Or are they like straight guys and don't care?

Should I pretend like I care less?

But I do care.

I care a lot.

Is that bad?

What's that smell?

We had been talking via text for weeks, never hearing each other's voice. Then, we mustered the courage for a phone call, never seeing each other's face. Then, we FaceTimed, never touching each other's bodies.

But *now* ... now it is time; now he's on his way; now we're going to finally meet, and now ... I'm panicking!

What if he grabs my hand?

Do I grab it back?

What will people think if we hold hands?

What about kissing?

People get uncomfortable with kissing.

Besides, do I even like kissing?
I didn't like kissing girls.
But do I like kissing boys?
I can't believe I'm doing this.
Do I wanna do this?
What if this is a mistake?
What happens if it all goes wrong?
Or worse, what happens if it all goes right?

As red, white, and blue whip and wave outside the prayer house, murky memories surface…

⌒๑

…We step out of the car. Tonight, there is only one flag at the prayer house, not hundreds. Just one, and it sags at half-mast.

There's barely any wind. Just enough for the cleats to knock gently against the metal pole.

Dad leads me forward. His pace is quick and determined.

"Pick it up." He calls but doesn't look back. His gaze is fixed on the door.

I quicken my pace, but I don't look up. *My* gaze is fixed on the ground.

He ushers me forward, speed-walking down the foyer. We're both anxious. Anxious that we might run into someone we know.

We enter the main prayer room where he points to a chair, telling me to take a seat.

Still no eye contact.

He exits the room, leaving me alone with nothing for company but a massive globe dominating the majority of the room and a pungent smell dominating the air.

It's hard to describe. But anyone who's been to the prayer house knows it well.

It's sort of clean. And yet not. Like clean sweat or sweaty cleaner. Makes perfect sense.

For decades, thousands of men and women have laid prostrate in this room, sobbing into the floor. For decades, desperate teens have danced and paced, sweat flailing from their bodies.

Tears and sweat. Both have found a final resting place in that dated carpet.

Day after day, faithful custodians attempt to remove it, but it never works. The smell refuses to leave; the musk now dressed in cleaner.

It evokes a comforting promise: through hard labor, you too could be cleansed; by tears and sweat, you too may bring about purification.

That's why my dad had brought me here: to purify me, to make me clean, to make me whole...

To make me straight.

That's right. My dad brought me here, to the house of prayer, to "pray the gay away."

It was the only thing he could think of after catching his son looking at gay porn just moments prior.

"What are you looking at, son?"

The screen had frozen while my heart did nothing of the sort. It threatened to burst out of my chest, just like my secret, a secret so dark and shameful, a secret I had been hiding for as long as I could remember.

But here it was...

Frozen...

In the open...

For all to see...

But more importantly...

For my *dad* to see...

And I was terrified.

"Brandon. What. *Is.* That?!" His finger pointed to the screen, shaking in rage. He kept asking the same question over and over and over again as if asking it enough times would somehow change the answer. But the answer was always the same: his son was looking at gay porn; his son was a faggot.

After his relentless questioning didn't resolve the problem, he decided he needed to try a different approach: the prayer house.

A magical, mystic place created by Pastor Ted Haggard before his fall. It would stay open every day. Every night. Every hour. National flags would surround its walls, reminding its supplicants the heathen world needed their God. Needed to be saved. So the faithful would pray. They'd worship. They'd seek their God. And God would answer.

Yes, the prayer house would fix this. The prayer house would fix his gay son.

My dad returns to the room with its big globe and steadfast smell.

Our eyes still don't meet. It's as though he believes my sins are his, and by meeting my gaze, he would be confronted with his guilt: "Failed father," the eyes would read. "You weren't man enough," they would say.

He doesn't utter a word. He touches me on the shoulder and motions me to follow, leading me out of the main room into a side corridor.

He opens a closet and closes it behind us.

And here he prays...

Here he makes his petition...

Here his prayers would be answered...

With just enough sweat...

With just enough tears...

This would work...

This *had* to work...

Just like the smell promised.

He closes his eyes. He looks deep within his soul, searching for the reality he wants to see—a straight son—and maybe, if he prayed long enough, believed hard enough; maybe, if he sweated from zeal and cried with passion, maybe if he squeezed his eyes tight, tight enough to block out the world, tight enough to block out the reality he didn't want, then maybe, just maybe the vision in his mind would somehow become real; maybe, just maybe his son would be cleansed of his filth, the filth of homosexuality, though he never says the word because saying the word would make it real, and this can't be real.

But just like that clean musk refused to go away, my gay refused to go away. My dad was stuck with it. I was stuck with it. No matter how hard and persistent the prayers; the gay refused to go.

A father's prayers would go unanswered...

And his son would shake from the shock...

Frozen...

Exposed...

Like the men on the screen...

But now it's him...

Sitting in a closet...

Again.

❧

…Colors of Zimbabwe and Sri Lanka dance on her olive skin, as the flags flap and flick outside.

We sit here, with coffee between us, at the bookstore hidden in the prayer house.

Further in the building, diligent worshipers pace, kneel, and cry, adding their tears to the carpet.

But we are not pacing. We are not kneeling.

However, we will be crying.

We've been laughing about nothing and everything for at least an hour. I have something important to say, but I push it off. I don't want this moment to end. It's too sweet and the future too bitter. Just a little while longer.

But slowly coffee turns cold; the exchange dies down, and the only thing that drowns out the silence is the screeching milk and cherished memories…

…Kidnapping my best friend on his birthday to watch one of the most disappointing sunrises.

…Napping on a miniature golf bridge after watching the elderly power walk through the mall.

…Competing at a cook-off where my best friend slaughtered his pig, impressing the judges, and the girls complaining it was cheating.

…Dancing beside a pond after bailing on homecoming—the bright moon above and discarded Chick-fil-A wrappers far better company than the thrumming music and throbbing bodies.

I smile as the memories return. Every moment, meaning so much…

…*meant* so much.

I begin to speak without looking up from my cold coffee.

"This has to end. We're going in separate directions."

The words come out as if an adult said them. But I'm not an adult. I'm sixteen.

You don't think about mature things like "going separate directions" or marriage and kids or careers and passions and all those heavy but lovely things at sixteen. You're barely thinking about *college* at sixteen. Instead, you should be thinking about the latest video game, the acne that refuses to go away, the cliques at school that you both hate and yet want to be a part of, the homework you forgot about over the weekend, and, most importantly: cute, annoying, immature, impulsive love.

But not for me. It's always been heavy—love. It's no joking matter. It's for keeps. It's for a future together. It's for marriage. It's for propagating the world with more of your acne-ridden spawn. And if it didn't end in marriage, if it didn't end in forever, you shouldn't entertain it, you shouldn't let it even come into your mind.

This *had* to end.

We had to end.

I take a deep breath. I muster courage. I act like an adult. And I say the adult words.

"You want to move to Africa and be a missionary. I want to move to the city. I love you, but we're eventually going to have to part ways, and that's not fair to either of us. We need to stop now before this hurts worse than it already will. I can't be your boyfriend, but the man who gets to be your boyfriend will be so lucky because you're amazing! You really are! We're just not going in the same direction, so this needs to end now."

Silence floats between us. Then comes the foreshadowed crying.

Through soggy eyes and a weak smile, she looks back at me. "Thank you … of *all* the things you've done, *this* is the moment I have felt *most* loved and cared for by you, because you fought for my heart."

I smile back at her, matching her tears.

Of all the moments…

Of all those unforgettable moments…

This is the one where she feels the most cared for…

The moment we say goodbye.

∽

The memories fade as my present sinks in.

Of *course*, this is where two men on Grindr would meet. Of *course*, this is where my gay love story would begin. Of course. It *had* to be the prayer house. It had to be. It was where my dad tried to pray the gay away. It was where I broke up with my first girlfriend. And now, now it is where I would rendezvous with some guy to go on my first gay date. Of course, this is where it begins. It just made sense.

What doesn't *make sense is that smell!*

Did I forget to put on deodorant?

Do gay guys care if you wear deodorant?
Do they want you to smell nice like girls do?
Or do they want you to smell rank like a man?
Am I supposed to feel like this?
Am I supposed to feel this much?
Care this much?
Ask this many questions?
The bees buzz. The flags whip. My car idles in silence.

Then his Jeep appears in the distance, and my stomach lurches.
I can't believe I'm doing this.
I can't believe I said yes.
What will everyone think?
How will my family respond?
How will my friends respond?
What if this blows everything up?
Is it worth it?
Do I even want this?
If I don't, why has this yearning never gone away?
What happens if it goes poorly?
What happens if it goes well*?*
WHAT HAPPENS IF IT GOES WELL?!
WHAT ON EARTH IS THAT HORRIBLE SMELL?!
He pulls up…
His Jeep adjacent to mine…
I force a nervous smile…
He smiles back…
A smile more confident than my own…
We roll down our windows…
"Hey…"
"Hey."
The bees stop.
The questions go unanswered.
    And all that can be heard is the thunder of the raging flags as they violently thrash about, while two gay men hold each other's gaze.

Electricity and Fire

I was saving it for marriage. Not sex. That wasn't enough. My first kiss.

While all those other horny teenage boys were unable to keep it in their pants, I would be better. I would do the hard thing that God asked us to do. I would be holy. I would be true. I would be the blessed virgin. And I wouldn't just offer my wife a virgin penis but virgin lips and a virgin mind. Look at me! I'm so clean I don't even watch porn with women in it...

I was saving myself for something better. Something beautiful! For love! And I loved love! It felt like something magical, and I love magic!

A spell would be cast with love's first sight; wars would end with star-crossed unions, and entitled princes would free sleeping beauties with a non-consensual kiss as fireworks and lanterns lit up the midnight sky.

Electricity. Fire.

So I threw myself at love. I'd wow my girlfriends with extreme gestures—keeping and pressing the rose from our first date, writing a fairy tale to display our love, dressing up as Aladdin while serenading on a rug strapped to my father's car. I'd write poems and pack surprise picnics and dance in foamy fountains. I'd compose letters to my future wife, and I'd pray for her like Rebecca St. James, the patron saint of Christian pop music, told me to.

I was the good and wholesome romantic virgin knight every Christian girl dreamed of!

Small problem: it wasn't for the girl. It was for beauty. It was for magic. It was for love.

Because I loved love! And in the end, I'd hurt any girl that got sucked into my too-good-to-be-true vortex.

I remember the first time I kissed a woman...

I was twenty-five (Yes, fucking twenty-five; perks of being a good-ol'-closeted-gay Christian boy), and I was planning yet-another-crazy-romantic gesture due to my love affair with love.

I took my then-girlfriend, Anna, to Helen Hunt Falls, a gorgeous waterfall named after the author, Helen Hunt Jackson, nestled at the base of a mountain, hidden in the back of a canyon. It was midnight as my car wove up the snaking two-lane road, the moon and stars smiling upon us.

"It's a good thing I trust you," she said, "because if I didn't, I'd say this is the perfect opening for a horror film!"

"*Or*! Maybe *because* you trust me, it's the perfect opening for a horror film!" I maniacally laughed as she glared at me with one of her fake glares, the kind where she tries to look intimidating, but you can't help but smile.

The two of us are some of the *least* intimidating people on the planet—I used to drive a red Vespa, and she carried a pink children's umbrella with little green frogs on it. She named it Matilda, and we'd take it on our adventures into the city. Her getting angry was like watching a beanie baby curse.

I parked the car and strode around to her door, opening it like some gentleman.

This had to be perfect. Every second. Leading up to the grand finale. Because this was a big deal. This was going to be my first kiss.

We skipped up the steps, as I held her hand, making sure she didn't fall.

We crossed the stone bridge where the water thundered underneath.

I turned to face her.

"Anna Elizabeth Poole," I declared like an adult version of Alfalfa. "It would be my great honor and privilege to share my first kiss with you."

"Are you sure?" She said to me, like a boy on prom night.

"Yes! I've never been more sure!" I said, like a nervous girl on prom night.

I leaned in.

She leaned in.

We kissed.

"How did I do?" I asked, eager.

"Typically, you open your mouth."

"Dammit! Dallas told me to open my mouth! Can we try again?"

We leaned back in.

We kissed.

Mouths now opened.

And then I pulled away.

"How was it?" she said with a beaming smile.

"There was more teeth than I expected," I said, like a girl on prom night.

As we walked back to the car, my then girlfriend deflated, I began to think.

Where was the magic? Where were the fireworks? Maybe the movies lied. Maybe this is what love actually is.

For years I thought I didn't like kissing or holding hands or cuddling or even being touched. It all felt like a chore, like something for *her*, like something you sucked up and did because *she* liked it, not because *you* liked it. Love wasn't about electricity and fire; it was about service; it was about duty; it was about sacrifice.

Then I kissed him...

It's December. Christmas is right around the corner, and, like a cheesy Hallmark movie, my town erected an ice rink downtown, equipped with laughing children wearing red mittens. Carols play over an old sound system, and snow gingerly falls on the ground, as we cup our hot chocolates to stay warm.

The moment is perfect.

But, *unlike* a cheesy Hallmark movie, we don't touch. Not even a little. We can't risk it. Not in our hometown. And definitely not with our internalized homophobia. We don't wanna look "too gay," as if it's some competition.

So instead of leaning into each other like some cute couple, we stand close, oh so close, so close we can feel each other's warmth. And instead of holding hands, we walk down the street; our pinkies every so often "accidentally" caressing. And instead of staring into each other's eyes, we go to a costume shop and put on masks, so we could sneak in glances as the mask comes on and off, daring to drink in as much of the other person as possible with the store empty and bare.

Don't touch. Don't hold hands. Don't gaze. Don't do anything that might bring unwanted attention in this little Hallmark town.

So we go back to that dark parking lot, and we get back in his secure car.

We close the doors and seal ourselves in our own little world.

We say we had a great time.

And then we laugh.

And then we get quiet.

And then we laugh from the quiet.

Then quiet again.

Till the silence builds.
And the pressure builds.
Then he turns to me.
And I turn to him.
And we gaze.
Unapologetically gaze.
Pressure building.
Anticipation building.
Then he leans in.
And I lean in.
And then we kiss…

And in this moment…
I.
Love.
Kissing!
And I don't want it to stop.
So I don't stop.
I keep kissing and kissing and kissing, breathing and breathing, breathing him in, breathing as deep as I can, as hard as I can, lips locked, tongues locked, eyes locked, till my lungs burn for air, but I burn for him more, as our lips hold each other, and our *eyes* hold each other, as *we* hold each other, late into the night, forever into the night, because I never want this moment to end, never to end, safe in our little locked-Jeep world, safe in our dark parking lot.
Touch. Gaze.
Electricity. Fire.
Oh…
I get it now…
I get those horny teenagers…
I get why they couldn't stay pure…
Because this whole time I wasn't holy…
I was just gay.
But like all moments, whether holy or horny, imperfect or pure, they must come to an end.
So at two o'clock in the morning, we drove back, his hand holding mine the entire time, refusing to let go.

We pull up to my car, the car sitting in the parking lot of the local prayer center: home of ex-gay prayers and sad ex-girlfriends. Now home to my first gay date, where I learned I liked kissing and what the movies were all about.

He parks, and I take a deep breath, knowing our time is coming to an end.

"I had a really good time tonight," he says.

I blush, nervous if gay men are allowed to blush.

"Me too." I whisper.

I look down in embarrassment, then back up and into his dark brown eyes. They're brimming with excitement and tenderness.

"I wanna see you again. You free tomorrow? Is that too soon?" (For straights? Yes. For gays? No.)

"I am."

"Great! I'll text you."

"Sounds great!"

"Great!"

"You're great!"

"No, you're great!" (And now I get how cheesy love can truly be.)

He leans in again, and I kiss him again, only this time more tender and tame. Our eyes open as our lips touch, drinking in as much as we can before we say goodbye.

"Goodnight, Brandon."

"Goodnight, Henry."

I open the door…

Close it…

Then I open mine…

Close it…

I look out my window…

Over to him…

Over to him and his tender-tame brown eyes…

We smile…

Then drive away…

When I get home, I throw myself upon the bed, pulsating with life and pleasure.

Not terror. Not shame.

Just electricity and fire.

This is new.

Up until this moment, every night with a man ended with shame and regret.

But this ... this was different. It wasn't just two people using each other to make it through the night; it wasn't just two strangers metaphorically shaking each other's penis hands.

It was something more. It was something ... good?

I smile, falling toward sleep as my body pulsates with warmth, when that familiar building tension in my chest wakes me from descent.

How was it?

God? Universe? Imaginary best friend who I conjured up to gossip about a date?

I smile and roll with it, comforted that I can share my joy with someone since I have to hide it from the world.

It was really great. It felt like the movies. I get it now. I get why everyone goes crazy with love.

How did it feel when he held you?

I blush at the question, this time not caring if gay men are allowed to blush.

So good! So so good! It felt right! It felt safe!

I feel that voice inside is smiling at me, a selflessly blissful smile, a smile that comes when you see someone you love experiencing absolute joy.

Regardless of what happens, the voice says, *remember that no one will hold your heart like I do.*

I smile at the thought, peace befriending my joy.

I reach out and form a fist, holding hands with that stable anchor.

Maybe God had me. Maybe I was okay. Maybe this *was okay.*

And with that, I drifted to sleep, dreaming of Hallmark films, buzzing and burning with electricity and fire.

The Farm

"So you're driving to Utah?" my coworker asks.

"Yeah! Well, close to it. Like five miles from the border," I reply.

"Tonight?"

"Yep."

"To spend the next week with people you met online?"

"Yep. I met them through my blog."

"And you've *never* seen these people before?"

"Nope. She emailed me and said I should come, and I said yes."

"You just said yes?"

"Yep! Why not? Time away on a farm? Sounds like a dream!"

"With a woman and her husband you've never met?"

"Yeah! She seems lovely, though, based upon our emails."

"What time are you getting there?"

"Around 9:45 tonight."

"And where exactly are you meeting them? On their farm?"

"Well, not exactly. They said their farm is hard to find, so they're meeting me at the highway exit, and then we'll drive to the farm together."

"And this *all seems fine* to you?"

"Yeah!"

I have a habit of doing things I probably shouldn't.

My best childhood friend, Dan, and I used to joke that every year there would be a lottery for our guardian angels because a year was all an angel could take. We'd dramatize it, talking about how the previous angels would be standing on the lottery podium, hobbling on crutches and covered in bandages and scars. The head angel would thank them and congratulate them for surviving the year. The guardian angels would then leave the stage whimpering and stumbling while all the other angels anxiously held their breath as new names were drawn. (Dan and I also had a habit of being melodramatic.)

But in this moment, I didn't need a guardian angel. Because contrary to how this sounds, I didn't get abducted or raped or trafficked as a drug mule. Instead, I had a phenomenal week with a phenomenal new friend. The best of friends. The type of friend where you keep asking, "Where have you been hiding my whole life?"

Leah is a wonderful lesbian that ended up marrying a man. She grew up in evangelical Christianity, just like me, and also, just like me, she was heavily involved. Volunteering all the time. Leading in the youth ministry. Joining all the small groups.

And as she was coming out, embracing her sexuality, she fell in love…

…with a *man*.

"I'm not attracted to men, Brandon. But I *am* attracted to Zay. He's my person. I can't explain it. It just happened."

Their story is incredible, full of crazy moments like when Leah felt like she needed to confess her love of Zay to the girl Zay had just started dating, or like when Zay said yes to dating her knowing she was a lesbian, or like when she quit her teaching job to buy a farm with her new husband, or like when she invited a complete stranger to their farm to spend a week with them because they both happen to be gay and both happen to be kinda-sorta Christian.

One would think that Leah would be the type of person who would advocate for her story, telling the world that hers is the right one. "If you would but trust God, your life could look mine!" I think a piece of me even wanted her to be that way, to tell me to model my life off of hers, to tell me to trust God and get over myself.

But she didn't. She never did.

"This is *my* story and *my* story alone. It doesn't make sense to *me* some days, let alone the rest of the world. But I wouldn't trade it. Zay's my person. My story is *not* for everyone. The lesbian couple who runs the pizza shop in town is just as loved by God as I am. Your friend who is choosing to be a celibate gay man is just as loved by God as I am. Who am I to dictate their story? That's between them and God, and faith looks different for everyone."

Throughout our time together, I asked all the questions, like *all* of them. Thankfully, Leah and Zay weren't intimidated by my lack of boundaries.

"What's sex like?" "Are you going to have kids?" "Zay, do you ever get nervous about Leah being gay?" "Leah, do you ever feel like you're not enough?"

And then we'd share stories, stories that I always felt like I held alone.

"You thought God was telling you he wanted to give you life and life abundant? Me too! I thought I might be hearing voices!" "You fought for the LGBTQ+ community in the church before ever coming out? Me too! I thought I was just being a good ally!" "You argued with the pastor when he said something dumb? Me too! I thought I was just being an ass!" (I was definitely still an ass.)

My time with them was beautiful and redeeming, giving me hope.

Maybe I could date this guy and I could be okay. Maybe God is *actually for me.*

When I came home, I posted a horrifically long and repetitive coming-out video. (Literally forty-three minutes of me stammering about how I like a guy.)

I wanted to be authentic. I wanted to trust that *maybe* God was in this. And I felt that being honest about my journey was important. So I posted a video, saying I was dating a man.

And it all went to hell…

∽

…"I'm scared for you, Brandon." I'm sitting at Starbucks with a missionary friend who's stateside, raising funds. He made time in his busy schedule to "catch up." Except it wasn't to catch up. It was to jump me.

"Not only are you on a dangerous path that will lead you to hell, but you're playing with someone else's soul. You might be the reason this man" (he can't say the word "boyfriend") "spends eternity separated from God. Do you really want that responsibility? Do you really want to gamble with someone else's eternity?"

I squirm in my seat, staring at my coconut milk cappuccino. (This is why I still get anxious when someone asks me to coffee.)

∽

…A friend calls. "I can't support this, Brandon. I can't support you being with a man. The Bible is clear. You need to repent."

"Okay. Cool. Thanks." I awkwardly say as tears and panic crawl up my throat. "Listen, I have a meeting I have to get to. I'll call you back later."

I never call him back later. In fact, we never speak again.

❧

…My old boss/pastor/friend emails me. "I need to create some distance, Brandon. I'm in church leadership. I'm a pastor. I need to be mindful of how it could come across if I'm seen spending too much time with you."

What would it look like, Joseph? How would it come across, exactly? Do tell. Could it maybe look like you cared? Like you're for people regardless of if you disagree?

And I would later learn that "some distance" roughly translates to "never see or speak to you ever again."

❧

…My dad texts me. "Do you really want to give up God's plan for your life? You're letting the Devil rob you. Don't let him win."

He and my mom had been fighting. I had offered we could go get coffee to get out of the house, in order to get some space from it all.

He was running late, so I texted him, asking him where he was.

Queue text above about God's plan.

I had been living with them for a few months after the friends I was staying with asked me to move out after they learned I was hooking up. But I couldn't spend another night with my parents after reading that text.

I went to the house, packed a backpack, and left, unsure of where I'd be sleeping that night.

❧

When all was said and done, I lost my entire support system—my friends went silent, the church I worked for pretended I never existed, my parents refused to let me move my furniture out of their house.

I had to start over. All because I came out. Because I got honest. Because I tried to live authentically.

When people think being gay is a choice, I think of these moments; I think of what being honest with myself and the world cost me, and the price tag is pretty fucking high, especially when you come from a religious background like myself.

According to the American Journal of Preventive Medicine, queer teens from religious backgrounds are far more likely to commit suicide than their non-religious counterparts, and it makes sense as to why.[1]

Armed with verses, parents, pastors, and lay people believe it's their job to "teach you a lesson in love," and "in love" I've been called "unnatural," "demon possessed," "immoral," "wrong," "deceived." "In love," I've been argued with, silenced, and mocked—not from atheists, but from those who "Love the sinner, but hate the sin." They are the ones who caused me the most pain—the ones who apparently serve a God whose name is Love—and they took everything from me, after I gave them the first twenty-five years of my life. That's the thanks. That's the repayment.

And we wonder why queer people never want to step foot in a church ever again.

⌒

Maybe I'm horribly wrong. Maybe everyone else is right. After all, there are so many of them and only one of me. Who am I to say that I know better? Who am I to question God?

I'm standing in Leah and Zay's field, staring at the purple-orange sky, paralyzed by fear.

Desperate, scared, and alone, I went back to the last place I felt safe, back to the farm.

Sheep bleat in the distance. The desert hill turns gold as the sun sets.

And all the conversations over the past few days weigh upon me...

⌒

"...I'm not sure what to do, Henry. Maybe we should break up. Maybe we should just be friends. I'm just so scared. What if everyone else is right? What if this is wrong?"

"I knew you'd do this! I knew you'd run! I saw it in your eyes the first time I met you."

"I'm sorry, Henry! I'm just scared. What if what the Bible says is right? What if we're going to hell?"

"What is *so wrong* with loving someone? I don't understand, Brandon. Sure, the Bible says that gays are going to hell. But it also says liars and thieves and hypocrites are going to hell too. That rules out all those shitty Christians. If they're not making it in, who is?"

"But what if God said gay people won't inherit the kingdom of heaven because it's actually bad. Like maybe there's a reason. Maybe it's bad for us somehow. Like a dad telling his kid to not touch the hot stove. Maybe being gay is…"

"Stop it! Just stop it! I can't keep doing this anymore, Brandon! If you can't date me, fine. I get that. But you need to decide because I can't do this again. I *won't* do this again."

"I thought you said that you'd be there for me no matter what I decide."

"I can't keep doing this rollercoaster with you, Brandon. You need to make a choice."

∽

"…What if I get hurt? What if I hurt *him*? What if this turns out *really* bad?"

"What if it does? Sometimes pain is the best teacher." It's Greg and his wife, Tiffany, from the perky-smile horde place, the ones who let me sleep in their basement when I couldn't find anywhere else to stay. "I say go for it. Even if it all goes wrong, you now learned something. Besides, do you think you'll spend the rest of your life looking over your shoulder if you don't do this now?"

"Absolutely. I *know* I'd regret it. I know I'd wonder for the rest of my life what could have happened. I *need* to know."

"Well, then I think you have your answer."

"But what about hell and God and sin and all that?"

"If it is wrong, I think God is capable of intervening. I think a loving father would save his son if he was ruining his life. You're gonna be okay. Regardless of how this turns out."

"Thanks, you guys. Thanks for being there for me. It means a lot."

∽

The cold of the desert night crawls on the air as the final sunbeams disappear over the horizon.

I can't take it anymore. I can't go blindly forward. I can't just accept that this is not okay. How could loving someone be bad?

I begin to pace down the freshly tilled field, talking aloud for the sheep to hear.

"God, I can't *not* do this. I need to try. I'm not able to say goodbye to Henry. I've tried and tried and tried. And I just can't! I need to try! I'm gonna date Henry."

And there in the field, I made another deal with God.

"If this is horribly wrong, if this is going to send me to hell, blow it up, destroy it beyond repair because I've tried to walk away, I've tried to end this, and I just can't. I can't…"

I fall to my knees and cry. It feels like I'm mourning everything I've ever known to try and make this work, and that reality wrenches my stomach.

Nearly swallowed up by the feeling, I force it down, wiping away my tears.

I stand, a new determination set within me. My eyes glare at the golden horizon.

"But if I'm *not* going to hell, I want this, and I'm going for it."

I turn from the field and head towards the house.

The sun sets.

The bleating sheep quiet.

And the stars come out to shine.

Ammonia

Ammonia is a vital resource. It's an explosive fertilizer that supports 60 percent of all food production in the world. Without it, we'd die, which is crazy because it's composed of hydrogen and nitrogen—two of the most abundant resources on the planet. You are breathing both right now.

But in order to change abundant nitrogen and hydrogen into an explosive fertilizer, a very strong bond must first be forged. To do so, shove nitrogen and hydrogen in a vacuum, create intense pressure, add heat, and then, introduce the catalyst: iron.

Before the catalyst, you just have a bunch of hydrogen and nitrogen, heat, and pressure.

But once the iron is introduced, nothing will ever be the same. Something new is made.

Henry was my iron.

After Henry was introduced to my life—a life of building pressure to be there for everyone in my family, a life of feeling utterly alone in a vacuum after being abandoned and hurt, a life of burning passion and rage as I jumped from body to body—I was forever changed. I was forged into something new, and there was no going back. Moving forward, my life was either going to be enriched or blown to kingdom come.

Before Henry, I could clearly tell myself that homosexuality was wrong. I was putting ads on Craigslist and building a profile on Grindr, sleeping with stranger after stranger, cutting them off the second I shut the door behind me.

Of course, this was wrong! No wonder the Bible says it's bad. Look at all the sex gays have! Look at all the sex I have! This can't *be good! This* can't *be right! Because sex is bad! Sex is wrong!* (Thanks, purity culture!)

So every night, I'd get back online, forgetting my qualms with homosexuality, to find a willing stranger, to have sex, to wake up, to pretend nothing happened, and then to go about my life as if everything was fine, lying to myself and everyone else, lying about where I was every night, lying that this would be the last time, lying that tomorrow I'd repent and be a good boy.

That, my friends, is what we call denial, and it was working *really well* for me, and by "really well," I mean slowly eroding me from the inside out.

That is until I met a guy on Grindr who simply said, "Can I take you on a date?"

Of course, the answer was no. Of course, I couldn't let this happen. Because it couldn't happen. Because if it *did* happen, and I started dating the guy, now I was *committing* to a life of sin. Now there was no hope for me.

A hookup is just a mistake. A hookup is just a one-time thing. An oddity. You can repent of *that*.

You can't repent of a relationship. *That's* something you carry with you. *That's* something you commit to. It's not a one-time immoral crime you can pretend to repent of on Sunday morning then return to Saturday night. That was a "lifestyle I was choosing," as the angry pastor would preach from the pulpit.

So I'd say no. I'd say no because if I went on a date, then the guy would have a name, and if he had a name, it would be really hard to pretend he's not a person, and if he was a person, it would be really hard to pretend that the night didn't happen, especially when you enjoyed the night, every single second of the night, every beautiful, luscious second.

So that's why you say no; that's why you say no to the date.

Emotions complicate things. Better to just keep hooking up and keep pretending I'll eventually end up with a woman. Then I can pretend this was all one big bad dream. One horrible nightmare. Maybe I can even share a testimony of it one day. I can be like one of those drug-addict preachers. You know, the ones who are special guests and always get a lot of people to come down to the altar. One of those! I'd inspire people! I'd show them what their lives can be like if they would but give their lives to Jesus, if they would but come down to the altar, pray a prayer, believe.

(And how many times did that work for me?)

And that's why you say no to the date. That's why you say no. So that this can *definitely* just be bad. So that this can *definitely* just be sex. Forgotten with the morning. So that I can never ask the question: Why is loving someone evil? Why is loving a man wrong?

But I *didn't* say no to the date.

I said *yes*.

And then I went on the date.

And I liked it.

And I went on another date.

And I got a boyfriend.

And I liked him.

And he made me laugh.

And I liked kissing him.

And cuddling him.

And he began to feel like home.

And I didn't want to lose my home.

Not after I lost everything.

And I stopped hooking up.

Because I didn't want to hook up.

Because I didn't want a stranger.

I wanted *him*.

And I wanted a future with *him*.

And it's really hard to pretend that this wasn't going to go anywhere when you want to go everywhere with *him*.

And it's really hard to pretend that this is all just a bad dream when it's not a bad dream.

It's a good dream—scratch that—a good reality.

And you wanna keep that reality.

And suddenly it becomes really hard to imagine loving someone was ever bad.

Why is loving someone bad?

It was a question I could no longer afford to *not* answer, and boy did I try to find the answer...

After every cute moment with Henry, I'd hold my breath, waiting for something to go wrong. Because it *had* to go wrong. Because God said it was wrong. It's in the Bible. It's clear! Can't you read? It's black and white! It's right *here*! And God wouldn't just say something was wrong just for shits and giggles. Right? He wouldn't just take something beautiful from us just to be cruel. Right? Something had to be wrong with it. Something had to be broken about it.

But what was wrong with this? What was wrong with loving a man?

I would get anxious about gender roles in the relationship. "Who's the woman? Who's the man? Am I too feminine? Am I too manly?"

This is the reason God said no: gender roles!

I would panic when my boyfriend would make sexual advances, terrified he'd want me to bottom, and I hated bottoming.

This is the reason God said no: anal sex!

I would freak out over children we didn't even have; I'd freak out about how in the world we'd even *make* these children we didn't have, how they'd take sides because they only biologically belonged to one of us, how they would be bullied in school because they'd have two dads, how they wouldn't have a mother, and everyone needs a mother, right? And if we didn't have a mother, who would talk to our girls about their periods and explain sex to them and help them when they have their own kids that come out of their vagina? I don't have a vagina; do you have a vagina? Who's going to talk to them about their vaginas?

This is the reason God said no: raising kids! (And having to explain vaginas.)

Any time there was a blemish—whether present, future, or imagined—I would point to it and say, "That's it! That's the reason God said no! It's in the Bible. It's clear! Can't you read? It's black and white! It's right *here!*"

That's the reason. Because there must be a reason. God isn't just some dick who commands us to not do things we like because he hates us. He's looking out for us like a good dad, right? Like a good dad that tells you not to cross the street. That's what they told me in church. He's a good dad telling me not to cross the homosexual street. Because the homosexual street is dangerous. The homosexual street is bad. It's bad because there's a car. There's a gay car. A gay car that wants to smash you. But where's the gay car? Where's the rain-bow-painted gay car? There has to be a rainbow-painted gay car? Where is it? Where is it? When am I gonna get hit?

In the end, we broke up.

I hadn't done the work to put my sexuality and faith together (or to figure out what the hell even was my faith or lack thereof). I'd oscillate between gay Brandon and kinda-sorta-Christian Brandon, even though I wasn't even sure there was a God, even though I hadn't read my Bible in years. I was too scared to. What if I bumped into a verse that made me feel like I was horrible, sending me into a spiral of shame and fear, blowing up everything? After all, didn't I ask God to blow my relationship up if it was evil and wrong and sending me to hell? I couldn't let it blow up. I had to protect it.

So I put the Bible away.

And what about churches? None of them wanted me. Besides, what if there was a sermon that talked about how homosexuals were going to hell, and I freaked out, and it ruined everything?

Can't go to churches.

And what about the friends I grew up with? The ones I went to Bible school with and worked in ministry with? What if they wanted to "catch up," but in reality, they wanted to "warn me in love" over another cup of blasted coffee? And then I freak out, and I ruin everything?

Best to hide from everyone. Best to just do life alone. Best to isolate. That could be safe.

So I pulled away. I pulled away from it all. Pulled away from anything that could potentially trigger me and ruin my relationship. I insulated myself from the world, trying to save myself, trying to save my relationship from being blown up by God.

But after pulling away from the world, after doing everything in my power to defend the relationship, it still blew up ... because in the words of Henry, I was "too emotional," I was "too sensitive," I was "too spiritual," "too Christian," too "you-overthink-anything-and-everything-and-ruin-everything."

Too much. *I* was too much. That's what Henry told me when we broke up for the twentieth time.

But then he'd come back around after a few weeks, pretend like nothing was wrong, and I'd pretend like nothing was wrong, and we'd get back together because we needed to get back together. After all, this is who I sacrificed everything for. This *needed* to work out. *He* needed to work out. Regardless of what he said. Regardless of how he treated me.

So I got small. And grew dim. Because according to the partner who claimed to love me, *I* was too much. So I became small. Because small is never too much. But apparently, I was still too heavy because *I* was the reason it kept breaking. So I walked cautiously. I anxiously lived life, trying to not break anything. Because this needed to work; because if it didn't work, it meant that God was answering my prayer; it meant God was destroying my relationship; it meant I was going to hell.

But it *did* end.

Like a lot of relationships do.

Because sometimes relationships just end.

Because sometimes they *need* to end.

Because sometimes they're toxic.

Because sometimes they make you feel small.

Because sometimes, when you're a bundle of anxiety, trying to not make a mistake, you become afraid to live, afraid to be, and you should leave the relationship.

So sometimes, relationships *need* to end.

And that's normal.

Ending a relationship is normal.

But then the questions came…

Am I going to hell? What did I do? My heart has betrayed me. I dared to chase what my heart wanted, and it was wrong; it was so wrong, just like those Christians said. And now I've lost everything! I have no friends or family. They're all gone. They all left me. I left them. Was it all for nothing? Was it worth it? What did I gain by coming out? I lost everyone and myself and the partner I burned it all for. How do I fix this? How do I make this better? Who do I turn to? Pastors would tell me to repent. Friends would say they were right. Family would pretend the last two years didn't happen. And where have they been anyway? Where have they been for the last two years of my life? I'm all alone. I'm all alone in the world, and I have nothing to show for it. What have I done? Where is God? Where am I? I'm lost. How do I get back? Can I get back? Where even is "back"? Do I date a girl? Do I date a man? Can I date a man? Didn't I pray for God to blow up my relationship if it was going to send me to hell? Does that mean dating a man will send me to hell? Am I going to hell? Am I damned? Is this wrong? Am I wrong? Stupid, filthy heart! Stupid, filthy, deceitful heart! How do I fix this? How do I "ungay" myself? Can I ungay myself? Is that possible? Do I want that? What do I do? WHAT DO I DO???

And the questions piled…

One after the heavy other…

And the terror mounted…

Weight upon unbearable weight…

Till I was crushed…

Till I was frozen…

Too scared to proceed…

Till the tunnel called my name.

The Tunnel

"It's been a while. Where have you been?" The tunnel calls.

"I found love."

"How did that turn out for you?"

"Horrible."

"I won't let you down."

"You *always* let me down."

"But that's why you *love* me. You can keep your expectations low. You know what you're getting. It's familiar. You know how to handle *this* letdown. And you can forget it all come morning. All of it. But for *now*, pursue pleasure, feel pleasure, *be* pleasure. If only for a moment. If only for a sweet and savored moment. Yes, the world will come with the morning. Yes, your problems will still be there. But you escaped. You escaped for a moment. A blissful moment. Don't you want a moment? A breath? A break? It's just a hookup. It's just one night. You're not committing to this. You don't even have to know his name. And come morning, you can repent. You can pretend that was the last time. But *tonight*. Tonight, you can *feel. Feel* the touch. *Feel* them with you. *Feel* like you're not alone in the world. *Feel* like only this moment matters. Only this moment exists. You. With this person. This stranger. Together. Not alone. You can figure it out tomorrow. You can begin again tomorrow. But today. Today is too much. Far too much."

"Today is too much. Far too much."

"Give me your pain. Give me your fear. Give me your loneliness. Give me all that weight. All that tension. I'll hold it for you. I'll give you reprieve. While you step into me. Into the tunnel. While you enter my mouth. My wide open hopeful mouth. Only this matters. Only I matter. The tunnel."

I pull out my phone. That faithful siren. That faithful whore.

The Church

I decided to go back to the church. And not just any church. The church where I was a youth pastor.

I woke up smelling like guy number forty-two, and I thought that maybe, if I could just rewind time, just go back to where I was before guy number one, I could fix things. I could go back to where it all made sense. Back to where everything was clean and right. Back to easy black and white. To meaning. To community. To where I was a part of something bigger than myself.

I'll behave this time. I promise. I'll listen to what you have to say and not ask questions. I'll clean up my mess. Bottle it all up. Lock it away. Just let me come back. Let me come home.

…*But isn't this the place where everyone went silent after I came out?*

…*Isn't this the place where congregants pretended I didn't exist when they ran into me?*

…*Isn't this the place where my friend and pastor told me he couldn't mentor me anymore because of "how it would look"?*

…*Isn't this the place that excommunicated every person that was involved in that perky-smile place the second they started getting love from somewhere else?*

…*Isn't this the place that sent me off as a missionary, saying they'd take care of me, that I wouldn't lack for anything while "doing the LORD's work," then stopped giving me money soon after leaving?*

Isn't this the place?

Years later, a counselor would help me figure out this psychotic behavior: a behavior of returning to my abusers.

Despite Henry being emotionally unavailable, despite him lying and cheating, despite him going silent the second I didn't behave the way he wanted, despite him making me believe everything was my fault, despite it all, I *always* came back. He had broken up with me countless times. But I always welcomed him back the second he texted me, acting like nothing happened.

The reason?

Because he felt like home. And contrary to the cliché, home is *not* where the heart is; home is what feels familiar, even if familiar is abuse.

In a study by Kolk and associates, they explore why scared animals return to their usual shelter, even if it lacks resources or produces pain, e.g. electric shock. The re-exposure to familiar trauma produces a "paradoxical sense of calm and control due to endogenous opioid release."[1] Their minds have become addicted to what is familiar, and in the words of James Baldwin, "home is not a place but simply an irrevocable condition."[2]

Terrified, I had come back, back to the painful familiar, back to the endogenous opioids, trying to get my fix and fix all that was broken. I came back because ultimately, I believed this was *my* fault, *I* was the problem, just like Henry said, just like the church said, and *I* needed to beg for forgiveness. *I* needed to make this right.

Home sweet home.

So I sit in yet another car, parked in yet another parking lot, because cars, for some reason, always feel safe. You can lock the doors, roll up the windows, drive away, all while taking in the world from a safe distance, my safe little vacuum.

So let me stay in my little vacuum, dammit!

Problem: my magical vacuum wouldn't fix the mess I made. I had to go in. Into the church that had hurt me.

I'll go in at five past. That should be enough time, right? Worship will be going, and I can sneak in. Maybe I should go in at ten past. Just to be safe. But what if I miss something? What if I need to be there right *as it starts? What if God gives me a sign at the beginning of worship, and I miss it, making yet another mistake? I just keep making so many mistakes! I can't make another! But if I go in before it starts, I'd likely run into* people. *And people scare me. Because people are mean. Especially Christian people. What if they* glare *at me? What if they ask me to leave? Or worse! What if they want me to stay?*

Breathe. You're gonna be okay. Breathe. You're gonna make it through.

I begin lying to myself all over again.

I open my car door, leaving the safe vacuum, and briskly make my way toward the entrance.

I look down at my feet, avoiding eye contact, which proves to be impossibly hard since churches are notorious for having greeters whose *only* job is to *make* eye contact, to *make* sure "everyone feels safe and welcome."

Well, I do *not* feel safe and welcome. I feel judged. I feel scrutinized. I feel like everyone has stopped what they're doing just to look at me. To call me out with their gaze. Objectify me. No longer a person. A thing. A filthy thing. A filthy prodigal.

"Is that Brandon?"

"Why do you think *he's* here?"

"Hopefully he's finally seen the error of his ways."

"You know I heard he had a *boyfriend*. No wonder he stopped coming to church. Picking sin over God! And to think we let him lead our children."

"Maybe he's finally come to beg for forgiveness. To grovel to the church for all the pain he caused us! Serves him right!"

"Keep your head down, you little sinner! You dirty rotten little sinner! You know how much fear you caused me and my teenagers? How much confusion?"

"What if he did something to the youth while on those retreats? If he likes guys, who knows where the perversion ends!"

"It's a slippery slope!"

"Let's keep an eye on him to make sure he doesn't go towards the *children's* area."

"Good idea! He can't be trusted. Disgusting!"

"He's *so* disgusting!"

"Brandon?"

Keep walking. Those voices aren't real.

"Brandon!"

Wait. That voice is real.

I look up.

"Chris? Hey! Good to see you!"

Lies.

"Haven't seen you in ages, Brandon! Let me introduce you to my wife!"

A woman is ushered before me. Chris tells me her name. I immediately forget. Because I can't think about her name. All I can think about is how I *don't* want to be here, how I just want to get into the stupid sanctuary and have a stupid encounter with a stupid God who I don't even know if I believe in but maybe, if there is a God, he can make my stupid life better because my stupid life is a fucking stupid shit show. So move out of the way nameless-Chris's-wife! I've got a stupid miracle to find!

"How have you been?" Chris asks.

"Been good! Just working at a tech company."

More lies.

"I'm so happy to hear! I was wondering what you were up to after everything."

After everything? Is that what we're calling it? Is that what we're calling me getting ghosted by the church after I came out?

He takes a breath to keep talking, but an electric guitar begins to swell in the distance.

"Ope! Gotta get inside! Wouldn't wanna miss worship."

More lies.

I would very much like to actually miss worship. To miss all of it. To miss the sermon too. Why the hell *am I here?*

"No worries! Hey," Chris grabs my hand and intentionally looks into my eyes. (Remember your training, welcome team.) "I'm *really* happy to see you."

In his defense, he actually *does* look happy to see me, and that *does* make me feel a little more "safe and welcome."

Blasted Christians!

I rush into the sanctuary. I hide in the back. In the darkness. Where I can feel comfortable in the shadows. Just like those "unbelievers and backsliders."

Wait! I'm the backslider! I'm the unbeliever! Gasp! I used to judge them! I used to judge people who stood in the back. But now I'm the guy standing in the back! I'm the unbelieving backslider! Shun the unbeliever! Shun!

The worship pastor begins to speak.

"Well, good morning church! Thank you so much for being here. Isn't it a great morning to be worshiping the Lord together?" (I puked in my mouth writing this. If you've been to any evangelical church ever in your life, you can predict what happens next. We all know it.) "Let's go ahead and stand up together for worship as we pray. God, we ask you to come and enter this place."

I thought your Bible says he's everywhere.[3] *Be consistent, you hypocritical asshole.*

Fuck. We're not even one song in, and I'm already a cynical piece of shit. Stop being a cynical piece of shit, Brandon. It doesn't help. You came here to get a miracle. Be a good little boy, so you can get your miracle!

The band holds a long chord, letting it rise and fall as the worship pastor continues to pray.

Worship is like a science of emotions, and there are formulas for it all. Synth swells, building and diminishing, as a trendy pastor "welcomes all." After that, you open up with an energetic song, one that everyone knows and gets people excited. By the end, you slow it down with a heavy song, making people emotional and primed for the pastor. For an altar call, use one with a building bridge, one with the classic six, four, one, five progression—makes people feel like they're climbing a ladder, like they're accomplishing something.

Formula. It's all a holy, blessed formula. One that magically makes God move, that makes him "enter this place." Glory, glory, hallelujah! May the chords be praised!

Right on queue, after people danced at the front to a song about freedom, the musicians transition to a heavy song about how holy God is, a cello humming in the background to move the hearts of the worshipers, and oh how they're moving.

Many in the audience look up to heaven with closed eyes and soft smiles. Others hang their heads, looking like they're in pain. Still, others lift their hands and sway, like some whimsical Rafiki from *The Lion King*. The more fervent worshipers, the ones who believe volume equates to holiness, begin to shout louder than the music. "Yes, LOOOOORD. Yehhhhhs, Gawwwwwd. We ask you to cooooome LOOOOORD. Fill this plaaaaaace. Yes, Gawwwwwd. Yes, LOOOOOORD." (You know you're holy when your vowels get long.)

While the Rafikis sway and chant, I begin to pace.

I always did that growing up. Ever since I was a teenager. I don't know why. The music would start, and I would go to the sides of the sanctuary, pacing back and forth, back and forth. It somehow helped me, helped me feel like I was doing something rather than just sitting still or standing in place. Like I was accomplishing something important, and today, I *needed* to accomplish something important. My miracle. My holy stupid miracle.

But beyond miracle making, pacing helps with my anxious thoughts:

These people look ridiculous. Some of them probably cheated on their partner earlier this week. That guy definitely *cheated on his partner earlier this week. Look at that face. Look at him cry. Cheater! Hypocrite!*

And what about that one? She's smiling and swaying like this is some Florence + The Machine concert. Would she be swaying if she were terminally ill? Would she be swaying if she lost her leg? Doubt it. Fraud! Hypocrite! Fake Florence!

The criticisms rage—crashing into me, foaming white.

But underneath the waves, a piece of me genuinely *wants* to be like them. Wants to sway like the Rafikis. To cry with bowed head. To have faith. To trust. To hope. To believe. Believe that God is my friend and not my enemy. Believe there's meaning to the universe and my pathetic existence. Believe there's more to live for than the next trip or next purchase or next job or next random stranger I'm gonna sleep with.

A tension pushes and pulls within me, rises and falls with the music, making me nauseous. (Worship science.)

I used to be one of them. Maybe still *one of them?*

But not really.

I can't unsee what I have seen. I can't unhear what I have heard.

In the Deaf community, there's a volatile tension. While the doctors and researchers view deafness as something to be cured, consistently conjuring up new ways of making people "normal," the Deaf community doesn't see themselves that way. They see themselves as simply different. Not broken. Not needing to be cured. They're whole and beautiful, and they've fought for a community that is rich and dynamic, one that refuses to be "fixed."

But there are parents. And politicians. And healthcare professionals. And parents and politicians and healthcare professionals hear. They belong to a hearing world, and they want their kids to belong to it too. Belong with them. Besides, how could anyone *not* want to hear? How could anyone function without knowing the sound of their lover? How could anyone go on without hearing the voice of their friend? We need to help them. We need to help those Deaf people hear. And we need to do it fast!

So parents refuse to learn to sign and subjugate their children to dangerous and expensive surgeries, forcing cochlear implants upon non-consenting children, all so we can cry at the latest YouTube video where a kid hears their parent's voice for the first time.

And politicians pass legislation to make them look good but never enforce it, and the only way they'll listen is when Deaf advocates make them listen, make them listen by sitting in capitals and hiring lawyers and talking to senators, all so they'll listen, but they never listen.

Instead, professionals advise oralism, where you make your child read lips and not learn ASL, because the child needs to learn how to function in *our* world because we don't want them to be different. We want them to be normal. We want them to be like us. So surgeries and oralism for all!

And Deaf kids are robbed of Deaf culture because they're no longer Deaf. Not truly. But then again, they're also not quite hearing. They're in this odd in-between, and they can't go back. They can never go back. They're caught in the middle. Caught between.

And I can't go back. I'm caught in-between.

For my ears have heard the heart-wrenching stories of my friends raised in the church who will never feel like they're enough, who will always feel like a failure. My eyes have seen the racism, sexism, homophobia, and nationalism that refuses to be laid down at the feet of Jesus. My skin has quaked at the abuse that I and other queer folx have experienced in the name of God, in the name of holiness, in the name of preserving this "Christian" nation.

I can't go back. I can't unsee. I can't unhear. I can't unfeel.

And yet … there's this piece of me that *yearns* to unhear … to unsee … to untouch. To be caught up in the rapture of these worshipers, to get swallowed by the waves. I want to feel what they feel, sucked down by the one they call the Holy Spirit.

If it wasn't the Holy Spirit, what was it? Who was it? Was it me? Was it my brain? Was it groupthink? Groupfeel? Is that a thing? Maybe it's that formulaic worship music! Maybe that's been it all along. And even if I could unhear, they wouldn't let me back. I've gone too far. I've done too much. I'm forgotten. Cast aside. Damaged goods.

I dance between longing and denial. I churn between belief and unbelief. Because, at the end of the day, I *did* experience something in these walls. At the end of the day, I *did* taste something that I can't get out of my mouth.

I want it again, whatever it was. But what was it? How do I get it back? Can I get it back? But do I want it if it means looking like them*? I refuse* to look like *them. I can't. I won't. They've hurt me and so many others. I can't go back to looking like* them*. I refuse. If being a Christian means becoming them, I don't want it. I* can't *want it.*

When dialoguing with C.S. Lewis about why he doesn't want to be a Christian, Sheldon Vanauken wrote in his journal, "[The] strongest argument against Christianity is also Christians—when they are somber and joyless, when they are self-righteous and smug in complacent consecration, when they are narrow and repressive, then Christianity dies a thousand deaths."[4]

When Christians are bigoted, hypocritical, loveless, defensive, xenophobic, sexist, homophobic, all while crying the victim when someone calls them out, then Christianity is brutally murdered millions of times. It loses all power, loses all luster … a horrific mess seeping into the floor.

Christians are the number one reason people don't want to be a Christian.[5]

A God who chose to become man, a God who chose to suffer, to experience what we experience and feel what we feel, to showcase his radical love through a life of servitude and saving us from the mess we've made is one of the most powerful stories of all time. It's beautiful, lovely, and ultimately attractive.

But a good story needs to have a good ending, and this ending looks like a Greek tragedy.

Here's this God, who gives it all to the world, and in return, his people wear their Brighton bracelets and Nike sneakers, caring *only* about themselves. Here's this God, who dies a brutal death, and in return, his people pray for the victory of Trump and the deportation of foreign bodies. Here's this God, who loves the unlovable, and in return, his people say "AIDS is the due penance for homosexuality," and "They had a choice—the choice to not have sex." Here are these people whose history is the Crusades, the Inquisition, and Manifest Destiny—a history they refuse to own, or worse, a history they choose to justify. Here are these people who refused to speak to me the moment I publicly said I'm attracted to men, the moment I became honest.

Baldwin, the inimitable, Black, gay writer, wrote about his own time in the church, wrote about how he became a minister to feel safe, to belong, to find that problematic place called home. Eventually, he left, tired of the cruelty and immorality, the masked imperialism and control.

"It is not too much to say that whoever wants to become a truly moral human being … must first divorce himself from all the prohibitions, crimes, and hypocrisies of the Christian church. If the concept of God has any validity or any use, it can only be to make us larger, freer, and more loving. If God cannot do this, then it is time we got rid of him."[6]

And as I pace, looking at the holy hands raised and downtrodden heads bowed, I squirm and squeal.

These people are not larger and freer and more loving. They're small and afraid and hurtful. And I can't do it. I can't do this. I can't become them.

I stop pacing and begin to cry, missing the God I loved as a little kid. The God who I met under the stars. The God who healed dying kids and barren mothers. The God who electrified me in a pool with holy pleasure. The God who would lead me to cute coffee shops just because he likes me and knows I like cute coffee shops. The God who trapped me in a car and opened a door to a real home. The God who held my hand.

I miss him … I miss him so much…

But I *can't* become these people. I *won't* become these people.

And I leave.

The Bible

I open up my Bible.

It may seem odd, especially after my experience with church, but there was this itching inside me, a missing.

I was that dork growing up that would *genuinely* enjoy sitting down at a coffee shop with a journal and Bible, devouring as much as I could, ravenously attempting to find some truth that the millions of people before me hadn't discovered over the past two thousand years.

So when the church didn't help, I decided to pull out my Bible. And instead of starting from the beginning like any normal person, or randomly opening it up like some Bible roulette, I went straight for the verses about homosexuality. (In case you were wondering, yes, I'm that person who's horrible with small talk. I go straight for the issue at hand, and can't think about anything else till I clear the air.)

I turn to 1 Corinthians 6. It's one of the "clobber" passages: a term coined by ex-Christian gays because Christians have used these verses to "clobber" and abuse us. I wanted to get right after it and not fuck around.

"Do you not know that the unrighteous will not inherit the kingdom of God? Do not be deceived. Neither fornicators, nor idolaters, nor adulterers, nor homosexuals, nor sodomites, nor thieves, nor covetous, nor drunkards, nor revilers, nor extortioners will inherit the kingdom of God."[1]

Wait. It says "homosexuals" and "sodomites"? What's the difference? Why two different words for gay?

I reach back into my youth-pastor past and retrieve my handy-dandy theology tools for making sense of the Bible. Today's tool: looking up the Greek. (When you don't like something in the Bible, always go to the Greek.)

Okay, one word is "arsenokoitēs"[2] which means one who abuses himself or lies with a man as a woman. Okay. Got it. Gays won't inherit the kingdom of heaven. Cool, cool, cool. What's this other one? "Malakos."[3] Means soft, effeminate, a boy kept for homosexual relations, a male prostitute...

Wait, so the guy who is being purchased for sex is going to hell? The boy, kept for sex, is being sent to hell after living a life of sex slavery...

What the actual hell? This is bullshit!

And that was it. That's all it took. All of a sudden, I started to look at the Bible with these new eyes, no longer making excuses for things that seemed wrong, no longer doing intellectual somersaults to make things make sense. I decided to read the Bible as if I were reading it for the first time, and it changed everything...

Wait ... did y'all know this book commands genocide?[4] Like, according to this book, God demands that men, women, children, and even livestock should be utterly destroyed. Like, he wanted full-on nations utterly wiped out. Except for the virgins. You know, for like, spoils of war and shit like that because that's cool. Did y'all know that? Oh, you did know that? And we're all okay with God commanding genocide? Oh, there's context to why God wiped out men, women, children, and livestock! Oh, they were evil and needed to be utterly destroyed! But God doesn't do that anymore, even though there's a verse that says he's the same yesterday, today, and forever? How about the Crusades, the Inquisition, and Manifest Destiny? Didn't Christians use these verses to validate murder? Oh, they misinterpreted the Bible! Oh, but you have the right interpretation of the Bible! Got it, got it. Cool, cool, cool.

Wait ... did y'all know this book instructs women to shut their mouths in the church?[5] How do you women feel about that? You're cool with just keeping your mouths shut during service till you get home, so you can ask your questions to your husband because you can't be trusted to talk in church? Oh, you're not okay with that! Oh, there's context! Oh, it's cultural! So do we do that with homosexuality? Oh, we don't do that with homosexuality! Oh, because that doesn't need context! Oh, because that one isn't cultural. It's black and white. Got it, got it. Cool, cool, cool.

Wait ... did y'all know this book has errors between the Gospels?[6] Like Luke totally fucks up who the king is during Jesus's birth, and it doesn't fit with the other Gospels. Oh, there's a reason for that! Oh, translators must have made a mistake! Things got lost in translation over thousands of years. But the Bible is still perfect somehow? Oh, I just need to trust it. Got it, got it. Cool, cool, cool.

Wait … did y'all know this book celebrates prostitutes and polyamorous couples and kings who kept brothels as agents of faith?[7] Oh, but that's not okay anymore. Oh, because it was a different time. Why is that? Oh, because God works in mysterious ways and he uses anyone and anything for his glory! How about me? Can he use me for his glory? Is he able to use a faggot? Oh, he's not able to use a faggot. Oh, that's something totally different. Got it, got it. Cool, cool, cool.

Wait … did y'all know that the disciples weren't sure what to do with the Gentiles, so they scrapped the whole law and just gave them three laws?[8] They literally just rewrote morality. Did you know about this? Oh, you didn't know this! Why has no one talked about this? Oh, you're sure that your pastor has an answer for that because he always has answers for everything and can't be wrong. Got it, got it. Cool, cool, cool.

Wait … did y'all know this book has fucking dragons and unicorns and sea monsters in it?[9]

And just like that, it all came crashing down. One little thread that started with the gays and unraveled with genocide.

Maybe this is why you shouldn't be gay: makes you start actually looking at things.

I think of pastors from my past, "exhorting" (a nice religious term used to soften the phrase, "I'm ordering you!") his (because, let's be honest, it's always his and not her) congregation to "Trust God" and to "not doubt" or question the Bible. "Don't let the Devil deceive you," he'd say, spittle spewed on the microphone. "God will not be mocked!"

But he *is* being mocked. He's being mocked by what, when you objectively study it, turns out to be a pretty confounding, if not at times downright flimsy, book. And how can the Devil deceive me if my goal is truth? Is not God truth? Shouldn't truth *always* stand regardless of if I question or scrutinize it? Shouldn't truth remain steadfast? Shouldn't it stand against a gentle breeze? Shouldn't it resist fear because truth always wins? Why are we so scared to question truth if it's genuinely truth?

However, what if the book just isn't perfect? What if the book just isn't the "word of God" because the Bible never claims to be the word of God? It says *Jesus* is the word of God. What if this book was just scraped together by some men who took some letters and added them to the Old Testament because they were trying to support their agenda and then removed parts of the Old Testament that didn't fit said agenda? What if we don't need a Bible because the early church didn't have a Bible? What if it actually has flaws? What if it's actually *not* perfect?

Oh, but there's a reason those verses don't add up, and oh, there's a reason those verses command things we don't support anymore, and oh, there's a reason God commands us to be intolerant and judgmental and spiteful; there's a reason; there's always a reason.

Got it, got it. Cool, cool, cool.

Till it's not cool.

Till there are people marginalized by *your* interpretation of the Bible. Till I'm left paralyzed in a metaphorical corner, terrified to make one misstep because if I make one misstep, I'm going to hell. But it's okay if *I'm* going to hell. As long as *you* feel comfortable at the church picnic. As long as *you* get to keep your nationalism and white supremacy and misogyny and patriarchy and homophobia. Got it, got it. Cool, cool, cool.

I slam the book shut.

I'm out.

The Gays

"Don't end up with a dude, Zach. They're all terrible!" Matt blurts out, as Zach and I sit on the couch, drinking martinis.

Matt and Zach are roommates, gay/bi (respectively), and *not* partners: a fact Matt always has to bring up when introducing Zach. "So-and-so, meet Zach, my roommate. Yes, he's bi. No, we haven't had sex. No, I'm not lying." (As if it's something novel that two queer men haven't fucked each other.)

"I'm serious, Zach. All men are terrible! You're better off with a woman." Matt is on his third martini and is getting more and more vocal and more and more slap-happy. (I have red marks on my thighs to prove it.)

For a few months, Zach has been exploring all the colors of the sexual rainbow, trampling all over the spectrum. He's been with men, women; young, old; ugly, sexy. For Zach, it doesn't matter who it is; Zach just wants to have sex. He loves it.

However, Zach and Matt had just come back from Denver where Zach had a rough go with a group of gay men.

"I genuinely thought gay men were different," Zach says. "I thought I could be myself and be accepted, but these gays were assholes!"

"What Zach is *trying* to say," Matt elaborates, "is that he pissed these men off because he said, 'All gay men are easy,' and they tore. into. him!" Matt slaps Zach with each word for emphasis, laughing hysterically.

"What? It's true!" Zach says. "It's a whole lot easier to get in a guy's pants than a girl's."

"You think that's true, Matt?" I pipe up from the other end of the couch.

"Most homosexual men I meet are trying to become sexual as quickly as possible," Matt says. "Even with my ex, we had sex on the second date. I thought that was going a bit fast, but he didn't."

I had experienced the same thing, but I tried to be open to the idea that I was the exception or that maybe it was because I was meeting men on a hookup app.

But it's broader…

There's this book called *Faggots*. It's considered a critical piece of queer culture and history, written in the late '70s, right before the AIDS epidemic. It opens up with one of the characters being propositioned at a sex club to fletch: to suck cum out of another man's asshole.[1]

I thought the author was trying to shock me with a visceral scene, opening up the book with something crazy.

Surely, the content would change. It can't all be intense gay sex scenes.

It was.

Gloryholes. Sex parties. Meth. Cruising. Bathhouses. Orgies. All while the book focuses on depressed characters desperately wanting love and never finding it.

The book is so horrifically sad and abrasive, I quit reading halfway through. My body literally couldn't handle the intensity of the book, and I became frustrated and convinced that this is just our lot as gay men. I mean, after all, we're nearly fifty years removed from *Faggots*, and a lot of it is the same, except now we're terrified of catching HIV.

Or, maybe this is what you get, queer or straight, when you date men—a fierce hunger for sex that consumes body after body of which we have no control over.

In *I'm Afraid of Men*, Vivek Shraya, a trans woman, shares how, regardless of being in what was perceived as a man or woman's body, men assumed authority over her body. Grabbing her ass. Taking her clothes off without permission. Calling her a tease when she didn't "put out." At one point she dated a woman, not because she was exactly attracted to her, but because she felt safe. And when she finally decided to date a man again, the trauma of men followed her into a stable relationship, causing her to doubt her boyfriend's intentions at every moment.[2]

At my Bible college, in our "Godly Men" class (barf), the teacher would often talk about how much sex we'd have once married. The boys would yip and holler, pumping each other up to keep it in their pants because "one day it'll be worth it," one day you'll get to have all the sex you want, and it won't matter what your wife wants because there are verses you can beat her with that say to give it to you (and it's not like Christian men are taught to pleasure women anyway).

Men are consumed by sex, and when another man isn't, it's confusing.

When I go on dates and say I don't want sex on the first night, I always have to explain myself.

"What do you mean? You want to wait? Are you not into me?"

"You got trauma or something?"

"I mean, I'm a dude. You're a dude. We both know what all dudes want."

And that's when you're actually *trying* to date someone. Outside of dating, I could get a hookup with a guy a whole lot faster than with a girl (not that I've tried). All it took was downloading an app or opening a browser, and I could have sex within a few hours, if not minutes. And, not only could I have sex as soon as I wanted, but I could have sex with exactly the type of person I was craving, as if humans were consumables, as if they were treats.

If you're ever curious about how shallow and racist and ageist and ableist and misogynist the gay community can be, just download Grindr (or don't because you'll never unsee what you see, and you'll see *a lot*).

"Masc for masc." "Only into fit guys." "Only into white guys." "Not into Asians." "Not into fatties." "Not into hair." "Not into sissies." "Cum use me." "Ass up, head down." "Just looking to dump a load in a sexy bubble butt." "Just looking to get anonymous head." "Just looking for a workout/fuck buddy."

All *actual* profile headers I've come across during my use of the app.

And it goes beyond the users—it's also the app itself.

A filter for age. A filter for ethnicity (removed from Grindr after the Black Lives Matter protests of 2020). A filter for height. A filter for weight. A filter for body type. A filter for tribes. A filter for marriage. A filter for kinks.

You can "build your own boyfriend," except, we're all kidding ourselves if we believe it's a boyfriend—it's "build your own sexual fantasy." If we end up with a boyfriend, it always starts as a hookup, and then maybe we'll catch feelings, and then maybe we'll end up together, but then we'll likely ghost each other, then maybe come back, and then maybe get married, but if we get married, we'll eventually have an open marriage, because men are men, and we all know what men want. (According to a survey by Compare Camp, one in three gay men are in an open relationship while their straight counterparts report one in ten.)[3]

"Why bend to that heteronormative ethic?" they say. "Why bind yourself by cultural norms?"

So let's open up the marriage. Let's see other people. Let's not deprive our-selves. In fact, you know what? Let's share a boy. Let's have a threesome. That could save our marriage. That could fix things. After all, we both want sex, right? We both are never satisfied, right? It's like a never-ending hunger, and we need to keep feeding. Right? It's never enough. You're never enough. More. More. More.

I say this as someone in the culture, not above it—I've used the filters; I've had those Grindr profile names; I've been the third boy!

But I'm not the only one who feels this anger and resentment toward the culture we're both trapped in and yet contribute to, all while hoping things might be different.

But we're all let down.

"Do you have any gay role models, Matt?"

I'm back with Matt, attempting to eat ice cream while driving, failing mis-erably. The steering wheel is covered in sticky liquid sugar.

Meanwhile, Matt gracefully laps his; napkin neatly folded on his lap.

He's a lot better at this than I am.

"*Gay role models*??? I feel like that's an oxymoron." Matt crunches down on the last bit of cone, slapping his hands free of crumbs.

"We're all damaged goods. How are we supposed to be a role model to anyone?"

Many of my gay friends and gay strangers alike have used this exact phrase on multiple occasions: "damaged goods." It's always said so matter-of-factly, as if it's some reality we just learn to live with.

On the one rare occasion my ex wasn't experiencing internalized homopho-bia, he'd get tipsy enough to want to check out the local gay club. (Yes, there was only one in my lovely town of Colorado Springs. Trust me, it adds up.)

Despite his willingness, my boyfriend was not willing to dance because that, ladies and gentlemen, was "too gay," and he needed to draw the line some-where. After all, he "wasn't a faggot," (or so he said to my mother at the family barbeque; she liked the guy). So instead of dancing, we played pool—a game he barely knew but was the "straightest" thing he could find.

While we pathetically tried to sink the balls (you'd think that would come easy for two gay guys), a pride of lesbians watched us, judging every move, ready to pounce.

We were truly terrible at this.

Frustrated, I stared off into the crowd. I didn't want to be playing pool. I wanted to be dancing. But I didn't want to risk making my boyfriend mad, or worse, make him less attracted to me because now I was like "one of them."

Instead, I broodingly gazed upon the crowd.

Bartenders in jockstraps pouring shots upon shots. Strangers dancing on strangers, sweat covering the floor. Brooding onlookers standing in corners wishing they were dancing on sweaty bodies. Lights flashing and pulsating. Music thrumming with heavy bass.

I frowned.

In a place brimming with booze and bodies, there was so much sadness. Everyone looked depressed.

"What's wrong?" My boyfriend approached me.

"Everyone looks so sad."

"I mean ... makes sense."

I looked at him with curiosity.

"I mean, you shove a bunch of people who have experienced the same trauma and bullshit, and you're bound to create a sad place."

The thought was revolutionary for me.

Of course, they were sad, we all have the same brokenness.

In Alan Downs's culturally critical book, *The Velvet Rage,* he writes extensively about how gay men have the highest rates of suicide, depression, and sexually transmitted diseases of any demographic, while simultaneously having the most expendable income and the most sex. "When you look around, it becomes somewhat undeniable that we are a wounded lot."[4]

Damaged goods.

Is this what I want? Do I even have a choice? Is this my lot after daring to come out of the closet? Didn't people say it was worth it? Didn't people tell me it gets better? When does it get better? Because this is not better. I hate this. I have to try something different. I have to.

Straight Date

I decided to go on a straight date. I've hated dating men (or rather, not dating men because the majority of my interactions with men are via casual sex), so why not give it a try! What could go wrong?

"I just really love Jesus. He's the real love of my life."
Apparently, a lot.
"Like, don't get me wrong, I want a husband. But until then, Jesus is my husband."
Jesus Christ! I used to say the same thing! Did it always sound this bad? I'm so turned off right now.
Give her a chance, Brandon. You just met her.
"So how did you end up working at this coffee shop?"
"Well, I used to be a YWAMer…"
Oh shit! This was a bad idea. Well, maybe we had a similar experience, and we can talk about how traumatic it was. That could be nice! Yay trauma!
"…and I really miss it! It was really transformative!"
Fuck! We absolutely do not *have shared trauma! She* liked *it? What's* wrong *with her? What's wrong with* me? *Am I into trauma now? Is that my turn on? Oh Jesus! Am I* that *broken that now I like brokenness?*
"Oh wow! I did YWAM too. Very different experience I think. What would you like to drink? I'll snag you something?"
Even though I think it's dumb that I have to pay just because I'm a dude. Gender rules are dumb. Why do I have to pay just because I'm a man and she's a woman? Who decided this? Aren't we all about equality and egalitarianism these days? Besides, she wanted this date just as much as I did. Likely more, since I'm hating every second of this. Why is it expected that I pay?

"Oh no, I'll pay. I'm the one that invited you out for coffee."

Oh! Well that's unexpected. Go female empowerment!

"Hey, thanks! That's so kind of you. So where did you go to school in town?"

"Oh! I was homeschooled! I know what you're thinking, 'Oh no! She must be horribly awkward…'"

Yep.

"…But it was really good for me. Helped me not get caught up in the wrong crowds."

Jesus Christ! I'm the bad crowd her mother protected her from. Does she even know what sex is or how to have it? *When she hears how many people—scratch that, how many* men *I've had sex with—she is going to lose her shit—scratch that, she won't lose her shit because there's no way in* hell *I'm telling her. This was a terrible idea! Horrible idea! A terrible, horrible idea! What the hell was I thinking?*

"So what's life like now that you're back from YWAM?"

"Well, I found this really amazing church! It's so different from any church I've ever been to. Truly refreshing!"

Said. Every. Church. That. Is. Exactly. Like. Every. Other. Church. Nope. Can't do this. I can't. I'm out. Abort. Aboooooort!

"Well, I have to run off. It was *so* nice meeting you!"

"We should do this again sometime!"

"Sure…"

Welp. That didn't work. Guess we're back to square one.

No Man's Land

In Lady Montagu's *The Turkish Embassy Letters* she describes a type of foot soldier in southeastern Europe belonging to the Ottomans—the *Arnounts*. Physically located at the border of Christendom and Islam, they would keep *both* holy days out of fear.

"They are utterly unable to judge which religion is best; but to be certain of not entirely rejecting the truth, they very prudently follow both, and go to the mosque on Fridays and the church on Sundays, saying for their excuse that on the day of judgment they are sure of protection from the true prophet, but which that is, they are unable to determine in this world."[1]

I resonate with that—binding yourself so intimately to fear you live in two worlds, caught at both a literal and spiritual crossroad.

Commitment means risk, so you give yourself to both, and in the end, you become a citizen to this new place, a place between countries: No Man's Land, and now, with borders on both sides, you are always at war.

I've been out for two-and-a-half years, and if I'm honest, it hasn't "gotten better," like the older gays say. It's gotten worse.

Being gay isn't easy. There are some days I wish I never came out. Not because I want to hide the truth of who I am but because most days I just don't like being gay.

The culture feels toxic and painful and sexual and broken and hurting. I try to put it on, to make it work, but it doesn't fit, like an oversized, hand-me-down sweater. It wasn't made for me. It's been forced into my hands, and I'm tired of wearing it because it's heavy, and I'm clumsy in it. (Not to mention it doesn't accentuate my figure!)

But I get it. I get pushing down your sexuality for so long that it comes bursting out at the seams. I get wanting to be held and desired and touched even if it's by a stranger. I get dancing and drinking like there's no tomorrow because today was a bit rough and an escape feels nice. I get the internalized homophobia that makes me squirm from acting "too gay" or "not gay enough." I get the shallow desire that wants someone sexy and young because that's what we're sold, and we're told we're hopeless and dead at thirty, so you might as well get what you can get before your time is up.

I get the closet … and how it still haunts us.

I truly get all of it.

I just don't want it.

And then I attend an old church, and it's too small. It's shrunk in the wash.

I itch with the every-head-bowed-and-every-eye-closed faith that doesn't amount to anything. I pull at the come-Lord-Jesus-comes when the Bible says, he'll never leave us nor forsake us. I squirm at the everyone-is-welcome-but-not-reallys, the bless-yous and the shake-the-hand-of-the-person-next-to-yous. I tear at the God-bless-Americas, the support-our-troops-at-all-costs, the slavery-was-hundreds-of-years-ago-can't-we-get-over-its.

It's all too small. Far too small. And it's hurting me. And others. Forcing the air out of our lungs. Binding us and smothering us.

I can't wear it anymore.

It's like when I came out of the closet, I looked behind the curtain of the church and saw them for what they really were. Now there's no going back.

Churches feel fake; the Bible feels like a weapon, and Christians feel like salesmen selling a product they don't even believe in but are terrified to not make their quota.[2]

But I get it.

I get the fear that cheers you on and makes you dig in your heels. I get the terror of hell and how it forces you to the altar week after week. I get the anxiety around making your life count for something eternal because your life was bought for you, and you better not waste it. I get the paralysis that takes hold of you when confronted with something foreign and new because it could shake everything you believed in. I get the chosen intellectual blindness because you're afraid of what you may find. I get the resistance to stories that contradict your own idea of reality because they don't fit in the box you've been sold.

I get it.

I truly get it all.

I just don't want it.

So I honor Friday and Sunday, except not really, because fuck Fridays and Sundays. They both suck. And I'm too exhausted and hurt to throw myself completely at either country: gay or Christian. They've been at war for millennia. We cannot sue for peace.

And there's no hypothetical Switzerland in this over-extended metaphor: a place where peace is found, a place where all my incongruencies fall into alignment, a country I might call my own. I'm placeless, wandering the hills for fear of invasion.

There's a word in German that embodies this feeling. It resonated with me the second I heard it.

Fernweh: to be homesick for a place you haven't found.[3]

It's like I'm a perpetual foreigner, an expat, uncertain of where to call home. It's probably why I'm most comfortable traveling or living abroad—it embodies a feeling deep within my bones and crafts a landscape to mirror my internal wandering.

Maybe it's time I surrender? Maybe it's time I leave the front? Because these warring identities are running out of resources, and I'm scared I'll die of exposure on these barren hills.

Part Five

Rising

This is plenty of miracle for me to rest in now.[1]

Anne Lamott

Spoiled Brat

You call me. Like you normally do when I'm doing something stupid. Like when I moved back in with my parents. Like when I tried to enlist in the army.

You have a habit of doing that—of speaking up when no one else will, when I've got everyone else fooled.

It's like you always know.

It's been years since we danced in that fountain, but somehow you always still know when my weight is off-balance, when I'm about to fall.

"I read your most recent blog."

You jump right into it. Neither of us care for small talk. It's one of the many reasons we dated.

"Hey, thanks!"

"Yeah, sure. It was beautifully written, as always, but I also can't help but feel you're a spoiled little brat."

I'm taken aback. But I'm also not crazy surprised. This is how our conversations usually go.

"What do you mean?"

"Remember when Don talks about how we're all spoiled kids?"

I don't know if I've ever heard you say an author's full name. It's too impersonal. So you call them by their first. As if they're your friend. As if you've spent thousands of hours together. Because you have spent thousands of hours together. And when I hold the books you've read—as I've often done—your secrets bleed on the page. You gush. You argue. You circle, underline, and heart every word you love or hate. You spill over the pages, sharing your feelings as if it's a diary.

"In *A Million Miles in a Thousand Years*," you continue, "Don talks about how we've become accustomed to miracles: sunsets and rainstorms, births and deaths.[1] But you've had more *actual* encounters with God than anyone I know. Including myself! And *now* in your blog post you give God an ultimatum. Show up, or else? Really, Brandon? I'm over here, daring to believe in him when I've never heard his voice. Meanwhile, you've heard him countless times, and you're threatening to walk away? You're spoiled!"

I think if anyone else told me those words, I'd tell them to fuck off.

But it's you, and you have a way of disarming me.

It's kinda hard to be mad at you. And it's not because of anything special we have. It's because of who you are—this embodiment of wind.

And can someone be mad at the breeze when it becomes a gale? No. It is what it is. You can either run away from it or lift your hands and face it, taking in the scent of summer rain.

You let it have its way. Because the wind always has its way, you breeze-turned-gale.

"I just feel like I'm crazy," I interrupt. "It's like all these Christians, these people who say they represent God, are telling me I'm wrong. It's like we're all in a desert, and I'm saying, 'The water is this way,' and everyone is going in a different direction, telling me to catch up or die in the desert."

"Well, do you even *want* to be like those people?"

"No. They're assholes! Which is another reason I'm confused: I want God, but not if it means looking like *them*."

"So then don't look like them. Why are you letting them take your faith? Why listen to a single word they say?"

"Because who else am I gonna listen to? How else do I get guidance on how to do this faith thing?"

"Yourself, Brandon. Your fucking self. You've had *so* many beautiful encounters with God. You *know* his voice. You *know* what he's saying. And only *you* can know the way forward. Only you. Fuck what Christians say. I still love God, but Christians piss me off. I don't go to church. You don't have to go to church to be a Christian. Just because you don't like Christians because they're *terrible*, doesn't mean you need to throw out God, and it doesn't mean you need to pout saying, 'God, if you don't show up again, I'm walking.' You can be pretty terrible too sometimes. We all can. But he's shown up for you again and again. When are you going to trust that he's there and that he's for you?"

Your words are brutal, but for some reason, I'm yearning to hear them, for someone to simply tell me I'm not crazy, for someone to push back against my raging. If I'm the bratty child, you're the mom refusing to let go.

"It just feels like I got off-course, like I took the wrong exit, and now I don't know how to get back on the freeway. Does that make any sense? It's the only way to explain it in my head."

"Brandon, you and I both know that you were *never* one to go where everyone else is going. Even at YWAM, you were always running off and calling out the leaders when you thought they were dumb—which was often. Is it any surprise that you feel like you're 'off course?' You're not. If anything, this makes the most sense for you. Honestly, I like that you've come out and you're not as Christian. You used to be so hoity-toity and judgmental. You're softer now. I actually think you look more like Jesus than less."

I begin to cry, but you don't hear it. I shove it down, even though your words feel like a warm hug. I can't let you feel the breaking inside, the desperation. Instead, I pivot to sarcasm, like I normally do when I get uncomfortable.

"So you're saying I was an asshole?"

"Oh my God, Brandon! After I pour my heart out, that's the only thing you hear?"

We laugh. Laugh hard. So hard we're snorting. Something you gave me permission to do. I didn't used to do that: snort. Not till I dated you. But somehow, you gave me permission, permission to laugh with all that I am, snorts and all. And as weird as it sounds, it adds saturation to the picture of life. Brighter pinks. Neon oranges. Seafoam blues.

And then we get silent. Because you know. You know what's going on beneath the deflecting humor and the snorting laugh. And you want me to know you know. You want me to know that you see me. So you tell me you see me with the lingering silence.

Then I start asking questions about you, uncomfortable with the spotlight on me—another strategy I use when I get scared.

You talk about how you used to be agnostic, about how you couldn't stand Christians. But now you've come to this beautiful trust in God. You believe he/she/they is a lot bigger than the Bible. You share how that "might be a bit New Agey" or even a bit agnostic, but you don't care; because deep down, you still love God; because deep down, you love how that being has given you so much hope and purpose and you're a better person when you're with him/her/them.

You: the woman who couldn't set me ablaze with a kiss, nor electrify me with a touch, now awakens me with a gale, blowing with the warmth of faith, carrying a scent of hope.

I turn to face the wind.

"Thanks for calling, Anna. Truly. It means a lot."

"You're welcome, friaaaaaand!"

Gold

I'm floating on Lake Shasta.

My friend's boat bobs beside me. The sun is beginning to set, chilling the hot California air. The steep hillsides transition from gold to black, becoming silhouettes scraped against the bright orange sky.

I close my eyes and drift, rising and falling with the gentle waves, weightless.

I decided to go to Redding. In my past, I traveled to Redding, a place that made me want to believe in God. There was a level of chaotic magic to it—praying for healing, dancing with flags, and screaming for joy when gold dust drifted in the rafters.

Yes, I'm talking about Bethel.

For those who are unfamiliar with Bethel, it's this megachurch that is intimately connected to the idea of the supernatural—hyper-charismatic, believing in the miraculous.

On a typical Sunday morning, one may experience anything from the preacher calling you out by name and declaring your liver cancer healed, to a random churchgoer barking in the corner and flailing on the ground.

Chaotic magic.

They're also hyper-conservative. They've created an ex-gay curriculum, preached from the pulpit about how men and women have distinct places in the world, and have endorsed worship leaders to run for local conservative public offices.

I know what you're thinking, "This place sounds insane." And true, it does. But after having sex with stranger after stranger and becoming frustrated with my old church and the Bible, I was desperately trying to grab onto *something*, *anything*, if it meant I had some semblance of direction. I felt like I was disoriented and adrift, lost at sea. I needed a metaphorical North Star to help me find my way, which is hilarious because now I'm *literally* adrift, rocked back and forth by the waves.

I came back to Bethel, looking for answers. Well, that and I tend to be masochistic. But I had good reason to trust Bethel despite all the insanity.

Right before becoming a missionary, I hitched my way to Bethel, curious about all the crazy stories I had heard over the years. But during that time, I didn't experience *anything* crazy. I didn't shake and fall on the floor. I didn't see angels aflame with fire. I didn't get some prophecy that shattered my view of the world. (Yes, all those things have happened to people there.)

What I did experience was God speaking to me through dumb, lame, every-day things. In a place known for the supernatural, I was experiencing the holy in … well, the natural—a book, a movie, a conversation, a walk. Through the mundane, God showed me the divine. Accustomed miracles, to steal Anna's words.

And in this place of disorientation, I needed the divine, even if it meant being told I was absolutely wrong, because deep down, underneath all the rage toward Christianity, I believed I *was* wrong, that I *was* going to hell, that I *was* damned and everyone else was right.

I sat through services, hoping the pastor would call me by name like some psychic. I prayed in their prayer garden, yearning for some Japanese maple to turn into a burning bush. I signed up for prophetic readings, desperately wanting a random stranger to tell me my fate like some fortune teller in Romania, not a megachurch in California.

But nothing extraordinary happened. There was no "voice from heaven." There was no gold dust. There was no uncontrollable "move of the spirit'" (as my Pentecostal friends would say). There was nothing. Just church. And that wasn't enough for me anymore.

So when the next Sunday rolled around, I wasn't eager to go. I was burned out and disillusioned and tired of trying, and when my friend Becca texted me, inviting me to her boat on a Sunday morning, I was eager to say yes, grateful for any excuse to not go back to this church I hoped and prayed had answers but wasn't delivering on the chaotic magic I was hoping for.

Becca and I go way back.

When I was a youth pastor, at the ripe age of nineteen (because having a nineteen-year-old mentor the most at-risk age is definitely a great idea), Becca was one of my first volunteers.

She had this hippie, granola vibe that was more than the trendy kind you see at Coachella. She'd talk of eating placentas and the benefits of homebirth. She'd rage against GMOs and share articles about the horrors of vaccines. She was the bona fide real-deal, wearing patchouli before Karens sold it to young Ashleys promising youth, health, and vitality (as long as they joined their multi-level marketing scheme).

Now, in the little town of Redding, she's a midwife, giving herself to all the things she loved and believed from the moment I met her. She's one of the most consistent people I ever met, and that rings true regarding our friendship.

When nearly every other Christian bailed, Becca stuck around after I came out. She wasn't scared. In fact, she was one of the first people to say that I was going to be okay.

"Brandon, yeah, this is hard. Yeah, I don't have the answers for you. But what I do know is that wrestling is an intimate act. It changes people. After you wrestle someone, you can't help but feel closer, even if it's a fight for your life. Regardless of how this ends, Brandon, you wrestling out your faith is intimacy, and I don't think God is scared of that; in fact, I think he loves it."

So here I am, floating on Lake Shasta, watching the sunset because one of the only friends that believed I was more than okay invited me out on the water. Well, that and the fact that I was exhausted and pissed from trying to make Bethel work.

It wasn't the chaotic magic I was hoping for, but there's a soft magic to floating, nothing but the water holding you. It slows down time, makes me present, forces me to stare up at the golden sky, body rising and falling, as gentle waves lap against my ears.

And as time slows, floating on water, my questions, concerns, and fears float to the surface. Well, really just one question ... one concern ... one fear:

God, I don't know. I don't know anything. Church sucks. The Bible sucks. Christians suck. But Anna says that doesn't matter. So I'm here. I've got nothing. But I'm here. And I need to know. I need to know what was so wrong about my love for Henry?

That gentle voice, that thing inside me that might be some creative act of my imagination or maybe a shard of the holy lodged deep inside my body, whispers, *Nothing.*

I begin to cry, tears joining the water.

Nothing?

Nothing was wrong with your love. In fact, I loved your love for Henry.
No holy prophet.
No divine preacher.
No chaotic magic to be seen or heard or felt.
Just a lake.
And a sunset.
And a stillness that allowed me to sink.
Allowed me to listen.

Glennon Doyle, a fellow queer ex-sorta-but-not-really-Christian woman, writes in her book *Untamed*, "It was as though I'd been drowning and in my panic I had been gasping for air, calling for rescue, and flailing on the surface. But what I really needed to do to save myself was let myself sink … What I learned (even though I am afraid to say it) is that God lives in this deepness inside me. When I recognize God's presence and guidance, God celebrates by flooding me with warm liquid gold."[1]

She goes on to share how she uses this "sinking," this "stillness," to help her navigate life.

When she gets scared and confused, she hides away and sinks. When there's a crisis or a big decision, instead of weighing pros and cons, she becomes quiet and listens to that inner voice. It guides her and gives her this golden strength to act.

The practice has revolutionized her life.

And of all the places, even though she too was hurt by Christians and ostracized from the church, she got the idea from the Bible.

"Be still and know that I am God."[2]

He wasn't in the howling hot wind of a preacher. He wasn't in the earth-shaking touch of the prophet. He wasn't in the burning zeal of a church.

He was in the stillness. In the quiet. In liquid gold.

And as I floated underneath a blazing sky and upon an inky deep, a deepness dwelling inside of me called my love…

Good.

Symptoms

It's two thirty in the morning.

I'm deep in the tunnel, driving around town while sending out messages.

"Hey, looking?"

"Hey, looking?"

"Hey, looking?"

My creativity is passed out in the passenger seat, and desperation is driving. I'm hoping for any bites. And I mean *any*.

"Yeah."

Yes!

I drive to his place.

Park.

Enter.

The deed is done in less than a half hour.

I get back in my car.

I take a deep, quivering breath.

I rest my head on the steering wheel and begin to cry.

Loneliness and shame assault me.

I pull out my phone to delete Grindr. (The classic purge.)

Don't delete it.

I pause. It's the voice from the lake. The liquid gold.

I ignore it and go to delete the app again.

Don't delete it.

My heart tightens, like it did under that willow and with the perky-smile people.

My initial reaction is to ignore the voice. There's no way that God would be saying to *not* delete an app that has made my current body count well over fifty. But then again, that same voice had told me to close the Bible and helped me find cute coffee shops; it had told me to root in Colorado Springs and asked about my gay first date. It had done a lot of things I wouldn't have expected, a lot of things Christians would label heresy.

Maybe it *was* God.

I stilled myself and sank.

Don't delete it. This is a symptom of something deeper. It's the cause that matters. When the cause is resolved, the symptoms will take care of themselves. Then you'll delete it. Then you'll walk away. Not because of shame. But because you won't *need it. You* won't *want it.*

My thumb pulls away from the dancing icon.

Alright. Let's give this a go.

12:45 a.m.

The next night.

I'm driving to a guy's house.

Google says I've arrived.

I park the car.

But before I go in, I notice a little red dot on WhatsApp.

(I'm that crazy person who can't have red dots. The fact that people have email notifications in the thousands gives me anxiety.)

I open up the app and play the voice memo.

"Hey B! Josh here. Just wanted to say that I love ya and miss ya. I'm looking forward to our road trip together. Can't wait to meet your friends and cuddle up with you every night. Let me know how you're doing, okay? Talk to you soon, buddy."

A tear wells up in my eye, and I quiver.

Someone I love wants to be close to me, wants to share life with me, is looking forward to cramming into the same bed during our road trip.

I smile at the phone then look at the door, the door of random man number seventy-something.

I look back at my phone.

My thumb hovers over Grindr.

It dances.

I hit delete.

Wasted Boobs

I got a wedding invite…

And I'm terrified…

It's been three years since I've come out, and a lot of my friendships have faded. They weren't these loud, violent endings. Some were, but most weren't. They just went quiet. Like when you slowly turn down the music, and you aren't sure when the song ended. But at some point, it did.

This was especially true with my Bible school friends.

Which is why I'm terrified—it's an invite to a *Bible* school friend's wedding.

Even if I decide to go, what would I say to these people? What do they think of me? Would they invite me out to a horrible cup of coffee? Where the hell would I stay?

In the past, my friends and I would simply crash at whoever's house was closest to whichever event or wedding or random reunion we were attending.

We'd fill up air mattresses, crash on couches, shove too many people in one bed. It was never a problem. We'd always find a place.

But now I'm out.

Now people aren't sure what to do with me.

And now I'm not too sure what to do with them.

"Are you coming to Amy's wedding?" my friend Arielle texts.

"I wasn't too sure. But I don't think I can miss it. I wanna be there on her big day, but I don't know where the hell I'd stay."

"Ummmm … with me. Rude! I thought that was a given. My house is *always* the Dallas house. It's been like that for years. I think the Morrises are coming too. So you'll be staying here with them and maybe Hannah. Amy will be around. Yeah, it's her wedding, but she told me she wants to see everyone. It's about time we all got back together! What's it been? Like two years?"

"Three ... it's been three."

Three silent years.

"That's *unacceptable*! I can't *believe* it's been that long! What time you getting in? I'll pick you up."

And before I could really think through the consequences of my actions, I was going back to Dallas—home of big toast, sweet tea, and Bible school trauma.

"So you're telling me that if I were to straddle you, sit on your crotch, grab your hands, and put them on my breasts, you wouldn't get turned on?"

I'm sitting in Arielle's living room. It's me and the girls—Arielle, Amy, and Hannah. Kameron, the only guy friend I have on this trip, and his wife are nowhere to be seen, which is probably for the best, considering he's got a three-year-old daughter and we're talking about sex.

"Nope!" I reply to Hannah. "I wouldn't get a boner. I wouldn't even get turned on. I've seen boobs in person, and I wasn't impressed."

"I'm waaaaasted on you!" Arielle, who apparently is well-endowed (I genuinely haven't noticed because, again, I'm gay), dramatically chimes in.

"So you're like *not* into women at *aaaaaaall*?" Hannah asks.

"Nope. Honestly, vaginas scare me."

"Reaaaaaaally? I mean, I'm biased, but I find mine quite nice. I wish you could take one for a test drive, just so you could know, you know?"

"That's called prostitution, Hannah."

We keep talking about straight sex and gay sex and boobs and butts. It feels nice. Instead of dodging around their questions, they address them head-on, deep-diving into all the details of what it's like being gay.

But it's been hours, and now we're starving. We have a habit of doing that—of losing track of time with each other. We've often stayed up till the sun rose, simply talking, catching up. We just feel so close and understood by each other. I guess that's trauma bonding for you.

We decide to pause our conversation (because it's always a pause and never a stop) and get some food.

"Brandon's riding with me!" Hannah says as she grabs my wrist and ushers me toward her car.

"Hannaaaaah!" Arielle yells after us. "You have to shaaaaaaare!"

I smile at the bickering. Being wanted feels nice.

Hannah is the best. She was the girl in Bible school that I could be my absolutely-most-dramatic self with and then quickly pivot to incredibly serious topics (my two favorite flavors of being, if that wasn't obvious by my style of writing).

We'd go from pretending we're old people to talking about childhood trauma, from shouting obnoxiously in the Sonic parking lot to intimate conversations over coffee (before coffee got tainted by Christians jumping me).

We flex and flow perfectly with each other, feeding off the other's energy.

As we get into the car, I'm torn, multiple emotions swirling within me.

Yes, I've missed her. Yes, she makes me come alive in so many ways. Yes, she makes me snort-laugh as we flail about. But she's also spent the last decade working in ministry. Like *deep* in ministry. Like *deep, evangelical, megachurch* ministry.

Now she wants to be alone with me in a car (which is one of my favorite places … when I'm *alone*. But add another human to the equation, and they transform into something nearly as bad as those dreaded coffee shops—it's hard to escape when you're moving forty miles per hour).

"Talk to me about you and Jesus and being gay."

Right to it. As always. How many times now have I mentioned that I hate small talk? It's genuinely not a wonder that the closest people in my life go straight for the hard, deep stuff.

I launch into my rehearsed soliloquy. "There are some great books out there about queer-affirming theology that will do a better job explaining this than me, but the verses in the Bible that condemn homosexuality are contextually about young boys being purchased by older men at the temple brothels. It was about power and exploitation, not love."[1,2,3,4] (I conveniently leave out the part that I'm not sure if I even believe in the Bible anymore or that I don't go to church anymore or that I'm not sure if God even exists anymore. But I did the research, so I could fight with Christians, using their book against them.)

We continue talking. She keeps asking questions, refusing to shy away. She's genuinely curious. Not defensive, and it feels nice. Feels like I might be safe, and the scream of my fears fade as the intimacy with my friends grows.

But she also hasn't said anything about how *she* feels … yet.

I hold my breath as the questions wind down, silence filling the space. My fears can be heard, muffled in the background.

She takes a deep breath and plunges.

"Brandon, I'll be honest with you. I think you were born gay. I don't think you can change that. But I also think acting on those feelings is a sin. Do I think you're going to hell for that sin? No. Just like I don't think I'm going to hell because I can be a prideful arrogant snot. But I still believe it's a sin. And at the end of the day, when we both die, we're going to get up to heaven, and we're going to find out who was right. Was it you? Was it me? Was it neither of us? Let's be honest, it's likely neither of us. But I don't need to be right, and I don't need you to be celibate to love you. I've seen God in your life, Brandon. I can't shake that. And I don't think you've been able to either. I truly believe he's got you, regardless of if I disagree with how you live your life. I'm not nervous."

I smile at her, a tear swelling in my eye.

Her faith feels safe. It's nice to know that *someone* believes I'm not going to hell.

This time, in the silence, my fears are muted, and I breathe a bit more easily.

"Yo!" Arielle knocks on the car window. I startle, breathing a little *less* easily. "We eating or not? I'm hungry! And you two have been in there for ages. My FOMO is kicking in! Hannah, quit hogging Brandon! He's not all yours!"

"Fiiiiine! Let me hug his neck and you can have him!"

Again, I smile.

Hannah turns towards me as Arielle walks away.

"I love you." Hannah looks right into my eyes with this tenderness that feels so refreshing.

But I get a little squirmy like I typically do when people make extended eye contact, so I look away.

"Thanks for being honest with me and giving me grace to talk this through with you when I know I'm gonna mess it up."

"Absolutely, Hannah. Thanks for ending the silence."

"Now let's get you in there before Arielle and Amy *murder* me."

We get out of the car. Arielle is waiting for me by the trunk, eagerly moving back and forth as if she has a tail, waiting to pounce. She launches, hugs me, then slips her arm into mine as we turn toward the restaurant where Amy and Kameron are waiting.

I missed this—being touched and not avoided, being brought near instead of pushed away.

We wrap up dinner, laughing and reminiscing the whole time. Afterward, Kameron fights to drive me back.

Kameron is that man that every girl secretly swoons over and every man secretly wants to be. He grew up in Oklahoma, was an Eagle Scout, has a strong build, plays all the sports, can talk to anyone, and has a shit-ton of character. He's the guy who would drive across the country if your car broke down and would *genuinely* not expect anything in return. He would just do it because it's the right thing to do. He fights for those he loves and owns his mistakes. He's a man's-man (why is that the phrase for a typically "straight" person; it sounds *sooooo* gay) but is humble and daring enough to join a dance team.

Yet despite all his goodness, I'm yet again scared to be trapped in a car. The fears are no longer muted.

Back in Bible school, we used to be close. He reminded me of my childhood best friend, Dan, and the familiarity made me trust him immediately. We'd sleep under the stars together, yell together, cry together, hold each other, and laugh at each other, knowing we were safe, which felt *so* redeeming because he represented the type of man that, growing up, I was terrified of.

But he was also one of the friends that went radio silent after I posted my horrific forty-five minute, stuttering-and-stammering coming out video on Facebook.

What will he say? Why does he want to talk to me alone? He's been awfully quiet. Is he going to say I'm going to hell? Is he going to say he can no longer be my friend?

"I owe you an apology." I'm taken aback by his words, but I still brace.

What is he sorry for? Is he sorry he didn't tell me to go to hell sooner?

"I didn't know what to say after you came out, so I didn't say anything, like a coward, which I think did more harm than good. I should have had the courage to step into conversation and own the fact that I didn't know what to say; I should have at least tried talking. I was a bad friend, and I'm really sorry. I'm so sorry, Brandon."

I stare in shock.

No one has *ever* apologized for how they responded after I came out. Most of them made it out to feel like it was *my* fault, that *I* made them react this way.

But not Kam.

Tears fill my eyes, for maybe the tenth time that night, perpetually surprised by the friends I feared.

As I soften, releasing a held breath, I realize I had been bracing myself not just since I decided to go on this trip, but for years, from the moment I came out.

Who am I going to lose? What are people going to say?

All the uncertainty puts you on edge, waiting for the other shoe to drop.

These old Bible school friends, these feared ones, represented my enemy. They represented not only my past, the past I no longer belonged to, but also all the Christians, the ones who went silent or angry the second I said I was gay.

But here they were, holding me—not perfectly, but gently—and it made my heart soften.

There's a verse in the Bible that talks about humanity being the hands and feet of God.[5] It's a beautiful sentiment. But often, instead of being caressed by hands, we're slapped; instead of sinking to contrite knees, we're kicked. We see Christians standing outside of abortion clinics with hateful signs; we watch YouTube videos with parents throwing out their children in the name of Jesus; we hear pastors preach about how "This nation is going to hell in a handbasket" because this "damned" nation is finally beginning to care about human rights and decency.

But here were these people, these Christians, taking their hands and holding my heart, using their feet and stepping into my story.

Years would pass, and that wedding would still affect me. Years would pass, and the afterglow images would refuse to fade:

The image of Amy's wedding invitation asking me to be there on her special day.

The image of Arielle's pouting face when she didn't get to hold my hand.

Hannah's eyes that truly didn't fear I was going to hell.

Kameron's tears when he said sorry for fucking up.

But most importantly, years would pass, and these friends would refuse to let the volume fade. They'd continue to sing, thrumming along, despite all the other noises and panics playing in the background.

They'd be there.

Always.

And it would mean the world.

A Bunch of Middle-Aged Men

I have an affinity for cults.

My Bible school was a cult.

My mission organization was a cult.

That worship place with the perky smiles was a cult.

1211? Probably a cult.

In fact, when I was a kid, of all the books I could nerd out on, I chose a book about religions and spent all my time reading the cult section: Scientology, Rajneeshees, Davidians, and apparently Mormonism (because that definitely fits with the rest). (An aside: Who gets to decide what's a cult? Like, most religions fit the same description. They're just larger. Yet they get a pass and avoid the label? It ultimately comes down to power of majority, and I don't think it's fair.)

I. Love. Cuuuuuults!

So I was immediately intrigued when my friend Wade introduced me to yet another one.

"You should do this men's retreat."

"Wade. You know how I feel about men's retreats—they're the absolute worst, and they're all the same. Everyone shows up, trying to act all macho, trying to out-man the other. In the sessions, they talk about how they should quit masturbating and stop looking at porn. After the sermon on porn, they watch *Braveheart* and talk about how they're going to be warriors for Jesus by not cheating on their wives, followed by some weird, awkward literal battle cry. Not to mention all the homophobia. It's all a bunch of horseshit."

"You know I feel the same way. Men's retreats are a joke. When I'm required to go to them because I'm on staff with the church, I make fun of the guys wearing camo and fishing gear. 'Nice costume, bud.' 'You going fishing, sport?' 'Did you bring your deer tags, champ?' Nothing gets a straight guy riled up like calling them 'sport,' 'bud,' or 'champ.' It's the best!"

And this is why I love Wade.

Wade was the worship pastor at the church that lied about being queer-accepting, the one with the gay glass ceiling. But, unlike the church, Wade actually loves gays. He thinks I'm just as lovely and annoying as the next guy, queerness a non-issue.

Before I gave up on churches altogether, I volunteered for the worship ministry, because Wade made me feel safe and because I like singing. And because of that safety, I listened to Wade when he told me about this men's retreat, a men's retreat I should, for some crazy reason, go to, even though we both criticize them.

"I'm telling you, Brandon, I know you. You'd love this."

"What do you do at this retreat?"

"I can't tell you."

"Well, that's sketchy as hell."

"Yes, it is."

"Is it a cult?"

"Kinda."

"Wade!"

"But it's a *good* cult."

"Said *every* cult *ever!*"

"K. Then don't go."

"Dammit, Wade!" I glare at him. "Now I'm intrigued."

"Of course you are. Because cults are intriguing."

"Where would one find information about this cult ... if one were interested ... hypothetically..."

"But only hypothetically, right Brandon?"

"Of course. Only hypothetically."

"Well, hypothetically, one would go to this website and register for a retreat. Hypothetically."

I went to the retreat. Because I trust Wade. And because I like cults.

༄

I'm standing in a circle of eighty men, mostly middle-aged. A man with a grizzly beard begins to speak with a commanding voice.

"We're going to check in. Still yourself. Get in touch with your body. What sensations are you experiencing? Is it a tightness in the chest? Is it a release in the shoulders? Now assign emotions to them. Sad. Angry. Scared. Happy. Excited. Tender. Once you've identified those emotions, assign them a story. *Why* are you happy? *Why* are you angry? When the first man is ready, you can share how you're feeling. Let's keep it to thirty seconds since there are so many of us."

Each man, each straight, middle-aged, Christian man, takes turns stepping forward and sharing how they're feeling ... willingly ... What the hell is this place?

"I'm feeling scared because this is my first retreat."

"I'm feeling sad because I looked at porn the other night while my wife slept next to me."

"I'm feeling angry because my friend killed himself."

Fuck ... for straight men, they're being fucking vulnerable. Shit.

Now it's my turn.

I anxiously take a breath.

"I'm feeling scared because I'm gay, and this room is full of evangelical, middle-aged men, and evangelical, middle-aged men have not treated me the best. I'm scared I'll have to hide this weekend or that most of you will reject me or react poorly to me because I'm gay."

Silence.

No one says a word.

Most just nod.

And then the next man steps forward and speaks, not missing a beat.

I don't hear what he says. Or the man after him. I don't hear anything. Because it's now out in the open. Because now I can't take the words back. And everyone now knows. And I'm even more terrified.

As everyone finishes, the circle disperses.

I go to leave the room, but a large man in camo—a man Wade would call "champ"—blocks me.

I shuffle to the right, avoiding eye contact.

He moves to his left.

I pivot to the left.

But he moves to his right.

Fuck.

I dare to meet his eyes, about to tell him to fucking move, but that's when I see it...

He's crying.

He doesn't say anything. He barely even moves. He just opens up his arms, wraps them around me, picks me up, and holds me in a bear hug for a solid thirty seconds.

My rigid body slowly relaxes, sinking into the man, head collapsing onto his shoulder.

I breathe the moment in, silently crying with him.

He puts me down.

"If anyone messes with you this weekend or says anything hurtful while you're here, you tell me. I'll kick their ass. What you said took balls, and if anyone says differently, I'll fucking beat the shit out of them."

The man leaves without another word.

I'm in shock.

No man, especially a *straight* one in camo, *especially* at a *Christian* men's retreat, has *ever* done *anything* like that before. This was the first. But it wouldn't be the last.

Man after man approaches me, pulling me aside.

"Thank you for being so vulnerable. It gave me permission to be vulnerable."

"I've never met someone with so much courage."

"I'm sorry for all the pain the church has caused you. I think it's really admirable that you've continued to try and have faith after coming out. That can't be easy."

I'm blown away, and as the strangers approach me, this hurt and distrust of men, especially *Christian* men, especially *middle-aged Christian* men, melts with every conversation, every hug, every second of uncomfortably prolonged eye contact.

I was safe here.

I was seen here.

I was wanted here.

With *men*!

With *Christian men*!

After the retreat, I decide to start meeting with a group of them. Week after week, I'm brutally honest. Week after week, I share who I am. And week after week, I brace for the inevitable rejection. But it never comes. Instead, they ask me with genuine curiosity, "What do *you* want?"

And I'm realizing, I don't know, which, come to find out, is actually quite common for gay men.

"Queer people don't grow up as ourselves," LGBTQ+ activist Alexander Leon writes, "we grow up playing a version of ourselves that sacrifices authenticity to minimise [sic] humiliation and prejudice. The massive task of our adult lives is to unpick which parts of ourselves are truly us and which parts we've created to protect us."[1]

So, with a divine irony, I begin to "unpick the parts" with these Christian men as we sit in an abandoned sanctuary.

I talk about how many men I've slept with. I talk about my cowardice and how I wish I would stand up for myself more. I talk about how I'm confused and how I'm not sure if I even believe in God, and *if* I believe in God, I'm angry with him; I'm angry at him because his people suck, and yet he made me this way, this way that his people hate, and I'm angry because it feels like the way he made me has cost me too much. Where's the payoff? Where's the happy ending? How do I move forward? Where do I go? What do I do? And all those other questions that have haunted me for years.

I talk about it all.

They listen to it all.

They nod.

They sigh.

They cry.

They smile.

They hug ... They hug me with those long hugs, the ones that make me feel uncomfortable. But it's uncomfortable because I love it, and I probably shouldn't, because I'm gay and all, because I'm a man and all, and we're not supposed to like hugs. So I squirm. I squirm while they hold me, refusing to let me go.

And then I cry.

And then *they* cry.

Cry with me.

Cry over me.

Hope for me.

Pray for me.

Curse with me.

They bear witness to my fears and shatter them with love.

They say I'm not too much.
That I'm more than enough.
They say I'm not broken.
Instead, I'm whole.
With a wholesome heart and good desires.
They're not bad.
I'm not bad.
I'm perfect.
Just the way I am.
Gay and all.
Human and all.
They: a bunch of straight, middle-aged, Christian men (sometimes in camo).
And I'm in.
I'm all in.

Thailand

"I don't need a partner to travel the world! I've got you!" my friend Adam drunkenly slurs on the other end of the phone.

Adam and I go way back. Like, *way*, way back. Like braces and pimples back. Back to when we ran a ministry together and believed we'd change the world. (You know, typical millennial evangelical bullshit.)

Youth has a way of doing that—of making you believe you could conquer the world for all the "right reasons"; that, although everyone has tried something before you, *you* would be the one to finally change things.

Adam and I had lost touch over the years, but we both came out within a few days of each other, and it felt like we were the only two people in the world that understood the questions that being raised in the church and coming out engender, of working in ministry and dating boys, of all the trauma before and after the closet.

It was all so messy and disorienting, but it felt like a kind mercy that we could at least be disoriented together.

"I wanna go to Barcelona. Let's go to Barcelona."

"Barcelona sounds great. Small problem: I'm poor."

"Bahhhhh! I'll pay for your trip!"

"Yeah yeah yeah … Adam, you're drunk. Let's maybe talk about this when you're sober."

"I'm not drunk! I've only had *one* bottle of wine!"

We end the call shortly after.

A few days pass, and as is our ritual, we'd call each other to talk about nothing and everything, feeling understood. Only this time, Adam is *not* drunk.

"Brandon! I'm planning a trip to Barcelona. I've always wanted to go, and I'm making it happen."

This is very déjà vu. He doesn't remember anything from our last conversation.

"Oh really? Who all is going?" I ask, knowing that I'm not going to be mentioned because he doesn't remember the night prior.

"David, Anthony, and a few friends from my church. I'm so excited! I need to get out of the Bay. I'm going crazy. And work is insane. It'll be so nice to just take a break from it all."

Called it.

"Adam, do you happen to remember our conversation from the other day?"

"Conversation? What conversation?" He gasps. "Oh nooooo! Did I promise to pay for your trip?"

"Yeaaaaah ... I'm not gonna hold you to it. You were drunk."

"Fuck. How about I pay for your flight and lodging and call it a deal?"

"Ummmm ... yeah! That sounds amazing! Are you sure?"

"I'm a man of my word. Even my drunken word."

The conversation leads to a trip, which leads to another trip, which takes Adam and me to Thailand.

Little did I know a vacation would impact me so much.

"I wanna go to Chiang Rai." I declare as we make our final plans.

"Why do you wanna go to Chiang Rai?"

"Because my friends who have spent a good chunk of time in Thailand say it's their favorite spot in Thailand, and you've picked all our destinations so far. I want to pick one."

"Fiiiiine! But how are we going to get there and what are we going to do?"

"I'm not sure. We'll figure it out."

Adam glares at me while he takes a sip of rosé. He hates ambiguity and spontaneity.

"I'll just keep an eye out for a bus or train or something. It's fairly close to Chiang Mai. We could do a day trip while we're there."

"Fiiiiine. But you need to figure it out. I'm not helping."

"Fiiiiine." I mock back.

It's the day before the trip, and Adam gets a text from his pastor, his gay-affirming pastor (yes, they exist). "Hey! Are you and your friend going to Thailand? You should totally connect with Rachel. She runs a ministry out there. You'd love it!" Rachel is a person from Adam's church.

"Brandon, do you want to spend some of *our vacation* visiting a *ministry*?" Adam says it in a way that basically translates to: "I don't want to do this."

Ministry is a really hard thing for Adam and me. We had both given years of our lives and thousands of dollars to them over the years. Then, when we came out, it was the ministries and churches that we poured our lives into that were the first to turn away. The idea of going back to one felt scary and hard.

"Uhhhh ... maybe ask where it is? If it's far away, that may make the decision for us." Which roughly translates to: "I don't actually want to do this, but I also don't want to say 'no' and be a jerk."

"K-k, let me reach out to this girl and find the details." Adam does his internet thing, the thing where he can find anyone after just seeing a picture, and in less than ten minutes, can tell you their social security number, traffic violations, and mother's favorite color. In two minutes, he's talking to this ministry woman in Thailand.

"She said it's in Chiang Rai?"

"Really?!"

"Why are you so excited?"

"That's the area my friends told me to check out! Maybe we should go! If anything, we get to see a cool part of Thailand where we know someone."

"Fiiiiine." Which roughly translates to: "I really hate this, but I'll go along with it because *you* want to."

Adam sends the text, and we sit in silence. There's this odd electric heaviness in the air as if saying "yes" to a stupid day trip to a ministry had bigger implications.

"I know this is weird and sounds *super* Christian," Adam finally breaks the silence. "But I think God may want to do something on this trip. Like, I think God may want to love on his two boys."

"That *does* sound *suuuuuper* Christian, Adam. Jesus Christ!"

"Whaaaaaaat?! I'm trying to not be a complete cynic! Besides, doesn't the Bible say something about, 'Where sin abounds, grace abounds all the more'? We're both gay. If that verse is true, we must have all the fucking grace because Christians say we're the absolute *worst* sinners."

Adam maniacally laughs like he usually does when he gets a crazy idea.

I simply giggle in response. I can't truly give myself to his thought, though. Sure, it sounds nice that God extends the most grace to the "chief of sinners," and sure, it sounds nice that Jesus loved spending time with those the religious rejected. But all I can think about and even believe is that I've been rejected because those who are called his hands and feet refuse to see and embrace all of me.

"Let's just enjoy our vacation," I say to change the subject.

"Thailaaaaaand!"

After getting the best ten dollar massages we've had in our entire lives, exploring temples and ruins like Tomb Raider, and drinking fancy cocktails on rooftop bars, Adam and I were on our fourth plane, bound for Chiang Mai.

"Where you girls off to?" Adam makes small talk with the ladies sitting across the aisle. (I do not make small talk with the random ladies sitting across the aisle. I stare at my book. Completely ignoring them. As mentioned previously, I hate small talk, and strangers scare me.)

"We're going to see the lantern festival."

"Wait…" I drop my book and chime in, "like *the* lantern festival?" (Suddenly I love small talk.)

"Yeah. It's today. Isn't that why you're here?"

Adam and I look at each other.

"We had no clue. We just picked this time of year because we found a cheap flight."

"Yeah, it's happening tonight."

Adam looks at me. "I told you God fucking loves the homosexuals."

After we land, we quickly hail a tuk-tuk, motorized rickshaw, and race to city center. It's 9 p.m., and we're nervous we'll miss it.

As the tuk-tuk crawls through traffic, Adam and I scan the sky.

There, in the distance, glowing lights float into the night by the thousands.

"AHHHHH!" We shake each other in excitement. This was happening. This was *actually* happening! And we didn't plan for it!

Suddenly, we're pulled from our euphoria when the tuk-tuk comes to a halt. Traffic was at a standstill. People are crowding the streets.

Adam looks at me. "You up for running?"

"Yup!"

Adam pays the tuk-tuk driver, and we race into the motionless traffic.

We slide and weave through the throngs of people, pushing to get to the clearing ahead.

But when we squeeze from the crowd, we find ourselves in the path of a parade!

Drummers pound their instruments as massive floats glide through the streets. Dancers tumble over and over as fire twirlers shoot flames into the sky.

We quickly push back into the crowd, embarrassed but bewildered.

Shirtless warriors carry a palanquin with someone in gold on top. Adam doesn't see the golden man. He only sees the shirtless men. And his eyes are huge.

"God *seriously* loves me." He smiles at me, and I roll my eyes.

After Adam regains composure, we maneuver through the streets, still unsure of where to go.

The city is madness, thrumming with energy like the drums. But ahead is another clearing.

It's the plaza of a Buddhist temple ... where they're selling lanterns!

Adam and I scream like two tween girls at a Harry Styles concert.

We fork over money and take a lantern from the monk. He hands us markers, and we scan the people around us; they're writing on their lanterns.

"Wishes." The monk says, noticing our curious eyes.

Adam and I go over to a nearby table with our Sharpie, about to write on our lantern when I have an idea.

"What if instead of wishes we write down things we want to let go of?"

The last few years had been rough for Adam and me. We had both lost a lot after coming out. Family. Friends. Support systems. Adam was even publicly "turned over to Satan" by his congregation for the "saving of his soul." Then, after coming out, we each got into our first gay relationships, relationships that ended up being super destructive.

It felt like standing in piles of rubble.

But here in this city, alive with celebration and joy, there was a renewed sense of hope. Maybe it was time to try and trust that the future might be bright, that it might be worth grabbing hold of.

But grabbing the future meant letting go of the past, a past that refused to let go.

Adam looks at me with soft eyes, the ones he gets when he feels vulnerable.

He nods in agreement to my question.

We begin writing...

"Unforgiveness." "Pride." "Doubt." "Anger." "Henry." "Dad." "Lorenzo."

Finished with our confessions, reading them to each other, the monk comes back and motions for us to raise our lantern.

He lights it, and we release it into the night.

As it slowly ascends, our gaze follows. We can't take our eyes off it.

Silent.

Thinking.

Maybe even praying.

After many minutes, it finally disappears, no longer distinguishable from the thousands of others.

Feeling content and light, we take a deep, cool breath, knowing this moment is somehow holy. Our gaze returns to the crowds and then each other. We nod and walk out, neither one of us speaking as we rejoin the throngs of celebrants.

The evening continues, somber yet joyful.

We eat all the street food and take in all the sights. We eventually arrive at the river, the heart of the lantern festival, and lean over the railing of the bridge.

In all directions, there are lights and booths and food and people. The city is brimming with light, but it's not harsh electric light—the kind found in secondary schools and Walmart warehouses. It's soft and glowing, like embers in a fire, warming and soothing, gently refusing to let us look away.

We communally stand in awe.

Awe of the flames in the sky.

Awe of the wishes released.

Awe of a shared experience that transcends language, religion, and creed.

Adam smiles at me. "I told you he wanted to love on us."

In response I simply smile, staring into the sky for the thousandth time because light has a way of doing that, of making humans lift their eyes.

Maybe he's right. Maybe God does want to love on his boys.

⁓

The next day is our Chiang Rai trip.

Rachel arranges for a car to come pick us up, taking us three hours north, away from the city, far into the mountains.

Ancient walls give way to houses. Houses give way to trees. Till we're lost amongst the jungle and farms.

There, across the street from a massive Monsanto farm, lies Rachel's ministry.

"I'm so glad you guys are here!" Rachel emerges from a concrete building. She has a brimming smile and sun-kissed brown hair. "How was the ride? Was it okay? And how was the lantern festival? Isn't it amazing? Truly magical."

She ushers us around, showing off her nonprofit with a proud smile as if it were a baby and not a complex.

"Through our research, we've identified different markers that make someone more susceptible to being trafficked. Lack of job skills. Internet illiteracy. Poor family relations. We then take those elements and create scores for each of our kids. Think of them like report cards. Through these reports, we can track and gauge how likely a child is to be trafficked when they graduate from our program."

The idea is truly brilliant—comprehensive and practical.

During my years in ministry, everyone simply *wanted* to "help" and never assigned measurements to determine if they *were* actually being effective. Because, in the end, it didn't matter if they were effective. It mattered if the missionaries felt good.

We'd hand out food. We'd dig wells. We'd drop off Bibles. Then get out, as quickly as possible, beaming with big smiles because we were such good and selfless people.

Look at us. Look at how good we are. Look at us making a difference.

When in actuality, we had no clue if we ever made a difference. When in actuality, we had no clue that buying a trendy pair of shoes for those poor Africans was destabilizing the economy in Johannesburg, bankrupting local shoemakers.

But this organization is holding itself accountable, and more importantly, it's *not* just a bunch of white guys patting themselves on the back. In fact, there's only one white employee. Everyone else is Thai, and the majority are men.

Over the years, I've always seen more women than men in the ministry world/nonprofit world/education world, especially when children are involved. It's as though only the feminine can stomach helping other humans.

But here are *men* choosing a career in helping and educating children.

We arrive at the main auditorium area, where music plays and the staff dance and sing with the students.

Three men grab Adam, Rachel, and me, pulling us into the circle.

At first, I'm anxious. I'm in a country I don't know with people I don't know being asked to awkwardly dance. Not the most comfortable situation.

But as the smiles of the staff and laughs of the children overwhelm me, I get caught up in the dance.

It's hard to *not* be happy with these people.

I begin to lift my hands and spin like some white girl at Coachella then stop and laugh with the kids nearby.

The music dies down, and Rachel brings us toward the back of the space.

"Who are all these men working for you? How did you find them?"

"They're our employees. We don't believe in volunteers. We wanted to make sure that we are not only helping the kids but also creating meaningful jobs for everyone involved; after all, people should get paid for meaningful work (what a concept). And one thing that I love about our org is that nearly every man is gay."

I stop watching the children and look at Rachel in confusion.

"Wait. What did you say?"

"All the men, minus that guy right there," she points to a man on the microphone, "are gay. We didn't plan it that way. We just hired the best people, and it turns out gay men are the best people for working with children. They've been amazing."

Gay men ... working in ministry ... with children ... and they aren't fired? They're allowed to work? Without being labeled as pedophiles??? In fact, they're celebrated????

The thoughts overwhelm me as I turn to Adam and smile. He knows *exactly* what I'm thinking because he's thinking the same thing.

Being gay had closed so many doors within ministry for the both of us, whether directly, like Adam getting excommunicated from his church, or indirectly, like when I was not allowed to lead worship or be with kids but was never told. Our sexuality had disqualified us, and that was a sore spot for me because I genuinely missed helping people in meaningful ways. The worst part? I think a piece of me believed them.

Yet here was this place, not only allowing gay men to work in ministry, to work with kids, but celebrating gay men working in ministry with kids, saying they did the *best* work.

"Of course they're amazing!" Adam snarks off. "They're gay men. We're fucking awesome!"

I laugh at Adam then turn back to the joyful staff dancing with the children.

I think God wants to love on us...

Maybe I can still do this as a gay man. Maybe I haven't been disqualified. Maybe all those churches and ministries were wrong.

Blessed Queers

A man wearing a rainbow cape ascends the stage and grabs the microphone. He begins to pray.

"Precious God, we thank you for your body and your blood."

Facing him are over two thousand LGBTQ+ people, holding bread and a cup of juice.

It's been a while since I've participated in this practice—this practice of our persecutors.

If anyone had a reason to raise a fist toward God and curse him, if anyone had a reason to say, "Fuck it!" and give up on any semblance of faith, if anyone had a reason to throw this bread and juice in the face of the nearest minister, it's these people...

A people cursed.

A people abused.

A people cast aside, cast out, and cast down.

A people told again and again that they are reprobates...

That they are perverts...

That they're abominations.

If anyone had a reason...

Yet here they stand, with the body and the blood.

Here they stand, saying God is good, that God is faithful.

Here they stand, holding the symbols of forgiveness and love.

Captain LGBTQ continues: "And just as you have forgiven us, forgive those who have sinned against us. Forgive those who have hurt us. For they knew not what they did. Forgive them, as you forgive us."

Whimpers and choked-back tears come from the audience.

Here are a people...

In spite of pain...

In spite of loss and exclusion...

Clinging to God, refusing to let him go, refusing to let "his people" rob them of his love.

"This is my body which is broken for you. Eat this in remembrance of me."

I chew on the bread, thinking of Jesus and how he was murdered and tortured by the religious and the pious. I think about how he chose to surround himself with people like me, people the religious called disgraced and unclean and unforgivable.

A verse comes to mind, taking on a new meaning:

"Blessed are you when people insult you, persecute you and falsely say all kinds of evil against you because of me."[1]

In the book of Matthew, the reader is confronted with a phrase: "Blessed are..."

To Christians, they've learned its name a *long* time ago, a name *not* originally found in the ancient text. It was added. The verses are called "The Beatitudes," and the name comes from this idea that these verses hold the *attitudes* we should *be*. (Any time Christians can shove words together to make them more memorable, they absolutely will. That, and alliteration and three points. Always three points. Never more. Again, branding.)

"Blessed are the poor in spirit, for theirs is the kingdom of heaven."

"Blessed are those who mourn, for they will be comforted."

"Blessed are the meek, for they will inherit the earth."

"And blessed are you when you are persecuted and falsely called evil."

But there's a problem with the name "Beatitudes": No one *wants* to be poor in spirit. No one *wants* to be in mourning. No one *wants* to be meek. Instead, we *find* ourselves poor; we *find* ourselves in mourning; we *find* ourselves meek.

They are places, horrible places, that we kick and scream and claw to avoid.

Yet these places are called holy. Holy, because they bless us, cultivating something within us as their shadow looms overhead.

They soften.

They break.

They make us realize life is not what was promised.

"Naked I came from my mother's womb, and naked I will depart."[2]

It's *these* places…

Places that bless us with their shadow…

Places where we are poor and don't have the answers…

Places where we mourn in pain and loss…

Places where we are humbled by our circumstances…

Places where we are persecuted and falsely called all kinds of evil.

With that in mind…

…Blessed are you, dear non-binary child, you who were poor of resources and language and support because churches refused to believe God made more than man and woman.

…Blessed are you, perfect trans boy, you who mourned alone as your body betrayed you and no one understood your loss.

…Blessed are you, beloved lesbian girl, you who were told to submit to authority after meekly questioning your youth pastor as to why girls never speak from the pulpit.

…Blessed are you, sweet gay boy, you who were removed from volunteering in children's church because you were falsely called a pervert and depraved.

Blessed are *you*…

You who will inherit heaven…

You who will be comforted…

You who will inherit the earth…

Beloved…

Queer…

Child of God.

You who were falsely called evil and wrong…

You who were called bad and broken.

Rainbow-cape man raises his cup.

"And this is the blood of the new covenant. Through which you are a new creation. Drink this in remembrance of me."

He swallows, and we follow suit, swallowing the blood.

Another verse comes to mind:

"Do not call anything impure that God has made clean."[3]

Blessed are you.

You who *have* been made clean.

You who *have* been called holy.

Blessed.

Are.

You.

When people persecute you and falsely call you all kinds of evil.

You…

Blessed are *you*.

"And all God's people said…"

"Amen."

When I Said Fuck in Church

I'm in church … again … but this time it's not because I'm reeking of shame, like when I smelled like guy forty-two.

It's because I'm captivated by hope.

A few months prior, I had learned of post-evangelical churches. They are these churches that have looked at the scriptures around homosexuality and decided that they could no longer, in good conscience, bar queer people from attending and being fully involved in church—volunteering, leading. Because they weren't just "welcomed" in this church in hopes that they would change; they were affirmed in all that they are.

And it moves beyond LGBTQ+ issues. These churches talk about racial justice and the problems of gentrification. They have women in all levels of leadership who are even allowed to teach men, carrying the title of pastor. (Gasp! Scandal!) They have open forums where anyone can question the Bible because they aren't scared of questions. They want to ultimately seek truth and understand that truth stands in spite of questions, and they own the fact that the Bible is a problematic book.

So I decided to take a risk. I decided to go back to church. Maybe this would be different. Unlikely. But maybe. After all, it's still a church. But today I woke up feeling spunky. Besides, I decided to let my resentment go in the Chiang Mai sky … at least for now…

A white woman who looks like she should be playing her guitar at the Washington memorial during the Vietnam War addresses the crowd from the stage.

"Hello everyone," she sounds like it too, her voice airy and dancing. "I'm so glad you're here. If it's your first time, welcome. We're happy to have you. Let's stand together as we worship."

My body tightens up with the familiar language. This greeting is unnervingly similar to all the churches that I grew up with, the churches that hurt me. *Fuck. Maybe this was a bad idea.*

I hold my breath, refusing to rise as everyone else stands. I wanna sit this one out. (And if I'm honest, I'm being a little testy to see how it would be received.)

"God, we thank you for your faithfulness," flower child says, "We thank you for your goodness to us. We humbly ask for you to fill this space and commune with us today."

I roll my eyes.

This again.

"He's already here. He's omnipresent."

I hear giggling nearby.

Oh shit! Did I say that out loud?

I look to my left and find a girl with dark brown hair smiling at me.

"I know, right?" she says. "Either he's omnipresent or he's not. Keep it consistent, people."

I smile back, feeling a little more comfortable.

The service continues, following the typical pattern of every other church I've been in—worship, announcements, tithes, sermon. However, when they do the tithing portion, it's not this big ordeal, this mini sermon to manipulate people to empty their wallets. They simply say, "If you'd like to give, here's how. We appreciate your help."

Well, that's refreshing.

During the sermon, the pastor brings up hard things.

"In Joshua, the text says that God commanded the destruction of an entire people. We have a term for this. It's called genocide. What do we do with that?"

"'Bout fucking time someone talked about that."

Shit! Did I just fucking cuss in church? Rein it in, Brandon.

But no one freaks out. Instead, there are more giggles.

Where the hell am I?

As the service progresses, I relax more and more.

"My name is Amanda," a white woman walks on stage. Less Creedence Clearwater Revival and more Norma Jean, especially with those tattoos. "I'm the teaching and adult ministry pastor."

"Oh praise Jesus. A woman pastor."

More giggles and smiles.

"I just wanted to remind you that tonight is our monthly Sunday night event called 'Question Everything.' Every first Sunday of the month we host these events where we encourage you to bring all your questions about God and Christianity and the church. We also use this time to answer any questions you may have about why we're affirming of LGBTQ+ and how we arrived there. If you haven't been yet, we would love to have you. Now, may the God of peace, who raised Jesus from the dead, strengthen you in your inner being for every good work. Grace and peace."

"Grace and peace." The congregation responds as the service ends.

Well, that wasn't completely terrible.

I grab my coat and head for the back door.

"Hey!" It's the brown-haired girl from earlier, the one that smiled at my cursing.

"Hi!"

"My name is Jackie. First time?"

"That obvious?"

"It's not every day that you hear 'fuck' in church."

"Yeahhhh … my bad. Kinda slipped out. But I was super surprised no one freaked out."

"That's DCC for you. It's pretty great. What are you doing right now?"

"Ummm … I was about to start my trek back down to Colorado Springs. Got an hour commute ahead of me, so I'll likely snag a bite before leaving Denver."

"Oh! There aren't any affirming churches down there?"

I start laughing, "An affirming church in Colorado Springs? You're funny. I'm guessing you haven't been down there."

"Not really. I just moved here a year ago. Well, before you start your trek, would you wanna come over to my place and make some pizzas? There's a group of us that always get together after church, and we'd love to have you."

This woman doesn't know me. I could be a serial killer or worse, a religious asshole, and she's inviting me over for pizza?

"Sure! That sounds great!"

From church, we all head to the grocery store to buy supplies together.

"Hi Brandon, I'm Elliot. Heard you're hanging with us today."

"Yessir. That okay with ya?"

"For sure! Happy to have ya. Where you from?"

The conversations continue with ease and comfort, ranging from who God is to being an LGBTQ-sorta Christian to the enneagram to childhood trauma. (My enneagram four heart is exploding.)

As we begin cooking, I decided to hide in the kitchen.

I've always found kitchens to be a soothing place, probably because food is naturally soothing to the body. But beyond that, people are distracted. People don't normally come to a kitchen to sit and talk. Instead, it's a place humming with activity, alleviating the pressure to talk and make awkward eye contact. And I hate both. Instead, you can sit there or do a task, talk or not talk, all while tasting that soothing food along the way. It's the icon of hospitality. (Plus, there's always a good counter to sit on, and I'm gay, so I love sitting on a good counter.)

Jackie is cutting vegetables next to this guy named Justin who happens to be gay and also happens to be very cute.

"So why are the two of you Christian?" I say as I snag one of the mushrooms Jackie was cutting.

Bad! At! Small! Talk!

A normal human, when meeting new humans, would usually ask questions like, "What's your name?" "What do you do for work?" "What are you up to these days?"

Not me. Instead, shortly after "Hi! My name is Brandon," I go for "How has the church hurt you?" "What are your thoughts around death?" "When was the last time you felt alive?" "Are there any areas of disappointment in your life?"

After the shock subsides, most people appreciate it. It's novel and makes people feel like I genuinely want to get to know them. And I *do* genuinely want to get to know them. People are fascinating, especially Jackie and Justin.

But in this moment, there's more than curiosity and fascination with the eternal mystery that is being human. I have ulterior motives.

Beneath this new budding hope, there's skepticism and judgment.

Passionate Christians hate *the gays. They can't tolerate sin. If these Christians like the gays, they probably don't even* like *God. He's probably just a nice philosophical idea that helps them cope with the world. They don't actually care about him.*

I think I got this from growing up at a hyper-charismatic megachurch.

We'd always go around trying to save other Christians because they weren't *actually* saved. I mean, if they were *actually* saved, they'd dance in worship, they'd speak in tongues, they'd try to save people from the fires of hell.

Years later, after coming out and having doubts in God, I would *still* look at progressive liturgical churches that were more mild and calm as a lesser version of Christianity, judging the caliber of their faith.

"I think it's 'cause he sees me," Justin responds to my question.

My heart skips a beat.

"Like, I feel at times like I've got everyone fooled. But not him. He sees me. Even when I've tried to hide. He always finds me. And it means the world."

I'm speechless. (And also a bit turned on. Apparently, having an intimate connection with Jesus is a turn-on for me? Who knew?)

"Jackie?"

"Because he loved me when no one else would." She continues to chop mushrooms. "Like, I have a lot of self-hate. But he broke through it all and called me loved and beautiful when I never could. I'm not sure where I'd be without him if I'm honest. My mind and heart can be pretty dark sometimes."

My mouth hangs open like some idiot.

"You okay, Brandon?"

"Ummm … yeah … that's just really refreshing to hear."

"How about you?"

"Ha! Ummm … some days I'm not sure if I even *am* a Christian."

"Ain't that the truth!" Jackie laughs and slams the knife down dramatically into a mushroom, scaring me a little.

"Like Christians can be rough for me. I'm not sure if I want to be one. Most of them are assholes."

"Okay, so then change the question: Do you believe in Jesus? Scrap the Christian part."

I smile.

Good strategy, Jackie.

"Yeah … yeah, I think I do. I didn't for a while. But I think I'm beginning to believe in him again."

"Why?"

"Because he's chased me. Like I've *tried* to lose him, and somehow, he still catches up to me. Stubborn fucker."

I'm reminded of that time in the car, the time God trapped me. My hand reaches out and forms a fist, as my feet dangle off the counter.

They laugh, and I smile for the hundredth time today. Because maybe I found my people. Maybe you *can* be Christian and decent. Scratch that. Maybe there are people that believe in Jesus and are decent. Maybe they love like he loved. Maybe they aren't some religious prudes that care more about stupid rules than grace.

But more importantly, because I can be selfish, maybe I'm not alone.

Maybe I've been found.

Vessels

I'm an external processor. It's probably why I can't shut my mouth and probably why I can't help but write. It has to get out of me. It has to become not-me for me to make sense of it. And it is in those times when ink drops onto a page or when words plop out of my mouth that I realize, "No wait! That's not it!" or "Wait! Do I actually feel that way? I think I do!"

I envy internal processors. They can make a mess in their minds, then bring out their stories and convictions with ornate wrappers and classy bows. So concise. So methodical.

Not me. It's messy in here. And when it initially comes out, there are *absolutely* no bows. It's just spewed out on paper or people.

"Wait! I didn't mean that! I take it back! I put it outside of me, and now I can clearly see it. It's not me! That's something else. It's fear. It's worry. Shit! Let me clean this up. Let me clean *you* up." As if I'm vomiting on the person listening.

But every so often, I say something, something I've never thought about, and it becomes an epiphany the second it leaves my lips.

౷

"So how do you make sense of the fact that you've encountered God in these places that have hurt you?"

I'm sitting with my friend Andrew and his wife Bethany.

Bethany and I used to date in high school, you know, when I was in love with love. Now, after some complicated years and hard conversations, we're best friends. Sure, they still work at a church, and yes, that freaks me the fuck out some days, but they also ask about my dating life. They met my Henry. They dared to step into a space they didn't understand. And it helped. Mistakes and all. Messiness and all.

But in *this* conversation, I sense an ulterior motive from Andrew. Like he's not asking the question out of curiosity. Instead, he's asking it to redirect me, to convince me churches can't be *that* bad if God is moving there.

It's the exact same rhetoric that allowed people like Mark Driscoll to get a pass while abusing staff and congregants.

"But God is moving!" his elders would say. "Thousands are coming to Christ!" "This must mean that God approves of Mark and his tactics, regardless of what people are telling us." "Like the Bible says, 'A good tree can't produce bad fruit.'"[1]

And now thousands of "bad fruits" are going to counseling.

This all-or-nothing mentality, this either/or mindset, is damaging on both fronts.

On the Christian side, it dismisses trauma and hides mistakes, cultivating a culture where leaders can do no wrong. And as a result, abuse will continue to be covered up for "the glory of God."

On the ex-Christian side, everything experienced within the walls of the church now becomes suspect and tainted. A beautiful moment with the divine is now called under scrutiny. A word of wisdom from the pulpit is now thrown out. *All* of it was bad; *all* of it has to go. The result is an overwhelming disorientation and loss of identity caused by fierce spiritual bankruptcy.

This mindset has robbed us all.

In contrast, "If we are open," Brennan Manning writes, "we rarely resort to either/or—either creation or evolution, liberty or law, sacred or secular, Beethoven or Madonna. We focus on both/and, fully aware that God's truth cannot be imprisoned in a small definition."[2]

And in doing, maybe we can feel a little less lost, a little more whole, enriching our lives, not with black or white, but the bountiful gray.

So what might the gray look like here with Andrew's not-so-curious question?

I'd find the answer in the vomit, spewed on the Cantrells and the floor.

"I mean, do you believe God moves through people?" I ask Andrew.

"Sure!"

"But you believe people are broken?"

"Absolutely!" he says.

"A vessel's a vessel. Whether it's human or not. I see a bunch of verses that make it look like God likes using broken things. Like Corinthians: 'We now have this light shining in our hearts, but we ourselves are like fragile clay jars…'[3] And in the church, we talk about it all the time, but it's only in relation to people. A preacher will often say before an emotional altar call, 'God loves using broken people! He loves using you!' Which is funny because the church *doesn't* love using broken people. They want everything clean and put together. But I think God also likes using broken things. Institutions and communities. And in the end, aren't those things simply broken people gathered together? And doesn't God say he shows up when people get together in his name?[4] Even if they're fuck-ups? So it makes sense.

"I've experienced God in some pretty fucked up institutions and communities, institutions that don't believe right, that don't love like Jesus loves; in fact, they cause hurt and pain. Why? Because they're composed of fucked up people. Really fucked up people. Just because it's now an institution, doesn't mean it's magically not fucked up. It's likely more fucked up because people seem to get more stupid the more people there are. You'd think more brains would mean more intelligence, but it rarely turns out that way.

"But for some reason, I think God uses broken things, and he says he likes it when we get together. Even when we're more stupid together.

"I think God does this because of his humility," I continue. "Like, he isn't too proud to live in a broken and dirty container. He just jumps in as long as there's an invitation, regardless of holes or cracks, maybe even *because* there are holes and cracks. As long as someone or something is willing to invite him, I think he comes, and I think he shines, and I think broken and cracked people are desperate and humble enough to ask him to come. And I think the reason he likes it when stupid, fucked up people get together is so we can behold him through the cracks of the people around us. Like that cheesy moment at an Easter service with all the candles. Little weak and wavering flames somehow light up a massive sanctuary, allowing us to behold something beautiful, reminding us that he's here, here in the person next to us.

"At the end of the day, I think he just wants to be with us. And I think he takes whatever home that genuinely wants him."

"Yaaas, Brandon! Preach!" Bethany pipes in. "That's- so- good!" She claps between the words.

"Thanks! Just comes from trauma!"

While Bethany is this vibrant energy demanding to be seen (one time she *literally demanded* a red carpet for a murder mystery party, feeling *way* too into the character), Andrew's this calm and soothing energy, bringing peace to a room. Together, they're this gorgeous yin and yang, push and pull, black and white—both/and—and it's their both-ness, their *and*-ness that has added so much color to me, themselves, and the world around them. They're better together.

Bountiful gray.

While Bethany pulls out her metaphorical hanky for my metaphorical preaching, Andrew simply sits there, sipping and savoring, gently nodding with that look he gets when he's processing something.

"That's gooood, maaaan." He says it like a California-surfer bro, even though he was born and raised in Colorado.

That was *good, wasn't it? Where the hell did that come from? Do I actually believe that? I think I do. I think I do believe that!*

My answer in the verbal vomit mess.

Bethany gets up, excited and bubbly.

"Who wants more wine?" She holds up the bottle and pours us all another round.

Gas Chambers and Sovereignty

"Who are we to decide what is evil?"

I'm sitting with my new good friend, Caleb. A friend I just met on Grindr.

While I was eager for sex, deep in the tunnel, a profile, with an actual face, messaged me.

"Brandon Flanery!? I've been wanting to meet you for ages! We were supposed to be friends at least five years ago. We run in all the same circles and keep missing each other. I'm Caleb. When you free?"

Duh fuck? I don't know you like that! Coming at me with all that intensity. (Is this how everyone feels about me? If so, I'm fucking insane.)

"Ummm ... would you wanna snag coffee in the morning?"

"I'm more of a tea guy, but that sounds great! Meet at your place?"

A tea guy? Ugh!

I know it shouldn't be this way, but when someone tells me they drink tea, I have judgments that they're pretentious, believing they're more enlightened or something, like they've transcended and look down on those pathetic coffee drinkers. "Oh! You drink coffee? How does it feel to be addicted to a beverage to cope with life? I don't need to cope with life. I embrace it. With tea!" Insert British laugh as they hold their leaf water with pinky out, monocle fastened to their eye. (When in actuality, the vast majority of them don't drink coffee simply because it makes them anxious and shake. So instead of them being the judgmental asshole, it's me. I'm the judgmental asshole. But I don't have a cool accent.)

"Sure. See you then!"

I honestly disregarded the interaction. People are flakes on Grindr. You make plans, and 90 percent of the time they fall through. So when Caleb *actually* rings my doorbell at eight in the god-awful morning, I quickly had to throw on pants and tame my hair.

The next thing I know, I'm in the throes of a conversation about the sovereignty of God and the definition of evil with a guy I just met on a hookup app, all while desperately trying to find any blasted tea in a house of unenlightened coffee drinkers.

What the hell is going on?

"Who are we to put God in a box, saying, 'You're evil if you do this to me!'" Caleb says. "Maybe the death of your child *is* the best thing that could happen to you. If we're all going to die, who cares how it happens as long as it's used by God for something good, and it's always good because he's good and he's orchestrating everything. I believe that God, whether I was born gay or made gay as a result of my circumstances, made me this way to teach me and the people around me things he could never teach if I was straight. And that's God's ultimate goal: to teach us. Life is a school, a school where we learn to trust God and believe that he's good, no matter what. I believe that our meeting on Grindr was no accident—it was orchestrated by God for us to have this conversation. Do you think we just met by accident?"

"Yes. I absolutely do. Is black tea okay?"

"I'm more of an herbal guy."

Of course, he's more of an herbal guy.

"Uhhhh … there's mint?"

"Perfect!"

"Anyway, back to Grindr. I've been on it a lot because I have no control over my sex impulses. It was just a matter of time before I met you. It's like evolution: just give something enough time, and coincidences form reality. We think it's destiny or something, but it's just the way it is because it's the way it is. Besides, if you believe God orchestrated us getting together, where's the line of what he's in control of?"

"What do you mean 'Where's the line?' I don't believe there's a line. He's orchestrating everything, and our poor and flawed concepts of good and evil are limiting our ideas of who God is and what he can do in our lives. We put him in a box when we say, 'That can't be God because that's evil, and if God is doing that, it makes *him* evil.' He transcends our pathetic ideas of morality."

"So you're telling me that you believe that as Jews were murdered in gas chambers, God was orchestrating it?"

"Absolutely! You don't know what those specific people needed to learn about faith. You also don't know how the Holocaust has forever changed how we relate to war and crimes against humanity. We're so finite in our understanding of the universe. God is bigger than that and knew the individual hearts of every person in those chambers and how that would shape them and our world. We're ultimately here to learn, learn to choose God rather than ourselves, and life's our teacher."

"So when your dad abused you, you would say that God was pulling the strings." (We had already chatted through trauma, now in the throes of existentialism because … again … I'm. Bad. At. Small. Talk.)

"Yes."

"Then what does accountability look like? If God is in control, who are we to punish people in the world for doing wrong? It's ultimately God's fault. Not theirs."

"Exactly!"

"What?! You *actually* believe that?"

"Who are we to judge people? Why is it so important to you that people are held accountable for their actions? Don't you realize that this means that you also must be held accountable for your actions?"

"Correct. I *should absolutely* be held accountable for my actions. If I kill someone, I *should* be held accountable for that choice. It's evil and should be called evil, and I should be locked away. Otherwise, society would crumble."

"Doesn't really sound like grace. If I believe God is in control, I can see the abuse of my father as something that made me more empathetic, more understanding. It's made me into the person I am today, and I can be thankful for that."

"Oh my God, Caleb. I can't believe that!"

"Well then what do you believe? If you believe in God, did he just make everything and float away."

"Kind of."

"Explain." He sips on his mint tea, peering over the lip like a British oligarch.

"I can believe there's a God that created everything. That makes sense to me. Whether he used evolution or not, I truly don't care. But every effect has a cause. It's a rule of science, and I think there must be a great cause that made this effect that is the universe. Then, he gave the earth to humans. We're the rulers. We have the keys. So he *literally* can't intervene. He's not sovereign here.

We are. I think he's powerless to move in the world. That would explain why it's such a shit show—humans are making a mess of it, and we're the ones driving this ship."

"So rather than thinking God allows bad things to happen, you think he is *literally* unable to stop bad things from happening?"

"Correct. Because even though we're stupid humans, *we* can even understand that if a person was standing at the edge of a dark alley and saw someone getting raped and did nothing, we would hold them accountable. We'd say they should share the blame. The same is true of God. If he's *able* to do something and *doesn't*, he *should* be held accountable; otherwise, he's not a good and just God."

"So how can you trust God for anything?"

"That's the problem! I don't think I can! I'm a pretty anxious person."

"What about the Bible? It has stories of God moving."

"Well, first off, I don't take the Bible literally anymore. I don't think it's perfect. If that's the case, God commanded genocide and the subjugation of women and the empowerment of the enslaver. I can't believe he would do that, and there are inconsistencies in the Bible. So I don't hold it as some holy, perfect thing. It's only recently that I started to think that *maybe* I can encounter God through it again. I view it like a window. It allows me to get glimpses of him. But it's not him. And a window can still get fucking dirty."

"So do you think that Jesus existed?"

"Yes. And honestly, I'm not sure about a lot. Truly. But I think I believe Jesus was a beautiful expression of God, a God who chose to suffer and become the embodiment of love. And I think God became man, Jesus, because humanity kept fucking up the image of God. For thousands of years, humanity was stumbling in the dark, putting their hands on something, trying to figure out what is life and who is God, and—"

"Like the parable of six blind men and an elephant?"

"Huh?"

"There's this theological metaphor that God is like an elephant and humans are like blind men with no previous knowledge of what an elephant is. One person is touching the trunk and describes a spout. Another is touching the leg and describes a pillar. We're all describing the same thing but touching different parts."

"I love that! That's exactly how I feel! And God got tired of people fucking it up. So he came to show humanity what he *actually* looks like. There enters

Jesus—the ultimate expression of God. It's why he says, 'If you've seen me, you've seen the Father.'"

"So then why didn't Jesus come sooner?"

"Because he couldn't come till someone trusted him. Again, he's bound to humans. I think there could have been thousands of Marys—women God approached to trust him with the miracle of carrying God incarnate through a virgin birth. But it took thousands of years for someone to say yes."

"So you think God is only able to act in the world as much as humans are willing to trust him?"

"I think so. I'm still working this whole thing out. But I think that's what I believe."

"That puts God in such a small box."

"Does it? Or does it free him to be good?"

"Maybe. But what can you trust him for if it's all up to *you*? And it also puts a lot of pressure on you. How can you rest if you're never sure that the next step or action you're making is the 'right' one?"

"Well, I can't. Duh. Again, I'm an anxious person." I take a sip of my black coffee and savor a moment of holy pleasure from my base caffeine addiction.

Caleb continues talking, fired up by one of his rants. I would quickly come to find out that he'd do this a lot—rant. And I would quickly find out that I loved it because it challenged me. And even though I would get pissed off and curse at him and call him out, a piece of me wanted to believe the same way he did, wanted to believe that God was in everything and controlled everything and that I could rest and trust in his goodness. As problematic as his theology was, I wanted to believe that purpose and destiny were real, that my life mattered and that God was writing a good story with it.

But this isn't a story.

This is real life.

So I would hold back and resist, refusing to fall into this reckless trust that Caleb had somehow found in the arms of a God who orchestrated the Holocaust.

The Alchemist

I'm not gonna lie—I hate this chapter. I hate that a silly book impacted me so deeply. That a fictitious book about a shepherd and fate and magic, of all things, somehow pushed me over the edge.

But then again, I'm a sucker for magic. And maybe, even though I resent a little book called *The Alchemist*, I'm also grateful because then maybe writing actually does matter. Maybe writing actually does change people. Maybe, in the words of John Green, "[a book] fills you with this weird evangelical zeal, and you become convinced that the shattered world will never be put back together unless and until all living humans read the book."[1]

But that terrifies me with responsibility as a writer, so I'll choose resentment and diminish the impact of writers so I can sleep at night.

∽

I'm in Durango—my favorite corner of Colorado—visiting the poor girl who asked this closeted gay boy out to Sadie Hawkins back in high school—Austin.

We had always stayed in touch over the years, even though I was a bad straight date.

A part of it was because she has always inspired me—living on sailboats, leading treks through Hawaii, teaching English in Italy. I love watching her life from a safe distance, vicariously savoring her risks.

Now she's what the locals endearingly call a dirtbag, someone who lives more out of their backpack than a house, romping through the deserts of Utah, working with teenagers to help them reconnect with their emotions.

She'd spend a week out in the field (as they call it) and then a week back in the "normal" world.

On one of those off weeks, she invites me down to take in the life of the desert, and oh how I cherish it.

Drinking beer while floating down the river. Tripping on shrooms while hiking in the desert. Laughing while covered in mud at a fancy winery.

There's an elusive magic to the desert I have never seen before, and it isn't because of the mushrooms, though they might have helped.

Maybe I can get behind this whole dirtbag thing.

Exhausted from a full day, we collapse on her couch, warming ourselves by the fire. And, because I'm a dingus and I love proving to everyone (mainly myself) that I can live off of barely anything, I didn't pack a book. Too much space. So I peruse her shelves and find one that has always stood out to me: *The Alchemist.*

"How's this?" I hold up the bright red cover to Austin.

"You've never read it?!"

"Nope. It's always felt like something that I *should* read, even though I know nothing about it. Does that sound weird?"

"Not at all, especially once you read the book. You should take it."

"You sure?"

"Positive."

Like the COVID test I would get a few weeks later.

∾

Lying sick in my bed, I call my recruiter.

She is not happy.

"What do you mean you got COVID? You're supposed to leave for Korea in a week. We have kids waiting for you, and you tested positive. This is not good, Brandon. Korea is very strict. You will not make it into the country. Let me talk to the school, but this is not good. They may need to find someone else."

I hang up the phone and begin to cry.

This may seem a bit dramatic but let me explain…

After losing everything once I came out, I formulated a plan: I loved living in Germany, why not live in another country forever? Sure, I could never be a missionary again—that felt like selling my soul, and they don't like the gays—but I could go teach! That could empower me to live as an expat, never begging for another dollar.

So I got my TESOL certification and went back to college at the age of twenty-six. I received a bachelor's degree in English and education. I student taught for a year in Colorado during a global pandemic. I worked with a recruiter to move to Korea and teach, signed a contract, and sold all my possessions to move in a few weeks.

What I fought to build after starting over was finally coming into fruition! I was finally getting my life together!

Till COVID…

As the weight of my recruiter's words hit me, I flip open my computer to watch another episode of *Schitt's Creek*.

Problem: my eyes are burning from looking at screens nonstop, unable to get out of bed from exhaustion.

Then I remember the book.

If not now, when?

So here, in bed, struggling to breathe, isolated from the world, I decide to read *The Alchemist* … and I'm hooked.

A shepherd in Spain. A shop in Morocco. An oasis in the desert. The pyramids of Egypt.

This book, one that so many raved about, is honestly quite basic and even childlike, just a kid on an adventure, looking for buried treasure. Yet somehow, while reading about Santiago traveling North Africa and finding his personal legend, following the omens and trusting his heart, that ugly and beautiful lady called Destiny tickles the corners of my soul…

"My heart is a traitor." the boy said to the alchemist, when they had paused to rest the horses. "It doesn't want me to go on."

"That makes sense," the alchemist answered. "Naturally it's afraid that, in pursuing your dreams, you might lose everything you've won."

"Well then why should I listen to my heart?"

"Because you will never again be able to keep it quiet. Even if you pretend not to have heard what it tells you, it will always be there inside of you, repeating to you what you're thinking about life and about the world."[2]

The story of Santiago empowers me to unroll the scroll of my life and inspect all the coincidences and happenstances.

The pages echo the words of that voice, that voice that might be God, the one that led me to coffee shops and warned me under a willow tree, trapped me in a car and called my love good. That voice whispers of how lovely life might be if Destiny were real. It sings of how even the horrible, terrible things might carry beauty and magic.

I think of my friend Caleb, of Holocausts and the divine. I think of Bethany and Andrew, of broken jars and broken hearts. I think of the middle-aged men, of brutal honesty and courageous acceptance. I think of lanterns. I think of countertops. I think of rainbow capes and wasted boobs.

No longer were they simple moments. No longer were they ordinary. They were omens. And for the first time in a long time, bed-ridden and quarantined from a pandemic, I decide that maybe it might be time to trust. That maybe it might be time to believe. Because *maybe*, I have my *own* personal legend, and the divine or God or whatever it is hasn't given up on me.

My recruiter calls.

"The school director said he's willing to wait for you. You're lucky. Most directors would not have done this. Keep testing. As soon as you get a negative test, we'll buy your airplane ticket."

Luck had nothing to do with it! This was Destiny! This was my own personal legend! And that legend is in Korea! And my heart is finally speaking up, telling me what it wants after years of being scared, and it wants to believe again! It wants to trust again! And all it took was a stupid book! All it took was me getting sick!

And just like that, a book became more than a book, a move became more than a move, and a pandemic became more than lying sick in bed, angry and alone.

"The boy and his heart had become friends."[3]

On a Plane Over the Pacific

I'm staring out the window as resiliently moonlit clouds float in an inky night, high above a raging Pacific.

I'm on my way to start a new life in Korea.

I can't sleep. There's too much in my head and heart, spinning and knocking about.

I think of the last time I lived abroad, back when I was a missionary, back when I believed in God and destiny and that I could be made straight with the right kind of love.

I think of how it all came crashing down. Of how miracles didn't happen, and leaders had affairs and God didn't lead me to a cute coffee shop.

I think of how a few beers here and a couple of well-delivered existential questions there made me panic and squirm.

I think of neuroplasticity and how it didn't change me.

I think of churches and pastors lying to their congregations and hurting the queer people in their pews.

I think of the boyfriend who I sacrificed everything for and then lost in the end.

I think of the friends who told me I was going to hell and the others that went silent.

But I also think of those who didn't.

I think of the ones who came back, the ones who said they were sorry and kept their promise of staying by my side no matter what.

I think of 1211 and the gift that it was.

I think of Lake Shasta.

I think of my ex-girlfriend and her willingness to tell me I was being a spoiled rotten brat when I was being a spoiled rotten brat.

I think of a bunch of middle-aged men bear-hugging me and saying I'm perfect just the way I am.

I think of heroes in rainbow capes, and vacations with floating lanterns.

I think of nice Christians who curse, and pizza talks on countertops.

I think of Caleb and the Holocaust, of sovereignty and destiny, and how the irony is juxtaposed to the fact that we met on a hookup app, both hankering for sex.

I think of silly books and silly words on silly pages.

I think of it all, and I think about how there was never some great miracle. Never some lightning in the clouds or a burning bush in a cave.

In fact, it was the opposite.

There were unanswered prayers and stubborn questions.

There were broken legs and broken promises.

And then there were normal moments inside normal days that somehow had a glow, that somehow had a warmth.

But they stacked and stacked, slowly and gently, eventually melting me like flames to wax.

"Light is incredibly generous," John O'Donohue writes, "but also gentle. When you attend to the way the dawn comes, you learn how light can coax the dark. The first fingers of light appear on the horizon, and ever so deftly and gradually, they pull the mantle of darkness away from the world."[1]

And that divine, warm, gentle light, like that of a candle, somehow coaxed my darkness.

There were still shadows. Of course there were. For this light was not the blazing glory of the dawn. They were candles, gathering in a dark room. They leave shadows and shapes in the inky black, questions and uncertainty in spite of their glow.

But here's the thing about uncertainty: its color changes depending on context. Let me explain…

You're blindfolded.

You can't see a thing.

You have no clue what is in front of you or where you are.

A hand reaches out. A voice calls your name.

If it's the voice of a stranger, terror seizes you.

What's going to happen? Where are they taking me?

But if the voice changes … If the voice is someone you know … If the voice is embedded with love and trust…

Then suddenly the scene changes.

Suddenly the questions take on a different hue.

What's going to happen? Where are they leading me?

Excitement. Eagerness.

For thousands of years, people have spent their lives trying to answer the unanswerable questions: Is there a God? Is that God one of love? If so, why is there pain? Why is there death? Why doesn't God answer prayers? Why doesn't he do anything?

But I don't think having the answers is the solution.

Maybe there *are* brilliant minds who have answered life's horrible and painful questions. Maybe they're out there, and I just haven't read them. Or maybe one day, in the near or distant future, some algorithm will come up with the answer, and life will be good and right; technology will have saved the day!

Maybe…

But tell those answers to a grieving mother who lost her child to leukemia at the age of eleven…

Tell those answers to a gay teen thrown out by the family who claimed to love God…

Tell those answers to a child raped by someone they trusted, someone who should have protected them, not ravaged them…

Tell those answers to a lonely Indian woman with a missing leg, pedaling around on a pathetic piece of wood, surrounded by the clinically insane and over-stretched nuns, all because one fateful day she slipped in front of a bus…

Tell your answers to them.

They won't be enough.

Because answers don't heal.

And maybe God knew that.

Maybe he knew that "If you keep shining the neon light of analysis and accountability on the tender tissue of your belonging, you make it parched and barren."[2]

Maybe he knew that knowledge isn't sufficient; it's not enough, and maybe that's why he doesn't give answers.

Maybe knowing the *who* rather than the *what* is a better answer to grieving parents, to abandoned teens, to violated kids, and to maimed women.

Maybe trust, born of intimacy, is a better answer.

And maybe that was the reason I decided to fly across the planet—to find intimacy, to reclaim trust, to take a leap and hope I was caught by *someone*, not something.

I had this crazy idea that maybe, if I moved across the world, maybe, if I started over and left everything, maybe, if I took a year, gave it to God, away from everyone, then maybe he'd show up. Maybe he'd come through. Maybe he'd ride in on a Korean rainbow unicorn, and we'd disappear into the sunset, and I'd trust and believe, and all would be right and well, and the credits would roll, and I would be safe and held and loved.

After all, isn't there something poetic about losing your faith in another country and then finding it again on the other side of the world? Isn't *that* a good story? Isn't *that* something that maybe, if there is a cosmic author, he'd write?

But I didn't know…

I just got curious…

And maybe a little hopeful.

Sure, there were shadows…

Sure, this is but a weak and flickering flame…

But maybe God could be good.

Maybe God could be faithful.

Maybe he'd come through.

But as the legend goes, the heart isn't only a friend…

It is also a traitor…[3]

Part Six

Stumbling

We shall not cease from exploration
And the end of all our exploring
Will be to arrive where we started
And know the place for the first time.[1]

T.S. Eliot

The Aforementioned Death

"Ryan is trying to get in touch with you. It's urgent."

The message is from my friend Adam, the friend I went to Thailand with, the friend I haven't spoken to in nine months...

We had a falling out, like all friends who enter into business together do. We hadn't said a word since I left the company after being a co-founder ... Well ... No words of love or fraternity ... Just words about money and stocks ... Words that were for the lawyers and not for us ... Words that hurt...

If he's reaching out, it must be urgent.

I find Ryan on Instagram and tell him I am free to talk.

He doesn't reply, which leaves me time to squirm and panic about what is so urgent, knowing, beneath the panic, it isn't a what; it's a who.

My mind searches for someone that Adam, Ryan, and I know, someone who is important to us all.

"Andy!"

The former mentor's name is the only one I could think of.

I mean, I wouldn't be surprised, he does drink a ton of Diet Coke and has had cancer in the past. That makes sense, right? God, I hope it's not Andy. That would suck.

I pull up Facebook, trying to discover clues.

Nothing.

Looks like Andy is fine.

Relieved, I go to the bathroom to get ready for work—I have children to teach; I can't wait on Ryan forever, regardless of how urgent. Besides, who else—

Then it hits me...

Dan...

I grab my phone and begin to panic.

Please don't be Dan. Please don't be Dan.

I try to get to his page but then remember he deleted all forms of social media.

So I go to his wife's.

Nothing. Not a single thing.

Alright … not Dan…

My heart begins to slow.

Maybe we were okay. Maybe I'm just overreacting. I always assume the worst. Quit assuming the worst, Brandon. It's probably not that bad. Just to be safe and calm my anxieties, I'll go to his mom's page.

Then I see it…

"I'm so sorry for your loss."

"I'm praying for you and the family."

"If you need anything, let us know."

"I can't even imagine what you're going through right now."

My heart drops out, picking up pace as it falls to the floor.

Fuck. Fuck. Fuck. Please don't be Dan. Please don't be Dan. Please. I just texted him two days ago. It can't be Dan.

Earlier in the week, I couldn't sleep for two days in a row, and both days I was thinking of him.

Dan and I go way back. Back to high school.

One day, after obnoxiously singing, "I Put a Spell on You," Dan and I miraculously became friends: me, the awkward closeted kid; him, the promising athlete.

Despite our superficial differences, we realized we shared so much: a love of acting, being silly and dramatic, serving in ministry, and an incurable masochism that led us to do hard things for Jesus.

We did everything together (well, minus sportsball), calling each other twin and biting each other as a sign of affection.

For the last seven years, he had been a missionary in Africa, accomplishing all the things we dreamed of doing together. Meanwhile, I was the *ex*-missionary who came back, doubting everything I believed in and coming out as gay, (not to mention sleeping with a bunch of strangers). Needless to say, we didn't have a ton in common anymore.

Suddenly, he dropped everything and joined the army, and after years of drifting apart and living in different corners of the world, he was moving back to Colorado … right before I moved to Korea…

Waking up from cold-sweat-dream number two, I started to have so many questions, questions I should know the answers to: Why the army? Why abandon everything he'd ever dreamt of doing? Didn't he love Africa? Didn't he believe that's what he should be doing with his life? Didn't he want to get martyred as a missionary in the savannah or some crazy shit like that?

I reached for my phone and texted him.

"Why the army? I know I should know this. Fuck up on my end for not knowing, but what was the reason? Why enlist when you have three kids and a wife?"

First text: "Poor life choices…"

Second text: "Because I wanted to be the equivalent of a physician's assistant on the ground."

I chuckled at the text. It was classic Dan-Brandon banter. Sarcasm, reeking of truth, followed up by the "right" answer that we sometimes believed, sometimes didn't. Depends on the day. Depends on the minute.

But now, reading his mother's Facebook page, I'm not chuckling. Now I'm panicking.

Maybe I should have pushed. Maybe there was a reason I couldn't sleep for two days. Maybe I should have said more. Maybe I shouldn't have moved to the other side of the world. Maybe I fucked up. Again. After all, he had just moved back to Colorado. He had finally come home. We could have made more memories. We could have become close again. I could have gotten to know his children. I could have been that weird, not-family uncle. That guncle. I could have…

"Could have." A phrase I would come to hate.

My phone buzzes.

It's Ryan.

I force down my panic and pick up the phone.

"Hey, Ryan. How you doing?"

"Hey, Brandon. I'm doing good."

He's doing good? Maybe it's not as bad as I think it is. See, Brandon, you always overthink and assume the worst.

"Listen," Ryan's voice immediately changes. "There's no easy way to say this. Dan passed last night."

I can't speak. My throat has dried up, and my jaw has locked.

This has to be a dream. He's thirty-one. He just finished training and hasn't deployed yet. This has to be wrong. This has to be. This has to be a mistake. A terrible, horrible mistake.

"Ummm…" Tears fill my eyes, and I clear my throat to try and make it function. "Wha- What happened?"

"There was a training accident." (What a horrible word for someone's death. As if the fact that it wasn't intentional, as if the fact that it wasn't the military's intention to kill my friend makes it all better. Oops! Our bad! It was an accident. A mistake. A terrible, horrible mistake.) "His heart gave out during an exercise."

"His heart gave out? How? What was he doing?"

"You know everything I know. They're running an investigation to see what happened. After it's complete, they'll release the body for the funeral. I'll keep you posted as more details come."

Funeral. My best friend is dead, and now there's a funeral. Because of an accident. A fucking accident.

"Ummmm … thanks for calling me, Ryan."

"Yeah, man. I'm sorry that I'm reaching out under these circumstances. You need anything?"

Yeah … my friend back. I need my friend back, Ryan. Could you do that for me? Could you get my friend back, Ryan? Too much? How about for me to not be halfway across the world when he dies? Could you rewind time and tell me to not move to Korea? Could you do that for me, Ryan? How about telling me this is a horrible dream? A terrible, horrible dream. That I can wake up from. That I can shake myself from. That I can just forget over my morning coffee. Can you do that for me, Ryan? Can you?

"Ummmm … No. I'm gonna get off the phone. I don't want to talk anymore."

"Understandable. Reach out any time."

"Thanks."

I click off.

And in an instant, I'm alone. All alone.

It's crazy how in one second, you're so intimate with someone, sharing a deep pain, and in the next, you're utterly alone in a studio apartment on the other side of the world, away from everyone you love. It's crazy how in one second, you're slowly waking up, bracing for another day of teaching kids in Korea, and the next second you're frantically trying to find answers on Facebook, trying to understand how your life has changed forever.

One second…

That's all it takes…

For your life to change...
To feel alone...
To be clothed in silence...
And it's suffocating.

I need to call Bethany. I need to be the one who lets her know. She can't find out from someone else. I have to be the one to tell her.

I pull out my phone and text her to see if she's up.

Bethany, Lynn, Dan, and I were all best friends growing up. We called ourselves the "Core Four." Why? Because we were teenagers and dorks, and somehow that name seemed cool at the time. But more than that, because regardless of what life threw our way, regardless of how we changed, or where we went, no matter how much time had passed, we had each other, and we knew that, deeply. We always knew that. Regardless of what we did with our lives and where we were in the world, we had each other. We promised...

It was my senior year, and I was a year older than everyone. So when I left for college, I was going alone. I had to leave everyone behind.

At my goodbye party, we stayed up late, lying on each other's bellies, laughing and crying, taking turns recalling memory after memory...

...A cook-off where Dan slaughtered a pig so that the boys could win.

...The county fair where Dan was both embarrassed and proud of his city slicker friend, attempting to walk in boots.

...Bailing on prom to dance barefoot underneath the moon.

...Late night conversations over pie at Village Inn, pondering about spouses and babies and death...

"Who do you think will get married first?"

"Oh, definitely Lynn!"

"Why me?"

"Girl! You're so eager for marriage! It's ridiculous! Of course it's you! Then Brandon, then me."

"What about *me?*"

"Dan, we all know you'll likely run off to Haiti and be too busy with missions to get married. Quit glaring at me! You know I'm right!"

"Well, what about kids? Who will be the first person to have kids?"

"Brandon, the dude was made to be a father. Come on. Easy."

"Then Lynn! She's getting married first and there's only so long you can wait before marriage leads to babies."

"I'm last. I'm not having kids till I absolutely have to."

"What about who's dying first?"

"Dan!"

"Rude! You want me to die first?"

"Oh come on, Dan! You're always doing something reckless. You'll either die because you did something ridiculous, like jumping off a cliff, or as a martyr in Africa because you're obsessed with missions."

"And obsessed with being a martyr!"

"Rude!"

"But true! You're like *so* obsessed with being a martyr! The amount of times you've talked about dying for Jesus is well into the thousands!"

We laughed, talking and joking about death like it was some far-off thing…

Like it would be decades…

Like it would be far away…

In a distant time…

In a distant place…

Like Haiti…

Or Africa…

But it wasn't far away in some distant country.

It was here.

In the States.

And it wasn't decades later.

It was now.

At the ripe age of thirty-one.

And he wasn't a martyr.

He was a soldier.

Barely.

And he hadn't even gone to combat.

He didn't give his life in defense of his country while "being the equivalent of a physician's assistant on the ground."

It was a training accident.

A fucking.

Training.

Accident.

My phone vibrates.

It's a text message from Bethany.

"Hey! Sorry for the delay. Was putting Wells down for a nap. Feel free to FaceTime whenever."

I instantly call her and take a deep breath as the tone dials.

Heart skips a beat as she answers.

"Hey, Brandon! How's it going?"

"Not good. Dan passed."

I'm really bad at this whole delivering-bad-news thing. All I know is that I didn't want to whip Bethany around like I was whipped around by Ryan.

Oh, how are you? Good! By the way, your best friend fucking died. Have a great day! Click. Better just to come right out and say it. Right? That's better?

"Wait what? I think I heard you wrong. What did you say?"

Her voice is laced with anxiety, her pitch climbing. She heard me. She just can't believe it's true.

"Dan died."

"Wait what? What?! What do you mean he *died*? Who told you? How did you find out? What happened?"

I explain what I know—that I don't know anything, that I just found out, that I'm just as shocked as she is, that none of this makes sense and this isn't fair and it isn't right but it happened just the same because Dan's heart decided to give out during a dumb training exercise, and now we have to figure out how to live without him because we were right—Dan would die first, and he would die now.

She stares off the camera, eyes darting back and forth, looking for answers, knowing she won't find any. Then she looks back at me, eyes full of tears.

"It's *Dan*. He can't be dead."

But he is…

Regardless of what we think, he is…

He's gone.

We cry together…

No more words…

Just crying…

Because there's nothing left to say…

Nothing left to do…

Because even though it *can't* be Dan…

It is.

And he's gone…

Forever gone.

"Ummm … I need to go. I need to process this."

"I understand. I gotta call my mom anyway."

"She doesn't know yet?"

"No. You were the first person I called."

"She's gonna be devastated. He was like a fourth son to her."

"Yeah … I know … He spent more time at our house than his during my senior year of high school. My whole family is gonna be crushed. Do you wanna call Lynn or do you want me to call her?"

"I'll call her. She should hear it from me. Are you gonna come home for the funeral?"

"I don't know. I don't think I can. I've been here for barely six weeks, and I just started teaching four weeks ago. I doubt they'll give me the time off. But I'm going to talk to my boss today and see what my options are."

"Brandon, you *can't* miss Dan's funeral. He was your best friend. It'll haunt you the rest of your life."

"Yeah. I know, Bethany. I just don't know what my options are. But I'll keep you posted."

"Brandon, you need to come home. You need to mourn with those you love. You have a piece of Dan that no one else has. *We* need that piece. His *wife* needs that piece. You need to come home."

"Okay … Okay, Bethany. I'll keep you posted. I gotta call my mom before I head into school to teach."

"You're teaching today?!"

"Yeah. In less than an hour."

"Oh my God! Brandon…"

"Gotta teach those Korean kiddos English. No rest for the weary."

Or the dead.

"I'll talk to my boss today and let you know what he says."

"Okay … Love you…"

"Love you too…"

I hang up. That terrible loneliness there to greet me.

Call mom. You need to call mom. Then get to school. You have lessons to teach. You have kids to take care of. Oh! And you were meaning to finish up decorating the classroom today. You'll need to do that too. But first the boss. Then I need to figure things out…

Then I need to…

Then I need to…

I need to…

Responsibility is a lovely way to cope.

Too Much

I moved across the world to try and trust God again.

I moved across the world because it seemed poetic and right, and maybe, just maybe, God would see my faith, and all would be well.

All would be well.

This was going to be an adventure. This was going to be good. I was going to see God move in my life, and I was going to start trusting him again, and this was going to be good; really good; I can trust again...

Then I got COVID right before leaving, delaying my departure to Korea...

Then I missed my graduation, something that for years I had been fighting for after coming out and losing my job in ministry and starting my life all over...

Then I tested positive, again, in Korea, and was thrown into a $2,000 government-issued quarantine...

Then I was thrown into teaching, without any training, having no clue what I was doing, because there wasn't time for training because I spent the last two weeks in quarantine...

Then I would get glared at for being a foreigner because it was *my fault* that there was a global pandemic; it was *my fault* that anyone got COVID...

Then I would get anxious because my date would get anxious, because no one is publicly out in Korea and gay marriage is illegal, so I guess finding a spouse is out of the question while I'm here...

Then I'd see pictures of my best friends having kids, of them getting together for summer picnics, of them taking turns helping with the newborn, making memories, bringing their families together...

Then my childhood best friend would move back to our hometown for the first time in over a decade, right as I planned to move to the other side of the world...

Then I'd get texts from my other friends about meeting up for brunch, talking about how grateful they are that I introduced them to each other so they could become best friends without me...

So that I could be left behind...

So that everyone could move on with their lives...

Because that's what people do...

They live their lives...

And you're halfway across the world...

Without anyone...

Alone...

But I'm here for a reason. I'm here because maybe God is on the other side of the Pacific. Sure, things are hard. But often the good things are hard. Think of the stories we love. Good things happened because of the hard things. That's what makes a good story. Like The Alchemist. *Like Santiago. Think of how he got stuck in Morocco. Think of how he lost years in the desert. Think of how he nearly died. It sucked, but it was all for something good. It was all good. Even the bad. Because it was a part of something bigger. It was part of the plan. There's something good here. There's something bigger. On the other side of the world, despite all the ridiculousness, there's a plan. There's a plan.*

I was trying to trust God. Trying to pay attention to the omens, even though problem after problem, disappointment after disappointment kept piling on, forcing me into the ground.

But maybe there is a purpose to all the craziness. Maybe there is destiny. Maybe having a crisis of faith and coming out and all the bullshit that I had to deal with over the past six years will add up to something. Maybe all this craziness in Korea will add up to something.

And then my best friend died...

And what's the purpose in that?

What's the purpose in moving across the world, starting over, pushing through a bunch of bullshit, all alone, in a foreign nation, to have my friend die six weeks after moving? To die in a training accident? What's the purpose in that?

What.

Is.

The.

Purpose.

In.

That?

Where are the omens? Where's the plan? Where's destiny? Where is God?

I could handle getting COVID. I could handle expensive quarantine. I could handle not knowing what I was doing and being all alone and learning a new culture and language and alphabet and how to be a functioning human in a chaotic new country. I could deal with the xenophobia and homophobia and sexism and ageism and all the other cultural things that you're not supposed to hate but you end up hating and feel bad about hating because now you look like an ethnocentric asshole.

I could deal with *all* of that…

But my friend?

Not my best friend.

This was too much.

Far too much.

And I broke.

"Is anyone up?"

It's 11 p.m.

I text Bethany and Lynn. They're the only ones I want to talk to since learning the news.

I feel horrible, and I know they feel horrible, so I didn't have to explain that I feel horrible and *why* I feel horrible and talk, yet again, about my best friend's death. I could just be. I could just hurt. Because they got it. Because they were hurting too. And that's all I wanted. I wanted to hurt with someone. Anyone. Just don't let me hurt alone.

"I'm not doing well, and I'm about to do something stupid."

Since moving to Korea, the tunnel hadn't called. I was being a good little celibate slut, not sleeping with a single stranger. It was the first time in over four years, and it felt good. Really good. Hope was on the horizon.

Maybe this was the reason I moved to the other side of the Pacific. Maybe it literally took an ocean for me to not ho around.

But with the news of his death, I just wanted to escape; I just wanted to not be alone…

And the tunnel called…

"I'm up."

It's Lynn.

I FaceTime her.

Once the connection is made, her face appears. Her eyes are puffy.

"Hey."

That's it. That's all it takes. And I break.

"I can't do this. I can't. I wanted to be strong. I wanted to prove to myself that I could stay. That I was strong enough. But I'm not. I can't do this. It feels like some horrible test. Like I need to choose God over Dan, and choosing God means staying here to mourn alone. But it's too fucking hard. I really wanted to. I wanted to trust God and stay. But I can't. I just can't. I don't want to do this anymore. I don't want to be alone anymore. I don't."

"You don't have to, Brandon. You don't. And I don't think God faults you for that. It's okay to not be strong enough. How long will you be coming back for?"

"Indefinitely. My job won't give me the time off. I'll need to quit if I want to go to the funeral."

"So what will you do after the funeral?"

"I don't know. I really don't. This feels like quitting. But I can't do this. It's too painful. And I know that if I missed his funeral, I'd regret it for the rest of my life."

"Don't you get penalized by your job if you break contract?"

"Yep. They can charge me for my two quarantines and my plane ticket."

"How much is that?"

"Like over $4,000"

"And how much are flights home?"

"I found one for $900. But it'll take me like forty-two hours."

"Jesus! There isn't another one?"

"Not for under $1,000."

"And what about all your stuff? Didn't you just furnish your apartment?"

"Yep. I'll try to return what I can, but I'll have to give most of it away."

"Isn't this what you wanted, Brandon? Didn't you want to move to Korea? Like, hasn't this been a dream of yours for a while? To live abroad."

"Yep. Sure is. But I can't stay here. I haven't slept with anyone since I've gotten here, but all I want to do is invite a stranger over and fuck so I can feel nothing for a few minutes and not be utterly alone. And I don't want to mourn alone. It's the worst, Lynn. Some days I feel like I can't breathe. Besides, I can't miss his funeral. I'd regret that for the rest of my life. He's my best friend."

Was. Was my best friend.

I hate that word.

We get silent as I process it all … rather, attempt to process it all.

One phone call with Ryan, and now my whole life is falling apart.

"This really sucks…" I start crying fresh tears, choking.

"Yeah…"

"Like, I know that death is *never* convenient, but this genuinely *sucks*. On top of having to mourn my best friend, I have to start my life completely over. Again. After only being here for six weeks. I fucking hate this. And I'm truly scared."

"Why are you scared?"

"There's this verse I've been thinking about a lot lately: 'Where there is no vision, people perish.'"[1]

"Why does that make you scared?"

"Because I have vision here in Korea. Sure, it's been a shit show. But I was supposed to come here to trust God again, to work on myself, to try and trust. Even though it's hard, I feel like I have vision, and it's the first time, in a long time, that I'm not hooking up. Plus, I'm being truly authentic with people. Like, I'm sharing all parts of me, not hiding anything, and I don't care how people react. I wanna own all of it, all of me, and it feels really good, like I'm whole for the first time, like I'm genuinely authentic. If I go back, I'm scared I'll hide parts of me again, shove them down, and then I won't have vision for my life, and I'll start hooking up again. Or maybe something worse … like *actually* perish like the verse says…"

"Well, selfishly, you can't fucking die. It's too soon. I can't handle that."

I giggle through tears, my head pounding with each breath.

"I'm just scared, Lynn. I'm really scared."

"That's okay. It's okay to be scared. We grew up in a culture that said we needed to change the world for Jesus, and if we didn't, our life was a waste. We needed to try and figure out what God wanted from us, even though none of us had any fucking clue. It's okay to feel that. It makes sense. But, as harsh as this may sound, maybe God, if there is a God, doesn't care. Maybe he doesn't care if you stay in Korea or come back. Maybe he doesn't need us to find some mysterious calling that, for some reason, he's hiding from us. Maybe he's just supportive … regardless of what you choose."

I get quiet.

"Like, maybe God just wants you to live your life and to not be a dick. Maybe that's it. And if you do something dumb when you come back, we'll be here for you; we'll figure it out."

"Thanks, Lynn … I'm just confused as to why I even came here. Like, what was the point of moving to Korea? You know?"

"I think you were just trying your best, Brandon, and your best friend just happened to die while you were trying your best. That type of shit just happens. You tried something. It didn't work out, but at least you tried."

I hate that. It sounds horrible and pathetic. Like random chaos. And that scares me. Because if it's all random chaos, I *should* be scared. I *should* be anxious. Because *anything* could happen. *Anything*. Like training accidents and broken legs. And I was here trying to believe the world didn't work like that. Trying to believe there was more than chaos. That's why I came here. I came here to try and believe that maybe God was more involved in my life than I believed, that maybe I could trust him again, that maybe he was good and real and lovely and for me…

But if it's all just chaos…

The thought becomes too much, so I lighten the mood to give me a piece of sanity.

"Well, if I fuck it all up, at least I'll get to see you and Bethany."

She laughs.

"Exactly! And I'm *definitely* enough of a reason for you to stop your whole life and move back to Colorado!"

We giggle together, relieving the pressure. Then we slowly settle into the silence.

"Thanks, Lynn … love you."

"Love you too. It's going to be okay. We'll make it through. Together."

"Okay, thanks for answering. I really didn't want to be alone."

"Of course."

I say bye.

She says bye.

We hang up.

And that horrifying lonely silence is yet again there to greet me.

Yeah, Lynn, maybe we can make it through together. Maybe friends will help. Maybe there's this power in gathering. Maybe if we could just sing "Kumbaya" while sitting around a campfire, somehow all of this shit would somehow be well because at least we have each other. Maybe that's all true. But you're not here. You're not in Korea. You're on the other side of the planet. And I'm here. Alone. All alone. Because I tried. I tried, and my best friend died. And now I'm here alone…

The silence becomes deafening…

And all too heavy…
All too much…
I need to drown it out…
I need to drown the silence out…
The loneliness out…
And the tunnel's mouth opens wide…

On a Plane Over the Atlantic

I'm staring out the window, high above a brilliantly bright Atlantic.

I can't sleep. There's too much in my mind and heart, spinning and knocking about. It's keeping me up as this plane takes me back home ... back to Colorado ... after living in Korea ... for barely seven weeks...

Seven weeks of teaching. Seven weeks of adventure and new friends. Seven weeks of believing that maybe there was destiny and hope. Seven weeks of pushing through hard things because maybe God was in the hard things and maybe there would be glory and sunshine on the other side...

Seven weeks...

Seven.

Weeks.

What a waste.

What was the point? Why did it matter? Did it matter? Did I hear God wrong? Am I an idiot for attempting to believe in God again? Am I doomed to repeat this same mistake of believing in a being that just isn't there? Are we all just chaos in the night, and I'm scared to face the storm, grabbing onto anything before passing into utter darkness?

Should I have said more to Dan via text message the day before his death? Should I have picked up the phone and called him? Should I have said more before leaving Colorado? Should I have left Colorado? Should I now be leaving Korea? Am I a coward for leaving Korea? What difference is it even going to make if I go home? His wife has people. She's not alone. She doesn't need me. Why am I going home?

I remind myself that I decided to go home for *me*. This was for *me*. I was going back because, ultimately, I didn't want to mourn alone. I didn't want to miss his funeral. I wanted to be there.

But what's next? What's after the funeral? This is such a mess. Where is God in any of this?

No answers...

Like death, the questions float forever...

Endlessly in front of me...

But for now...

I stare out the window, as golden clouds shine to spite my pain, high above the raging Atlantic.

A Cheryl Strayed B-Film

I'm in the mountains. I flew across the world to mourn my best friend with people I love, and then, after the funeral, I decided that I couldn't handle being around the people I love, so I ran to the mountains, to get away, like some pathetic version of Cheryl Strayed.

If you haven't read *Wild* by Cheryl Strayed, stop reading this book and go read hers. (Maybe not; you're almost done with mine.) It's better. She's better. Because she's a bigger badass than me. And has more courage than me. And writes better than me. Writes words that stab into your skin and carve something of meaning into your bones. It's better.

Cheryl, after the death of her mother, slept with anyone and everyone, unable to stop, all while being married. The movie, based on the book, opens up with her and her husband getting matching divorce tattoos days before she decides to walk the Pacific Crest Trail.

She didn't know what to do to change things. Her life was spiraling out of control. She knew she needed to do something, she just didn't know what. In the end, she landed with hiking a trail, a trail that takes several months, even though she hadn't spent a single day backpacking in her entire life.

I read the book years ago, and it still haunts me, specifically one moment:

While on the trail, she meets another hiker who she starts flirting with. (Old habits die hard, even when you're on a vision quest.) As they sleep next to each other, each in their own tent, she counts how many layers are between her skin and his. Her underwear. Her pants. Her sleeping bag. Her tent. His tent. His sleeping bag. His pants. His underwear.

Here she is, trying to get away from everything, ultimately trying to get away from herself, but realizing she carries herself with her wherever she goes— the desire for sex, that blissful escape, refusing to leave her side.

Her fixation made me think of my tunnel, and it made me feel like I wasn't alone, that I wasn't crazy.

So here I am—a Cheryl Strayed B-film. Except it isn't a B; that's too kind. More like a C or even a D-film.

Sure, my best friend died, but it wasn't my mom.

Sure, I ruined everything going on in my life by quitting my job and moving back to Colorado, but I didn't blow up my marriage because of my sex addiction.

Sure, I was on a trail, but it wasn't the PCT; it wasn't even some semi-impressive trail—it was some random loop in the wilderness.

My original idea was to be like Cheryl and do a longer hike like the Colorado Trail—a trail that takes at least four weeks.

But I got scared.

I got scared that I wasn't prepared (because I wasn't). I got scared that I had no clue what I was doing (because I didn't). Scared I was incapable (which I was). That it would be too hard (because it would be). That I'd either die from a moose (because moose are terrifying) or from starvation (because I can never eat enough) or from simply being alone for far too long with only my thoughts; eventually I'd throw myself off the nearest cliff because I'm dramatic and overly emotional.

Regardless of how horribly it turned out, one thing was sure: I'd most definitely die.

I'd die on some stupid long trail because I got too emotional, because I didn't know how to cope with the stupid death of my stupid best friend and my stupid life. And now *I* would be dead in addition to my friend. Two for the price of one. One from a stupid training accident and the other from pure stupidity. (My emotions are most definitely rooted in logic.)

So I settled on a pathetic loop in some pathetic wilderness that would take me a few pathetic days even though I wanted to be brave like Cheryl, be free and alive like Cheryl, leave the civilized world behind to process life and death and all those heavy and horrible things.

But I got scared.

In the words of Cheryl, "I'm a free spirit who never had the balls to be free."[1] The woman had bigger balls than me, that's for sure.

So here I am, day three of being in the wilderness, and I'm just as clueless as I began.

How long does it take to get some life-changing epiphany? A couple hours? A few days? Weeks? Why is it taking so long? Where are my answers?

It's probably because I keep listening to this fantasy audiobook. I should be walking in the silence trying to listen to my heart or nature or whatever-the-fuck. Or maybe God or the universe or whatever-the-fuck.

Or maybe it's because I keep hanging out with strangers instead of being alone. Because being alone sucks. Because if I'm alone, I might hear God or the universe or whatever-the-fuck, and that sounds fucking scary.

Or maybe it's because I can't think straight because I have fucking blisters all over my fucking feet because I've never done this before because wandering off into the fucking wilderness seemed like a good idea at the time, even though I have absolutely no fucking clue what the hell I'm doing.

How the fuck did Cheryl-fucking-Strayed do this? She never backpacked, and she somehow made it. She was somehow fine.

But I'm not fine. I'm the opposite of fine.

And I'm not getting answers. I'm supposed to be getting answers. That's what happens to people who go into the wilderness. You get answers. And it's already been three days? Three fucking days! The same as Christ! Hurry up, answers! My fucking feet hurt!

"Wanna head back with us?" a hiker says.

While on the inside I'm raging, on the outside I'm smiling or quiet (a well-practiced skill, compliments of hiding my attraction to men), and the girls I'm hiking with so I don't feel alone, have no clue what's going on inside. Instead, they just want to hang out with me.

After hours of hiking a trail that crawls over East Maroon Pass, we stand at a crossroad. To the right is the way back to an alpine lake where our tents reside. To the left, is a terrifying cliff called Triangle Pass, over which is a lovely hot spring.

The day was gorgeous, full of wildflowers, majestic mountains, flowing rivers. We laughed and sang and swapped stories, and I didn't feel as scared because these women actually knew what they were doing (unlike me). Their presence was a welcome reprieve from the panicked voices in my head.

But I didn't need a reprieve…

I needed sadness…

And to be alone…

To process…

And stare into the existential void…

And get answers…

And become enlightened.

I didn't need to have an easy trip…

A joyful trip…

I needed to suffer…

To be in pain…

And get lost…

So that maybe I could be found … (or some other cliché phrase you hang over a toilet).

I look to the left. To the treacherous mountain pass.

It taunts in the distance, a barely visible trail crawling up its sheer summit, massive boulders precariously stooping overhead. They look like furious rock parents, parents looking down on their dumb climber children, asking, "What the hell are you doing?"

I swallow hard like I'm in some cheesy film, like the moment the protagonist decides to do the hard thing and musters courage for the difficult road ahead. In the end, they do the hard thing; all is well; the enemy is vanquished, and the credits roll. But it all came down to that hard swallow.

Gulp.

"I'm gonna hit the hot springs. It was lovely meeting the two of you! Have a great hike back into town!"

The two strangers smile, and we hug.

As the second girl pulls away, she looks at me with these intentional eyes. "It was really lovely meeting you, Brandon."

Even though we had only been together for two days, they somehow felt safe to me. It probably had something to do with the fact that they were both search and rescue EMTs. Kinda hard to die when you have two of those trekking the wilderness with you. But beyond that, there was a presence to them that made me breathe better.

Plus, when I told them I was up in the mountains because my friend died, there was a stillness about them. Instead of anxiously trying to make me feel better, instead of trying to move past the pain, they simply nodded, smiled, and handed me a beer.

"I hope you find answers." The other says as they turn to hike down the mountain.

"Me too."

I turn and face the threatening ascent, take another big gulp, and begin to climb.

Triangle Pass is this ridge between Crested Butte and the Maroon Bells—Colorado's most photographed mountain scape. There are other, safer passes that hikers can take over the mountains. But those don't have hot springs. And I want a hot spring. With naked bodies. Carrying my tunnel with me into the mountains. Just like Cheryl. So I climb.

Few problems:

One, to my right is a five hundred-foot drop. To my left is a five hundred-foot looming cliff. Before me, a kinda-sorta-but-not-really trail that balances between the two. It stretches out, skirting its way to the top of the pass, hundreds of feet in the distance. Here or there, the kinda-sorta-but-not-really trail slowly becomes a not-trail, just a pile of boulders from a landslide.

Two, there are eighty-mile-per-hour winds blasting through the mountain bowl.

Three, it's four o'clock in the afternoon. I only have a few hours of daylight left.

Four, I can't camp on the other side. I'm not allowed to. You had to plan for that, registering with Parks and Rec, and I don't plan. Like ever. Like ever ever. I'm crazy impulsive. It's a problem. So, because I didn't plan, I needed to come back over the pass. Back to my camp. Miles away. Yet again over this terrifying pass. All with only a few hours of daylight left.

Because I don't plan...

And I have no clue what I'm doing...

Think like Cheryl, Brandon. Think like Cheryl. If she could do it, you can do it. Just think like Wild. *Or is it* Into the Wild? *No, that's the one where the guy dies in the wilderness because he's dumb and doesn't prepare. Wait ... I didn't prepare! Am I dumb like that guy that died in Alaska? Am I living* Into the Wild *and not* Wild?

A gale nearly knocks me over, and I grab onto one of the precarious boulders.

Fuck! Definitely Into the Wild.

To get my mind off my inevitable death, I put in my headphones and play the fantasy audiobook.

"But the Immortal Words—these Ideals—guided everything they did..." The voice actor reads on.

Balance over teetering rock.

"The four later Ideals were said to be different for every order of Radiants..."

Shove fingers in crack for balance.

"But the First Ideal was the same for each of the ten…"

Hug boulder to brace against another gale, turning my face from its sandy blast.

"Life before death, strength before weakness, journey before destination."[2]

My destination is going to be the bottom of this fucking cliff!

Jesus Christ! I'm gonna die. I'm gonna fucking die. All my friends and family just mourned Dan, and now they're going to have to mourn me because I didn't know how to mourn Dan. And now I'm gonna die. I'm going to fucking die. Why do I always have to be so dramatic? Why can't I just mourn a friend's death like a normal person? Why does it have to be this big existential thing? Why does everything have to be some big existential thing?

Making anything about the meaning of the universe is very on-brand for Brandon Flanery. Someone cutting me off in traffic becomes an expression of the selfishness that is the human condition. Someone being late for a date means I'm not worthy of love. A fancy jar of peanut butter symbolizes the love of God.

It's all connected. Always.

So as Brandon Sanderson drones in my ears about life before death and *my* death is just a gust away, I begin to think about Dan and why this all happened.

His funeral was held in the church we grew up in—a megachurch with a sanctuary the size of a Walmart.

The typical sappy-sad slideshow flashed image after image of Dan and the life he lived. I wasn't in a single one. Predictable. That's kind of how our relationship was—a special thing that only we shared.

But more than that, I hadn't been involved in his life for years. I hadn't flown to Africa to see him as a missionary; I hadn't visited him in North Carolina during his two-year training after he joined the army.

After learning that he died, I looked over our text message thread. It was so easy to see our friendship drifting year after year. Shorter messages. Longer gaps. Missed video calls.

In the past, when we would connect, he would pour out his heart, while I remained cold.

I was too scared to look even *remotely* gay. Anytime I did, it always felt like my straight friends pulled away, like my gayness was some sickness they could catch. Wide girth, everybody, wide girth.

So I pretended to not care—guarded, calculated—always making sure Dan was the one to initiate any form of intimacy.

Don't sit too close on the couch. Never hug too long.

So as he'd message, "I miss you a ton … I crave my friendship with you…" I'd simply respond with, "Awww thanks! Love you too, bro." (Always include the bro.)

Every micro emotion, every tone of my voice, every gesture of my hand was calculated and planned because I couldn't risk exposing myself. I couldn't risk my friends realizing I was gay and have them pull away.

But when I came out, my fears were realized.

Dan and I barely talked anymore. We would only hang out when others were present. We'd never have one-on-one conversations about life and meaning and purpose like we did for hours on end when we were teenagers. It all shifted.

And no matter how many times I asked if something had changed since I came out, he reassured me that things were fine.

"It's just life, man." "I'm busy." "We're still good."

Regardless, it felt like I couldn't be trusted to be alone with him when never in a million years would I ever make a move on my best friend. He was like a brother.

Slowly and slowly, best friends became friends; friends became acquaintances, and then the acquaintance dies. However, as the slideshow played, even though there wasn't a single picture of us together, his memory still pierced me, and I didn't make it to the chair.

I fell to my knees and started sobbing. Right there in the middle of the aisle. Right there in the middle of Jesus Walmart. (Cleanup in the worship department!)

Bethany and Lynn came over, holding me and rubbing my back, carrying me to my chair as I heaved in and out. I couldn't catch my breath, like it kept running from me, and I would never catch it, like I would never catch Dan. He was simply gone. Punched from all our lungs.

Despite the time, despite the distance, despite how our relationship had changed after I came out, he mattered … and he always will.

Some pastor ascended the stage in somber silence. I had no clue who he was, but I didn't have a clue who anybody was anymore. Most of the people I grew up with had left. I guess that's what happens when a church has a scandal or two, an affair or two, a shooting or two.

"We gather here today," the unknown pastor said, "to remember and cele-brate the life of Dan. Before we have Dan's friends and family come up, we're going to spend some time in worship: something Dan requested for his funeral. Even in his death, Dan wanted to put the Lord first. Dan was a good man that loved his God and loved his country. Let's remember him today as we worship the Lord together."

The language was hard. It's the language of my persecutors, and I hadn't heard it in years.

But nameless pastor was right—worship *was* something Dan loved.

As teenagers, we'd jump and dance in worship, calling the area nearest the stage our "mosh pit of righteousness." (Yes, we were *that* kind of Christian.) Though it might seem weird, to us, it was this freeing expression that commu-nicated "I don't care what anyone else thinks. I'm here to 'give everything to Jesus.'" And I guess "everything" roughly translated to dancing till you clothes-lined the sweaty body next to you with your own sweaty body. And the sweatier the better. It was like sweat equated to how much you loved Jesus.

Are you just musky? Not enough. Is there moisture on your brow? Keep going. Come back when you're dripping.

The electric guitar began to swell, summoning us to worship.

I don't remember the song. I don't remember any of the songs. What I do remember was who stood first to worship: Dan's wife, now widow, Rose.

Everyone in that Walmart room quickly followed suit, standing to their feet. If this grieving mom was going to worship God despite her pain, you bet-ter get your ass out of that chair.

More out of muscle memory than cognitive choice, I drifted to the back of the massive sanctuary as the worship band began to play.

While Dan would be found in the mosh pit, I would often drift to the edges, frantically pacing and praying that God would make me straight, that God would somehow be pleased with me despite my attractions. But those prayers always went unanswered, even though I wanted to change, even though the Bible said he answers prayers, even though I would dare to dance and jump and flail and smash my sweaty body into the person next to me.

Nothing.

I guess there wasn't enough sweat.

When Christians use words like, "choice" and "lifestyle," it's torture. It's torture because I think of these moments, the moments where I screamed into the night through tears, where I came to the altar on bruised knees, where I pleaded to God to make me straight. Because I desperately didn't want to be gay. *Anything* but gay. *Anything* but that unspeakable word. That unforgivable sin. That hated sin. *Anything* but that.

Why would anyone choose this?

But despite my pleading, here I was, a raging homosexual.

From that familiar place on the fringes of the sanctuary, far from everyone, a place that somehow felt safe because it embodied how I felt in my deepest being—separate—I took in the scene.

The massive hexagon-shaped sanctuary. The towering stage. The vaulted ceilings. The laser lights. The cross-shaped baptismals.

So familiar...

And yet...

So foreign...

Amongst strangers...

Amongst hundreds of strangers Dan had touched.

Throughout his life, Dan impacted everyone he came into contact with, whether it was only once or for the thousandth time. Dan had a way of making sure *everyone* felt safe, seen, and loved.

I have this friend, Hannah, the one who talked about me grabbing her boobs. She only met Dan once. Once. But she called me, shaken by how much his death affected her.

"He was just *such* a good man. *Such* a good man. When we met that day for coffee," (always coffee), "I felt so seen and honored by him. He loved *sooooo* well. I miss him. Even though I barely knew him."

At the age of thirty-one, Dan died because of a training accident...

Because his heart stopped...

And if there is *anything* that makes sense about his death...

It's that he died because his heart stopped...

The heart that never stopped giving...

Giving all it could...

Till it couldn't anymore...

Because it gave it all...

And it stopped.

Dan impacted more lives than I have or likely ever will, likely more lives than the average person ever will.

Because he dared to care...

Because he dared to love...

Hard.

Till his heart gave out…

When the music finally ended, Rose ascended the stage.

"To be honest, I wasn't sure if I was gonna speak. The last few weeks have been the hardest of my entire life. But how could I not speak? If the roles were reversed, if I was lying there and he was standing here, I know he'd be honoring me, so I want to honor my husband.

"I've had lots of people reach out, asking, 'Aren't you angry? Aren't you mad?' And to be honest, I was, and some days still am. After Dan joined the military, we would pray every morning for God to let Dan live, to not let him die. We prayed the exact same prayer the morning he left for training.

"When I heard the news, it felt like God had betrayed me. But, earlier this week, I heard him say, 'I never promised Dan would live. I never promised you many years with him. I didn't. But I did promise I would be enough, and I did promise I would carry you through.' My God has not broken a single promise to me. He is still with me. He is still enough. And I hope and pray he'll carry me through."

Now, in the mountains, the bitter cold wind makes my eyes water, as I recall her speech, hauling my body over another boulder.

"It's too late," the audiobook continues. "I've failed. They're dead. They're all going to die, and there's no way out."[3]

Is God enough, Rose? Is he? He's left you all alone in the world with three kids, and God is somehow still enough? How can he still be enough? If he orchestrated this, God is an asshole! He's cruel! Not only did he kill Dan, but he killed him just after you gave birth to your third child. He killed him while I was on the other side of the planet. He killed him when I dared to trust, when I dared to hope. When I dared to believe again. That's when he had to take out your husband? That's when it was "God's timing"? If God did this, I want nothing to do with him.

Lynn's words over Facetime come to mind: "Sometimes shit just happens. And it sucks."

The rocks beneath me give out, and I jump to the nearest slab, holding on for dear life. Hundreds of feet below, the rocks crash and slide. I catch my breath and refuse to blink as if blinking would somehow be too much movement.

Shit just happens. And it sucks. Like me dying on this mountain. Because I needed to have a Cheryl Strayed moment. I'm an idiot, an absolute idiot! My best friend died because he went off and did stupid hard things because growing up we were told to do stupid hard things and now I'm gonna die because I still believe I need to do stupid hard things!

Growing up, Dan and I were a part of this flavor of Christianity that attached suffering and sacrifice to pleasing God.

"How much are you willing to give to Jesus?" the sweaty preacher would say.

That question had been a guiding force for so many of my decisions.

Instead of thinking about what *I* wanted or what makes practical sense, I didn't just pick the hard thing, but the *hardest* thing, the thing I *desperately didn't* want to do.

Don't go off to university like everyone else. Join a crazy-cult-Bible school that throws you in prison, feeds you pig intestine, deprives you of sleep, makes you roll in mud and vomit, all while working for them, all while paying them. But that's okay! Because it's for Jesus!

Don't go on tour and act and sing, things you absolutely adore. Pick up your life and move back home to be a youth pastor at the ripe age of nineteen when you have no clue what you're doing, and sacrifice the best years of your life for a pastor that makes over six figures while you can't even afford to leave your parents' basement. But that's okay! Because it's for Jesus!

Don't stay in 1211, this place that's become home. No! That's too easy. Pick up your life again and live alone in a basement and try to date a girl even though you don't like kissing her because you're gay. Yay Jesus!

Don't come out of the closet. Trust God that you'll be straight. Suffer in silence. Don't let anyone know. It'll eventually go away. Trust and believe. Jesus! Jesus! Jesus!

Don't give up and hike back down with the girls. Go climb Triangle Pass and risk your life for an existential moment that hopefully will somehow change everything because Jesus will see your trust and your pain and your panic, and he'll honor it and reward it because it's all for him; we do it all for him. Hallelujah!

Do it! Do it for Jesus! Do the hardest thing you can think of! The thing you hate the most! The thing that looks the most painful! Because it's all for the Lord! It's all for his glory! You dying on the side of a cliff in the middle of the mountains is all for his glory!

Finally arriving at the summit, I look down the other side. It's steep. Like, really steep. Like, take-one-misstep-and-tumble-all-the-way-down steep. And my legs are killing me. And I'm hungry. And I'm dehydrated. Because I didn't pack enough. Because I have no idea what I'm doing. And didn't plan. Like that guy who died in Alaska.

Do. The. Hard. Things.

I pull out my map, holding it desperately to the ground, the wind feverishly trying to rip it from my hands.

It's at least another two miles to the springs. That's four miles there and back. And then another two miles back to my camp. Six miles total. Six *rough* miles total. It's now five in the evening.

Maybe I can make it. Maybe there's enough sunlight. Let's just keep track of the time, and if I need to turn back, I can turn back. It's not that big of a deal. Just turn back. Plenty of people turn back. That's what smart hikers do, right? They turn back? But let's take the risk. Let's see if we can make it. Let's try! Try like I tried Korea. What's the harm?

I descend the mountain slowly, slipping here or there on the steep decline.

"And so, does the destination matter?" the audiobook continues. "Or is it the path we take? I declare that no accomplishment has substance nearly as great as the road used to achieve it."[4]

Well this road is fucking hell.

I wince with every step. My knees are swollen. My body was *not* ready for this.

But Cheryl never backpacked before, and she did a multi-month trail! Come on, Brandon! Don't be pathetic! Grow some balls and be a free spirit. Trust you can do this! Trust God. Give it all to God! Do it for Jesus!

Sidestep. Sidestep. Poles out. Lean back.

Sidestep. Sidestep. Poles out. Lean back.

Slip!

Fuck.

Sidestep…

Two men sprint past me, revealing just how slowly I'm going.

I look at my watch. It's 5:30 p.m. I've gone *maybe* a quarter mile.

I'm not gonna make it to the springs and back before sundown. How the fuck did Cheryl do this? How the hell did she not die?

I look back up. Gray clouds whip and whirl, sprinting over the mountaintop.

"We are not creatures of destinations." More audiobook. "It is the journey that shapes us. Our callused feet, our backs strong from carrying the weight of our travels, our eyes open with the fresh delight of experiences lived."[5]

I really need to turn back. My body can't take this; my pace is horrible, and I can't get caught on that pass after the sun sets. I'd absolutely die.

I turn around, facing defeat, bracing myself for the climb, a climb I had *just* descended moments prior.

So much for trying.

You're an idiot, Brandon! An absolute idiot! You should have headed out to the hot springs this morning instead of going with those girls. You should have been alone more. You shouldn't be listening to this audiobook. How the hell are you going to get answers if you're not alone? If you don't sit in silence? That's when God talks— when you're alone in the wilderness. When you're in the quiet. Don't you remember the song? Haven't you read the Bible? You keep making mistakes. You keep messing it up. Just like your choice to move back from Korea.

Then the should-haves got bigger.

You shouldn't have even moved to Korea. What was the point? Complete waste of time and money.

You should have gone to college earlier. You're thirty-one and you just got your bachelor's. You're so far behind.

You should have tried harder to make it work with your ex-girlfriend. Why couldn't you believe that God would perform a miracle?

You should have never hooked up. You started something that now controls you. You're pathetically powerless against it.

You should have never come out of the closet. Wasn't your life better before you came out? What have you gained? I bet you that's why Dan is dead. God killed him to get your attention, to break you down, to make you repent of your perverted ways. This is all your fault.

And in classic, over-analyzing-Brandon fashion, a stupid decision to hike to a stupid hot spring became a symbol for my entire stupid life.

When am I gonna learn?

I ascend the mountain; I hike over the pass; I carefully traverse the kinda-sorta-but-actually-not-really trail; I descend to my tent; I fall asleep exhausted; I wake up as soon as I can; I pack up everything, and I hike out of the wilderness with a feverish pace, a desperate, angry, feverish pace, thinking about how I keep fucking everything up, thinking about how I never learn, thinking about how I desperately wish life could just be better, how something, *anything* could just be better. But I keep fucking it up. Fucking everything up. Like that mountain trail.

I should have hiked more. If I had hiked more, I would have gotten answers. Cheryl hiked more, and she got answers. But you got scared, and didn't do the Colorado Trail, and didn't hike alone, and didn't do the hard thing, and now you didn't get answers, because you were too scared to do the hard thing, and this is all your fault!

I put my headphones back in to drown out the voice.

"The purpose of a storyteller is not to tell you how to think, but to give you questions to think upon."[6]

I leave the wilderness…

After three pathetic days…

I leave…

Because I can't make it the whole week…

Because it's too hard to be alone with my thoughts…

Because life is too hard to process…

Because I keep fucking everything up…

Because I'm too scared…

Because I have no balls to be a free spirit…

And the credits roll…

On a pathetic Cheryl Strayed B-film.

Maybe...

It happened at my sibling Jay's apartment.

I had spent the day in Denver, visiting friends, going on dates, pretending everything was fine.

Then I came back to my sibling's apartment...

And slowed down...

Just to pack...

But it was enough...

For the world to catch up...

And sitting there...

In my sibling's apartment...

I froze...

Unable to move...

Staring at a corner...

My mind was crashing...

A panic attack.

It was the second one in my entire life, the first one just a few days prior.

I went from never having them to every couple of days? How the hell does that happen? What the hell was happening to me? And what the hell do you do when you're having a panic attack? How do I stop having a panic attack?

I had no clue. And trying to figure out how to stop a panic attack made the panic attack worse.

So I just stared into the corner of my sibling's apartment...

Unable to move...

Waiting for my body to calm down...

But it didn't...

So I pulled out my phone...

While lying on the floor...
Staring at the wall...
And wrote...

⁓

I'm not a good writer.

If I were a good writer, my final chapter would have been "On a Plane Over the Pacific."

It's poetic, and it makes sense.

The book sleeve would read, *Stumbling: a story of redemption and hope.*

"Heartfelt," the reviews would read. "Inspiring," they'd say.

But it wouldn't be honest.

And while I'm not a good writer, I am an honest one...

And I feel like if I stopped the book there—where dreams may come true, and hope is right over the horizon—I'd be lying...

Because dreams didn't come true...

They got dashed...

And I got lost...

Again...

Really lost.

The death of my friend shook everything. I was daring to trust God, starting a new life on the opposite side of the planet.

Then his life ended.

And it came crashing down...

I quit my job. I moved back to the States. Back in with my non-affirming parents. At the age of thirty-one. After just getting my bachelor's degree. No career in sight. Not sure what to fucking do. Not sure where to fucking go.

I was aimless.

Maybe I was supposed to stay in Korea.

Maybe I was never supposed to go.

Maybe I shouldn't have come out.

Maybe I shouldn't have broken up with my girlfriend.

Maybe I shouldn't have become a missionary.

Maybe I shouldn't have hooked up.

Maybe I shouldn't have looked at porn.

Maybe I shouldn't have walked away from my faith.

Maybe I shouldn't have put my faith in God to begin with.

I read a stupid tweet-turned-meme the other day (yes, you know you're at an all-time low when you're using tweet-turned-memes for inspiration), and it said something to the effect that we all have moments we'd like to go back and change. We can't do that. But if future-you were to come to this moment, what choice would they make?

While the maybes are valid, they don't actually matter…

Because we don't have power over yesterday…

We can't change the maybes…

And the only power we have over tomorrow is held in today…

In this moment…

This frightening moment…

And the choices we make.

I have no idea what's next. I wanna make better choices with my life. I wanna make my friend's death mean something because maybe if it meant something, I wouldn't feel so lost, and maybe, if it meant something, this wouldn't hurt so bad, and maybe, if it meant something, God would be worth trusting, despite the pain. (And now I understand why there are so many organizations and nonprofits that pop up after someone dies—it somehow gives the death meaning; it somehow makes those we lost eternal.)

But maybe it has no meaning…

Maybe it just happened…

Like Lynn said…

Because life sometimes just sucks…

Because death just sucks…

And death is just another shitty thing in this shitty life that we somehow have to survive…

Maybe…

But here's a not-maybe: death.

We all fight and claw and break to get out of its grasp, but it comes for us, nonetheless. No matter how hard we fight, no matter how far we run, no matter how many trinkets and bodies and insurances we collect, it claims us all, consumes us all.

So does this mean that death is the ultimate victor? After all, life is never victorious. Every living thing on this planet eventually bends its knee to death. From the asshole millionaire to the starving child, from the ancient tree to the day-old fly, from the giant sun to the microscopic bacteria.

It. All. Dies. We all die. Swallowed up by darkness.

So why not give up? Why not yield to it now? I mean, after all, if death wins, what's the point? Why struggle? Why try and make something of yourself? Why not surrender to the tunnel because nothing else matters in the end? We're all just chaos in the night. Who cares if I marry someone? They'll eventually die or leave. We all eventually die or leave. And who cares if I have kids? They'll eventually follow me to the grave after attempting to survive life. Shouldn't it end with me? Do I dare, as Cioran puts it, commit every crime but that of being a father?[1] Why carry this on? Why let it continue? Instead, why not simply eat, drink, be merry? For tomorrow—nay—*today* we die?

Why not?

If we know how it ends, why begin reading the story?

At the beginning of this book, I told you how it ends: my best friend dies.

So *why* did you keep reading? Why did you turn the page? And keep turning? Till you made it here? Till you made it to the end? The end you always knew?

Because a good story has little to do with the ending...

"Journey before destination," as Brandon Sanderson says.

Sure, an ending matters, but it means *nothing* without the pages leading up to it.

When I realized that Dan was the end, that he was where this was all leading, I had a thought: *I need to go back and write more moments with Dan.*

Why?

Because without the pages of detail, without the wonderful moments where I show how wonderful Dan was, his death would likely mean nothing to you, because his life meant nothing to you. He was just some guy in some book. *He* meant nothing to you.

But his death meant so much to *me*.

Why?

Because of every moment we shared, every page we wrote.

Every book worth reading requires character growth and plot development, mystery and struggle. Does it need a good ending? Sure, but it is the pages leading up to that ending that make us keep reading. And if the ending is horrific and the main character brutally dies in the end, it only matters if we've fallen in love with the character along the way, if we've seen them fight and struggle for what they believed in, if we've felt them win *and* lose day after day, if we've journeyed with them, page after page.

That's when they matter.

And when they matter, their death matters.

A good story is ultimately composed of pages—scratch that—a good story is ultimately composed of sentences, well-written sentences.

It is the sum of its parts that creates value. It is the great accumulation of every moment, every blessed and vile moment, written well, that makes your story a good one, that makes *my* story a good one, one worth reading.

Does the plot twist? Of course. Every good one does.

Does he fail? Absolutely. Every good character fails.

Does she die? Most certainly. We all die.

But it's those pages…

Those sentences…

Those moments…

Leading up to that final breath that makes us shout for joy or weep in pain when the character finally closes their eyes.

It's the *moments*…

That make life worth reading…

That make life worth living…

And we carve another letter…

Carve it into our lives…

With every choice we make…

Or *don't* make…

Written for all eternity…

Never to be erased…

Should I have come back from Korea?

I don't know. But it is written.

Should I have restrained myself and never hooked up?

Likely. But it is written.

Should I have dared to hope and put trust in God and return from being a missionary "on fire for Jesus," whatever that means?

I don't even know if that was possible. But it is written.

We can't affect the past.

We can't undo it with should-haves or maybes.

We only have now.

And the pen is in our hand.

And every good story is not meant to be read alone.

When I was at 1211, all of us single people would crawl into bed together and read *Narnia*, voicing the different parts. Together. Because a book shared is a better book.

The best stories—the ones we share with friends and family, the ones that transcend the page, touching our lives and bringing us together—are never read alone.

Dan's life was not read alone.

In the sanctuary of my youth—the sanctuary that seats thousands, the sanctuary where I laughed and cried and sweat and begged for God to make me straight—we sat and savored a life well-written, a life well-lived, by Dan.

"When we strive to become better than we are, everything around us becomes better, too."[2]

What made his life worth reading, worth living, a life that brought hundreds of people to his coffin, was a life that gave.

The sun, despite its rage and fury, gives. It always gives. It never *stops* giving. And through the ages, we've written of it; we've lived life by it; we've worshiped it.

Because it gives...

Despite its unavoidable death, it perpetually gives...

And our lives are warmed by its glow...

In fact, our lives *exist* because of its glow...

When I came out, I stopped glowing. Not because I was disqualified for being gay. But because I *believed* I was disqualified for being gay.

After my family pretended "it" would go away, after friends faded into silence, after churches cast me out, I believed I deserved it all, that I did this to myself and that now I must suffer, suffer the consequences of my actions. And now, I had to fight for myself, because if I didn't, who would?

Family?

Friends?

Churches?

God?

Wounded, I began to take...

And take...

And take...

Because if I didn't take, who would feed me? Who would care for me?

I used to believe that no matter what, God would. God would take care of me. God would provide. After all, doesn't your father in heaven love you more than the lilies of the field or the birds of the air or whatever?

If he does, where is he?

Nowhere to be found.

So I needed to *not* share…

I needed to have *my* fill…

I needed to gobble up as many lovers and strangers as I could…

Because death was coming…

Coming for me…

Coming to swallow me whole…

And I needed more…

And more…

A black hole, with deep gravity and no light, takes. And takes. It never stops taking. And because of its taking, no one can see it. The only way we know black holes even exist is because they affect the light of other stars around them. They add nothing to the universe. They *just* take, and eventually, they destroy themselves and all the stars and planets around them…

But we never see it. We have no clue. Because they stopped shining. Stopped giving. And they vanished from sight.

That … is a rough story, a rough book, a rough life.

At the end of the day, *maybe* God spoke to me all those times, and *maybe* it wasn't a voice in my head. Maybe God *did* heal that girl of leukemia when I was a child and then didn't heal my brother's leg when I was an adult. Maybe God *did* trap me in a car and tell me I was chased and loved. Maybe he did give me 1211 and an ex that yelled at me and middle-aged men and Christians who cursed and old friends who apologized and new friends who I met through hookup apps and a dumb book all to warm my heart and help me believe and show me how much he loves me through the pain and the suffering, crying out to me through fear and doubt.

Maybe…

Or maybe he didn't…

Maybe there is no God…

Maybe it's all just happenstance and coincidence…

Molecules bouncing about till our light goes out.

"People break down into two groups," Graham from M. Night Shyamalan's *Signs* says. "When they experience something lucky, group number one sees it as more than luck, more than coincidence. They see it as a sign, evidence, that there is someone up there, watching out for them. Group number two sees it as just pure luck ... [and] deep down, they feel that whatever happens, they're on their own. And that fills them with fear. [But those in group number one] feel that whatever's going to happen, there will be someone there to help them. And that fills them with hope."[3]

When I reflect on my life, all those moments could have been simple coincidences...

They could have been...

But that doesn't fill me with hope.

It makes me panic and shake, frozen on the ground.

But the alternative isn't much better...

Because if there is destiny, if there is an author that wrote all those poetic and lovely moments, shouting through the universe that I am known and seen and loved...

Then that means he also killed my best friend...

Is that supposed to fill me with hope? Is that supposed to cause me to throw myself at the divine again?

In the end, the moments, those beautiful and also horrific moments, do and yet don't matter...

They help...

They give me *some* taste of hope, as Graham says...

But there's a bitter aftertaste...

And I'm left nervous in the dark...

Unsure of if I should trust and believe that there's a God...

After all, look at where that got me last time.

But there's something that claws at my chest, something that makes me want to trust after all the bullshit.

God's absence.

We forget air sometimes. We go about our day, our lungs doing what they do, what they have done since the moment we were pushed from the womb, perfectly oblivious there's this invisible substance all around us, keeping us alive...

Till it's gone.

Fill a house with smoke...

Shove your face underwater...

And all of a sudden...

You remember air…

You remember it…

And you remember that you *need* it.

At the end of the day, I *do* think God, the divine, the source, whoever or whatever it may be, *is* all around us. Despite all the bullshit, despite all the questions, I think God is somehow dancing and weaving in the mess.

He's knocking on our lungs and caressing our lips, yearning to enter. She never stops doing that. Never stops being that. Because it's their nature. It's who the divine is.

"If we are unfaithful, he remains faithful, for he cannot deny who he is."[4]

Regardless of pressure, air is always yearning to fill a space.

Regardless of the day or season, the wind will always blow.

And God can't stop blowing.

Regardless of how we respond.

But I *can* hold my breath…

I *can* shut up my lungs…

And when I do, quickly turning from white to purple, I remember air.

Maybe others have better lungs. Or maybe others have grown gills. But I can barely hold my breath these days.

I've tried to. Many times. Fighting for myself. Refusing air's aid.

And every time…

I crumble…

Every time…

I fall…

Till I open up…

Till I take it in…

Till I breathe that ever faithful breath.

God is not just the genie I get angry at when they don't give me my three wishes. Not anymore. She's become the wind that fills my life with life. He's become the light whose waves touch everything, giving them their hue.

Without the divine, death honestly sounds quite nice. Let's end the story. It's a bad one anyway. Let's slam the cover shut. Please.

But when I'm writing my story with God…

When I breathe them in and see the world by their light…

I want to exhale…

I want to give…

Like she gives…

Like the sun gives.

With God…

I wanna write a good story.

Yeah, my story is shit. Yes, it has a lot of pain. And I lose my way. And I have a lot of sex. And I easily forget who I am. And who God is. And what he's done.

But who likes reading about Prince Charming? He only shows up at the end.

We're not attached to him. We don't love him.

Instead, we love a hero who struggles. We love a woman who gets back up despite falling and failing again and again. We love a man whose demons still haunt him after trying and trying to shake them, trying and trying to lose them. We love a family who fights to stay together, though the world hasn't given them a single reason.

Because struggle doesn't *just* make a good story, it makes a good *character*. "If the point of life is the same as the point of a story, the point of life is character transformation."[5]

And maybe that's why Dan died. Maybe that's why my brother's leg didn't heal. Maybe that's why Angeline, that beautiful woman with a missing leg in Mumbai, cried in my arms…

Or maybe it's all just shit, and shit happens, and maybe this is all some scheme in my head to make sense of the world and help me cope with nihilism.

Maybe…

What is not a maybe is the fact that despite all the shit, despite all the pain, I somehow become my best self, a colorful one, a stable one, a hopeful one, when I dare to believe, when I dare to inhale.

Because when I do, I want to exhale; I want to give, offering what little light I have; and in doing, maybe bring warmth to another; and in doing, maybe bring hope to another; and in doing, maybe write a good story.

It sure as hell won't be perfect, but maybe it can be good…

༄

And at some point between "I'm not a good writer" and "but maybe it can be good," my body began to relax, and it became a little easier to breathe, and I stopped staring at the corner, and I stood up…

…and took a deep breath.

Moonlight on a Mountain Lake

I'm out in the mountains ... again.

No Cheryl Strayed agenda this time.

I gave up on that.

Seems like God prefers talking to me through panic attacks and people.

"You coming, Brandon?" a camper calls.

"Nah. I need a moment." I'm sitting on a massive rock, on the edge of an alpine lake as the group heads back to camp.

I don't want to follow. I'm a bit overwhelmed. Everyone is new except for one friend, and I get insecure with new people (hell, I get insecure with familiar people). Plus, they're all Christian, like *good* Christians, and for some reason I thought it was a great idea to talk about all the sex I've had. All the gay sex I've had.

Didn't really go over well. Shocker. (Again, I'm. Bad. At. Small. Talk.)

"You want my headlamp? The sun is gonna set soon."

"Nah. I'm good."

"You sure? It's starting to get *really* dark."

"Yep."

The final two campers look at each other, confused, then walk away.

Truth be told, I want to be in darkness. I want it to envelop me and hide me, hide me from those cleaned-up Christians who don't talk about sex. But more than hiding, I wanted to gamble. I want to gamble with God ... again.

You gonna get me back to camp, God? Or am I gonna get eaten by a bear like those bratty kids in the Bible who made fun of an old man? Lord knows I've made fun of you. And you're God. Not some crusty curmudgeon. Who the hell am I kidding? With my luck, it wouldn't be a bear. It would be a stick. I'd just trip over some stick, break my neck, and die alone in the dark where some toddler would eventually find my rotting corpse as she took her first steps. The parents would go from joy to horror as their child pokes my rotting nose. Not only would I pathetically die, but I'd pervert a beautiful memory.

(Always so dramatic.)

The final sounds of the campers fade, and the sun sets. Darkness crawls, and the water laps, as I lie down on the cold rock, staring up at the stars.

I'm reminded of that time, long ago, as a little kid, I made another gamble with God while staring at the stars—one for a baby brother—and how that prayer started it all.

Now, here I am again, barely holding onto any semblance of the divine, the majesty and wonder of blazing balls of gas burning billions of miles away explained away with facts and figures and science.

Somehow understanding robs us of magic.

I start to wiggle and squirm thinking of the fond-yet-confusing memory. To distract myself, I think of the cleaned-up Christians and how I'm going to clean up my sexscapade mess. After all, even though they're Christians, I still want them to like me.

Guys! Yes, I know I said I've slept with multiple guys, but it wasn't that great! In fact, it's exhausting, and I feel like I can't escape it. Like it controls me.

Wait, that sounds pathetic. We don't want to look pathetic? Or maybe we do! Pathetic could be good! Christians love that shit! I could grovel and say I'm bad and promise to be good. That kind of shtick always works with Christians. They can think their holiness somehow saved me; I can look like a repentant sinner, and we can all be friends! Perfect!

But I actually really like gay sex ... Could I give up gay sex?

I drop the thought, now exhausted by the need to manage how I appear to people.

Instead, I take a deep breath and let the darkness clothe me.

Being alone feels nice. It's like a soothing blanket. Like a cool gentle breeze. (Probably because there is a cool gentle breeze. But that's beside the point.)

My rib cage relaxes as the anxiety leaves. My heart slows as I begin to feel comfortable in my own skin again. Here, in the darkness, I feel cozy and safe and rested.

I really should head back before a bear actually does *eat me.*

I get up from the rock and stare into the forest. It's pitch black.

But when I jump off the rock, a bright moon crawls over the black mountain, lighting my path.

I smirk.

Thanks, God. Guess I won't break my neck and traumatize a toddler tonight.

I jump from rock to rock and skirt past the branch that would have definitely been my demise. I weave in and out of the woods with ease.

When I get to the other side of the lake, I stop.

A bright light shines through the thicket.

I push aside branches, thinking one of the campers was hiding in the bushes with a flashlight. When I emerge, I'm on the other side of the lake, its shore lapping before me. The bright light is the moon's reflection dancing on the water.

I sit back down and savor the night once more before retreating to camp where Christian criticism awaits me. (I'm *obviously* not in a rush.)

A mountain breeze caresses my skin and cools my sunburned face. It feels nice, and I smirk.

I begin to think of the day. Of how I love it. Of how it offers adventure and life, opportunity and beauty.

But as I smirk, I also love the night.

I love how it offers rest, hides me from the hard-to-please Christians, cools me with a soothing breeze, lights my way with the moon's gentle glow.

I think about how we'd all burn if there was only day.

I think about how we'd fail to live if we never slept.

I think about how death makes room for new life.

While O'Donohue was fascinated by light, writing about all the different kinds, he also loved the dark, because we humans, creatures of the clay, are made of both light and dark.

"Each thing creeps back into its own nature within the shelter of the dark. Darkness is the ancient womb. Nighttime is womb-time. Our souls come out to play. The darkness absolves everything; the struggle for identity and impression falls away. We rest in the night."[1]

In this moment, I am grateful for darkness.

I inhale it, drinking it in deep one final time before returning to the warmth and illumination of the fire. It hid me. Caressed me. Refreshed me. So that I may return to the light.

I turn and walk toward the Christians huddled around the campfire in the distance.

That night, I'd chat with strangers, anxiety melting from free-flowing bourbon. I'd finally fall asleep, grateful for its sweet release.

In the morning, the anxiety would return, scared a cute boy would discover I thought he was a cute boy, so instead of talking to the cute boy like a normal person, I drank coffee alone, letting the sun reheat my face. We'd head down the mountain, and I'd volunteer to sit in the hatch, because if it wasn't me, who else would it be, and the whole ride home I would feel anxious and forgotten because the one guy who said he had lots of gay sex to a bunch of Christians is now the one gay guy sitting in the hatch ... alone.

On the way down the mountain, my parents would text me. They'd say they wanted to talk, and I would get even more anxious. I'd come home, and our conversation would somehow oddly be decent. We'd talk of my fears and how I was having panic attacks and how scared I was of life. Again, they'd be decent. I'd talk about being gay and the church and how frustrated I was with Christians. Still, they'd somehow be decent.

Then my dad would give me a knife, and on the knife, it would read, "God doesn't waste pain." And I'd think about how I liked that, liked how assigning meaning to hard things somehow helps me breathe a little better, like the darkness on the mountain, and I'd be grateful for the knife and my parents and the night and the moon and the sun and coffee and booze. I would be grateful for it all, because somehow all of it made me breathe a little easier...

Sacrilege

I decided to pray to Dan.

Yeah that might sound sacrilegious, but the last few months have been rough, and I don't really care. Besides, I haven't sussed out what I believed, so sacrilege is the least of my worries.

A few months back, a friend who's a spiritual director and all-around-decent human being asked me, "What's spirituality look like for you? What do you believe these days?"

"I don't know, Tyler. I feel like I either need to scrap God altogether and become an atheist or God needs to become bigger, more encompassing, more inclusive."

"Why can't it be both?"

"No, Tyler. I'm not doing that. That makes zero logical sense."

Tyler just smiled coyly over his coffee while I rolled my eyes.

Atheist and more-broad God? What are you thinking, Tyler?

But just like my conversation with Bethany and Andrew, my thoughts came out, and then began to make sense. I was realizing, as Tyler smirked over his coffee, that I had been standing at this fork in the road for quite some time, maybe since I came back from Germany.

Should I leave God altogether or try to make God encompass more? I'm not sure. But what I do know is that I can't align with this evangelical God who loves people but condemns them to hell, who makes people gay but hates them, who says he's in control while the world is a mess. It doesn't work for me anymore, and I can't look like those Christians. I can't.

A few weeks after that, I met with my therapist, as one does when they've had paralyzing panic attacks because they can't make sense of the world.

Up until this point, my therapist, we'll call him Hubert, had been very nihilistic with me. We'd talk about how all is meaningless and it's all just chaos in the night. It was nice having someone recognize that the world seems like one big cosmic joke. It made me feel close to him and trust him.

The little fucker did a good job with that whole rapport thing because using that rapport Hubert went for the existential jugular.

"Brandon, in spite of everything, I don't think you're an actual atheist." I glared at him. "I think you still believe in God, and no matter how hard you try, you can't stop believing in him. You've tried. I think what's actually going on is you believe in God, you're just angry at him."

I sat there in silence, processing his words…

Then stopped attending therapy immediately after.

But both Tyler and Hubert got into my head, and I couldn't shake our conversations. Tyler had helped me see I had been standing at a crossroad for years, and my sessions with Hubert helped me understand the reason why I hadn't moved: anger.

And seething with that anger, I stand outside of the shower, cranking it up to as hot as it'll go, matching a boiling point that's been building within me.

On the brink of tears, that familiar pressure rises in my chest.

I turn inward to pray, but I can't do it. I'm too mad at God.

Trying to gaslight myself, I decide to pray to Jesus. I like him more. Might have something to do with the fact that he loved the sinner while God seemed to tear children apart for teasing old men.

But I can't do it. I can't pray to Jesus. He feels like a fraud.

I keep searching, desperate to form any type of safe spiritual connection with anyone or anything that might hear me.

That's when I think of Dan.

"Dan. I need help. I'm not sure how to move forward or what to do. All I know is that I need help. I feel stuck. Please help. And God, if Dan can't hear me, you can fucking forward a message. Just someone please answer me. I'm not sure how or what I'm even asking for, but please help."

The boiling hot water falls on my body. There's not a response, but I feel a little lighter.

I'm with the middle-aged men again. They're one of my few connections I still have to Christianity, and honestly, they've earned it.

For years, I've felt safe and seen by them, a bunch of middle-aged straight men, and today I wanted to go after something.

"I want confidence." I tell John, the older man leading the group.

The men around nod. Hands on chin. Eyes looking at mine as I stand in the middle of a circle.

"I feel paralyzed because I believe any choice I make is going to be the wrong one, and things will blow up. I went to Korea. Blew up. I came out. Blew up. I can point at every major choice I've made over the course of my life and tell you why I doubt it was right."

"So you want confidence?" John asks.

"I think so…" I lift my eyes and search the room, knowing it doesn't quite sit right, like I'm stumbling in the wrong shoes.

I choose to trust my gut.

"No. That's not it."

Now I search the floor, as if the answer will be there. Apparently it was.

"I'm not a confident person. I never have been. Instead, when I was little, I exported my confidence to God. He would tell me what to do, and I would just do it. My faith in him became my confidence. But when I started doubting God, not only did I get existential dread, but my confidence completely collapsed. While I know I need confidence, that feels lonely, and I don't want to be lonely anymore. As much as I hate to admit it, I miss him. I miss God. I miss going on walks with him and holding his hand. I miss knowing he's there for me even if everyone else abandons me. I miss him. And while I need confidence and I need to grow that for myself, the bigger work is that I miss him. I'm just angry at him. And! I also feel like he's judging every choice I make. Like no matter what I do, he thinks I'm a fuck up."

"Is that what he's saying to you? That you're a fuck up?" John asks.

"When I look at the Bible, it seems on-brand. In fact, God seems like a complete asshole, and I don't know if I can trust him or if I believe in him. Not to mention the world is a complete mess."

"Okay. That's fair. If that God exists, do you think that God is worth worshiping?"

"Absolutely not. I don't want anything to do with that God."

"Okay. If you could imagine any God, a God that's perfectly good and kind and lovely, what do you think he'd say to you?"

I search the carpet for more answers.

A forgotten memory comes—a memory of Dan…

I had just come out, and Dan had just returned from Africa, taking some time in Colorado before he enlisted in the army.

Walking around a lame movie theater, we talked, openly and honestly, not rushing to get on to the next thing. I missed this. I missed him. So many of my memories with Dan were simply this: talking and feeling at ease in each other's presence.

It would be the last one-on-one conversation we would ever have.

As I asked questions about his time in Africa and heard about his first year of marriage, my mind was buzzing, curious about how he felt toward me since coming out. Eventually I ran out of questions, and it got quiet.

"Dan, are you scared for me?"

Like me, he also looked at the floor for answers. When he finally got one, he smirked.

"You know, Rose asked me the same question just the other day."

"Really? What did she say?"

"She had just finished watching your coming out video or reading a post you wrote. I can't remember. Afterward, she asked me if I was scared for you."

"What did you say?"

"I told her I wasn't."

I looked down and smiled. "Why aren't you scared for me, Dan? Seems like everyone else is."

"Because you're Brandon!" He looked over at me and our eyes met. I smiled with tears in my eyes. "And I believe in you."

Hidden in that memory, I had John's answer.

"I think God, if there is one, and if he's perfectly good and kind and lovely, would say he believes in me."

The middle-aged men hum in approval. John smiles and nods at me. "Sounds like a pretty lovely God."

"Yeah … maybe he is."

Epilogue: Falling (Again)

I'm sitting on a couch. With a man. A man I've fallen for. And we're crying.

Two months before, I had moved to Washington. I was still having a hard time with being human, continuing to have panic attacks, unsure of what to do with the next minute, let alone the next week or month. So I decided that something needed to change, and apparently, I thought overcast skies and rainy days were exactly what my depression and anxiety needed. Plus, a friend in Tacoma offered me a free place to stay if I ever decided to write a book.

I guess it's a good thing I'm writing a book.

Then, in one of the messiest, most confusing moments of my life, I met *him*.

Pete.

And of all people, my mom was the one to set us up. (She had read a book, and somehow that changed her mind about homosexuality.[1] I guess I'm not the only one a book can change.)

"Brandon, I think you should meet Pete while you're up there. I think you two have so much in common."

"Mom, I'm not gonna let you play matchmaker after a few months of you being cool with me being gay. Besides, I don't trust your picker."

"I have a great picker! I've set up so many of my friends."

"And how'd they turn out?"

"It's not *my* fault people are stupid! Forget it. He's too good for you anyway."

"Oh, is he now?"

"Will you just meet him?"

Despite my better judgment, I got curious. *And why not?* I thought. *What did I have to lose?*

Apparently, more than I thought…

After a whirlwind of emotions, I fell. And I fell hard. And it's not like there was this one thing that swooned me into the river of desire. No crazy act of kindness or fortitude of character that won over my heart. It was a bunch of little things, a bunch of normal little things...

...It was the way he'd always reach for my hand even if it was for just a few seconds as we walked from the car to the grocery store.

...It was the way he listened to me.

...It was those hazel eyes.

...It was that genuine smile.

...It was the way he cared—cared for his family, cared for his friends, cared for every single cocktail he'd make for every single guest that entered his home. He just cared. A lot.

But more than all these things, I think what caused me to surrender to the gravity of affection was all that we shared...

...An absurd love for *Lord of the Rings*.

...A history of working in the church while living abroad.

...A deep commitment to community.

...Friends and family fading the second we came out of the closet.

...How we felt like God told us we'd experience "the goodness of God in the land of the living,"[2] even though our worlds were falling apart.

It was natural and easy, like slipping on a well-fit shoe. And in the dark land of the Northwest, I felt like God was maybe in control.

Sure, my life was falling apart.

Sure, I was disoriented from pain.

But here was this secret gift that the divine knew was there all along, waiting for me on the other side of the darkness, a pleasant surprise.

I started to apprehensively trust, trust God with something I never dared to trust him with before—my love life—because it always felt like if I handed it to him, if I handed him my heart, he'd dash it to the ground.

How dare you date a man and expect me to be involved? Didn't you read the Bible? Didn't you realize that you're all on your own? I will never be for this. You're on your own. Your heart is on its own.

But then I'd think of the night I came home from my first date with Henry...

And I'd think of that moment in Lake Shasta...

And I'd think of those moments deep in the tunnel when God would whisper that there was something more—more rich, more full, more right—than this twisting and turning in the dark.

Maybe the divine could be in this. Maybe they gave me Pete. Maybe they wanted to help write my romance story.

Unless you're a complete moron, like me, you should be able to guess what happens next and why we're crying. Because everything that falls eventually must smash into the ground.

"I look at you," Pete says while sitting across from me on his couch, "and I want to be there. I want to trust God like you're daring to trust him despite all that's going on. But I'm not there. And I think if I try to be there for you, I'll be doing you and myself a disservice. I mean, you pulled out your Bible the other day, and I was a nervous wreck. I wanted to be ready for you—I really did—but I'm not."

I stare at him, this person who woke things up in me I didn't know were there, and I know he's right. Despite this feeling so right and perfect, like maybe there was a God, and they were in this, Pete is right—this has to end, and it's breaking my heart.

"Do you feel like God betrayed you?" Pete asks with those listening hazel eyes.

I wince at the question.

Pete was good at this, at seeing what was going on beneath the surface. We both were. It's why this felt so nice. We'd feel things about each other before the other person even felt it, even though we had only known each other for eight weeks.

Before answering Pete's question, I think of Rose and the words she said at Dan's funeral…

It felt like God had betrayed me … But he never broke a single promise…

And in that moment, I think of my father's knife, the one that says God doesn't waste pain.

"Pete … when I look at you and where you're at, I see myself seven years ago when I came back from being a missionary overseas. I was angry and confused, trying to figure things out while stumbling out of the closet. I see it, and I don't fault you for it.

"To be honest, Pete, the Bible is still terrifying. It was used to hurt me so badly that I didn't touch it for years. I was scared I'd bump into some verse that would make me feel horrible. So I put it down and threw it away. The Bible I brought out the other day isn't even mine; it's one I found at my parents' house. I packed it on a whim, and me pulling it out and reading it is something new and terrifying. But I think, as scary as it is, I wanted to try and see if there was something in there for me today. That's it. But it's still terrifying, and I still hate it most days.

"But what made me want to pick up a Bible was, I feel like God has been grabbing hold of me for a long time, and over the years, I've kicked and thrashed about, wanting him to let me go. But he never did. And for the first time in a long time, I'm wanting to grab back."

My right hand instinctively reaches out underneath the cushions, forming a fist. I suddenly don't feel so alone.

"You're on your way out the door of faith," I continue, "and that totally makes sense. I get it. I really do. But I'm on my way back in, standing at the threshold.

"So do I think God betrayed me? No. Because if it wasn't for you and me dating, I wouldn't have realized that, and that's a truly wonderful gift. Thank you, Pete. Thank you for everything."

For months, Rose's words felt like salt to a wound. But now they feel like salve. And we do not have salve because we live in a world where pain and suffering do not exist. We have it because life bites and cuts, leaving us in pain.

But there's also joy…

And hope…

And most importantly…

Love…

No matter how brief…

And in this moment, I become grateful that I don't believe in a God that is high above everything, ordering it all, unphased and unmoved, detached from the bending and breaking of the world. Instead, I believe something beautiful, something I see hidden in the Bible—Jesus, a man who claimed the audacity of deity, also claimed the title of "suffering God," a God who is with us, one who chooses to not just hold our hand in our suffering but bare it in their bones, eventually turning it into something beautiful.

The suffering God…

I think that might be a God I can believe in.

Pete cries fresh tears, cocking his head to one side. "Brandon, despite us breaking up and this ending, you really were and are evidence of 'the goodness God in the land of the living' for me. Thank you for helping me look up and see him."

Now it's my turn to cry fresh tears…

And then we hug…

Crying into each other's shoulders…

Whether it was one second or a thousand, neither of us would know, but eventually, we pull away…

And stare into each other's eyes…

And say goodbye…

A goodbye so painful…

And yet so right…

Goodbye.

References

Before Reading
1. Henri J. M. Nouwen, *The Wounded Healer: Ministry in Contemporary Society*, 2nd ed. (New York City: Doubleday Religion, 2010), 77 & 79.

Part One—Finishing
1. T. S. Eliot, *Four Quartets Part II: East Coker* (New York City: Harcourt, Brace and Company, 1943), 23.

Part Two—Falling
1. E. M. Cioran, *The Trouble with Being Born* (New York City: Arcade Publishing, 2013), 6.

English Ales at the Fête
1. Peter Rollins, "Uncertainty Can Be a Guiding Light" (lecture, James W. White Lectureship & First Congregational Church, Colorado Springs, CO, May 12th, 2017).
2. Jeremiah 17:9 (KJV).
3. Donald Miller, *Blue Like Jazz* (Nashville, Tennessee: Thomas Nelson 2003), 29.
4. Proverbs 3:5-8 (KJV).

Legs
1. Paula Woodward, "Man claims 3-year sexual relationship with pastor," *9News* (Colorado Springs, CO), November 1st, 2006, https://www.9news.com/article/news/local/investigations/man-claims-3-year-sexual-relationship-with-pastor/73-344420260.
2. Haggard quoted in Woodward, "Man claims 3-year sexual relationship with pastor," 2006.
3. Felisa Cardona, Manny Gonzales & Eric Gorski, "Pastor takes leave amid allegations of gay sex," *The Denver Post* (Denver, CO), November 1st, 2006, https://www.denverpost.com/2006/11/01/pastor-takes-leave-amid-allegations-of-gay-sex/.

Plastic Brains
1. Norman Doidge, *The Brain that Changes Itself: Stories of Personal Triumph from the Frontiers of Brain Science* (New York City: Viking Press, 2007).
2. Sarah A. Raskin, *Neuroplasticity and Rehabilitation* (New York City: Guilford Press, 2011).
3. Genesis 21.

Gay Glass Ceiling
1. Ezekiel 36:26–27 (NIV).
2. Eugene Kennedy, *The Choice to be Human: Jesus Alive in the Gospel of Matthew* (New York City: Doubleday, 1985), 8–9.
3. Kennedy, *The Choice to Be Human*, 8–9.
4. Anton Szandor LaVey, *The Satanic Bible* (New York City: Avon Publishing, 1969), 26.
5. John 14:6 (NIV).
6. John 8:44 (NIV).

Part Three—Stopping
1. Brian Schell, *The Five-Minute Buddhist* (Scotts Valley, CA: CreateSpace Independent Publishing, 2013), http://www.dailybuddhism.com/archives/903.

Part Four—Stalling
1. Kate Chopin, *The Awakening* (Chicago: Herbert S. Stone & Co., 1899), 28.

Bodies
1. Alan Downs, *The Velvet Rage: Overcoming the Pain of Growing Up Gay in a Straight Man's World*, 2nd ed. (New York City: Hachette Go, 2012), 51.

The Farm
1. Megan C. Lytle, John R. Blosnich, Susan M. De Luca & Chris Brownson, "Association of Religiosity with Sexual Minority Suicide Ideation and Attempt," *American Journal of Preventive Medicine* 54, no. 5 (2018): 644–651. https://doi.org/10.1016/j.amepre.2018.01.019.

The Church
1. Bessel van der Kolk, Mark Greenberg, Helene Boyd, & John Krystal, "Inescapable shock, neurotransmitters, and addiction to trauma: toward a psychobiology of post traumatic stress," *Biological psychiatry* (1985), 20(3), 314–325. https://doi.org/10.1016/0006-3223(85)90061-7.
2. James Baldwin, *Giovanni's Room* (New York: Vintage Books, 2013), 88.
3. Psalm 139.

4. Sheldon Vanauken, *A Severe Mercy* (San Francisco: Harper and Rowe, 1977), 85.
5. Technically the behavior of Christians is the second reason why people are leaving Christianity. The first reason is the exclusion of LGBTQ+ people according to research I conducted. The full article can be found at *Baptist Global News*, "I asked people why they're leaving Christianity, and here's what I heard," December 13, 2022, https://baptistnews.com/article/i-asked-people-why-theyre-leaving-christianity-and-heres-what-i-heard/
6. James Baldwin, *The Fire Next Time* (New York City: Dial Press, 1963), 47.

The Bible
1. I Corinthians 6:9 (NKJV).
2. "G733—arsenokoitēs—Strong's Greek Lexicon (kjv)," *Blue Letter Bible*, accessed 25 May, 2022, https://www.blueletterbible.org/lexicon/g733/kjv/tr/0-1/.
3. "G3120—malakos—Strong's Greek Lexicon (kjv)," *Blue Letter Bible*, accessed 25 May, 2022, https://www.blueletterbible.org/lexicon/g3120/kjv/tr/0-1/.
4. Exodus 23, 34; Deuteronomy 7, 9, 12, 13, 20; Joshua 1.
5. I Timothy 2:11-12, 3:2; I Corinthians 14:35.
6. Bart D. Ehrman, *Jesus, Interrupted* (San Francisco: HarperOne, 2010).
7. Hebrews 11.
8. Acts 15.
9. Numbers 23, 24; Job 39, 41; Psalms 29, 74, 92, 148; Isaiah 27; Revelation 12, 20.

The Gays
1. Larry Kramer, *Faggots* (New York City: Random House, 1978).
2. Vivek Shraya, *I'm Afraid of Men* (Toronto: Penguin Canada, 2018).
3. Arthur Zuckerman, "30 Open marriage statistics: 2020/2021 demographics, popularity & health risks," *Compare Camp*, May 23rd, 2020, https://comparecamp.com/open-marriage-statistics/.
4. Alan Downs, *The Velvet Rage: Overcoming the Pain of Growing Up Gay in a Straight Man's World*, 2nd ed. (New York City: Hachette Go, 2012), 2.

No Man's Land
1. Lady Mary Wortley Montagu, *The Turkish Embassy Letters* (London: Virago, 1994), 63–64.
2. Donald Miller, *Blue Like Jazz* (Nashville: Thomas Nelson, 2003), 97.
3. Nele Schröder, "German word of the day: Das Fernweh," *The Local*, January 30th, 2019, https://www.thelocal.de/20190130/fernweh/.

Part Five—Rising
1. Anne Lamott, *Traveling Mercies: Some Thoughts on Faith* (New York City: Anchor Books, 2000), 67.

Spoiled Brat
1. Donald Miller, *A Million Miles in a Thousand Years: What I Learned While Editing My Own Life* (Nashville, TN: Thomas Nelson, 2009), 58.

Gold
1. Glennon Doyle, *Untamed* (New York City: The Dial Press, 2020), 57.
2. Psalm 46:10 (NIV).

Wasted Boobs
1. David P. Gushee, *Changing Our Mind: Definitive 3rd Edition of the Landmark Call for Inclusion of LGBTQ Christians with Response to Critics* (Canton, MI: Read the Spirit Books, 2017).
2. James V. Brownson, *Bible, Gender, Sexuality: Reframing the Church's Debate on Same-Sex Relationships* (Grand Rapids, MI: Wm. B. Eerdmans Publishing Co., 2013).
3. Colby Martin, *UnClobber* (Louisville, KY: Westminster John Knox Press, 2016).
4. Matthew Vines, *God and the Gay Christian: The Biblical Case in Support of Same-Sex Relationships* (Colorado Springs, CO: Convergent Books, 2015).
5. I Corinthians 12.

A Bunch of Middle-Aged Men
1. Alexander Leon (@alexand_erleon). "Queer people don't grow up as ourselves." Twitter, January 7, 2020, 3:11 a.m. https://twitter.com/alexand_erleon/status/1214459404575100928.

Blessed Queers
1. Matthew 5:11 (NIV).
2. Job 1:21 (NIV).
3. Acts 10:15 (NIV).

Vessels
1. Erik Petrik, Mike Cosper, and Joy Beth Smith, "Who Killed Mars Hill," June 21, 2021, in *The Rise and Fall of Mars Hill*, produced by *Christianity Today*, https://www.christianitytoday.com/ct/podcasts/rise-and-fall-of-mars-hill/who-killed-mars-hill-church-mark-driscoll-rise-fall.html.
2. Brennan Manning, *The Ragamuffin Gospel* (Colorado Springs, CO: Multnomah Books, 2005), 66.
3. II Corinthians 4:7 (NLT).
4. Matthew 18:20.

The Alchemist
1. John Green, *The Fault in Our Stars* (New York City: Penguin Books, 2014), 33.

2. Paulo Coelho, *The Alchemist* 25th-Anniversary ed. (New York City: HarperOne, 2014), 133.
3. Coelho, *The Alchemist*, 139.

On a Plane Over the Pacific
1. John O'Donohue, *Anam Cara: A Book of Celtic Wisdom* (New York City: Harper Perennial, 1998), 1.
2. O'Donohue, *Anam Cara: A Book of Celtic Wisdom*, 35.
3. Paulo Coelho, *The Alchemist* 25th-Anniversary ed. (New York City: HarperOne, 2014), 133.

Part Six—Stumbling
1. T.S. Eliot, *Four Quartets* (San Diego: Harcourt, Inc., 1971), 59.

Too Much
1. Proverbs 29:18 (KJV).

A Cheryl Strayed B-Film
1. Cheryl Strayed, *Wild: From Lost to Found on the Pacific Crest Trail* (New York City: Knopf, 2012), 73.
2. Brandon Sanderson, *The Way of Kings*, read by Kate Reading & Michael Kramer (New York City: Tor Books, 2010), audiobook, 45:30.
3. Sanderson, *The Way of Kings*.
4. Sanderson, *The Way of Kings*.
5. Sanderson, *The Way of Kings*.
6. Sanderson, *The Way of Kings*.

Maybe
1. E. M. Cioran, *The Trouble with Being Born* (New York City: Arcade Publishing, 2013), 4.
2. Paulo Coelho, *The Alchemist* 25th-Anniversary ed. (New York City: HarperOne, 2014), 155.
3. *Signs,* directed by M. Night Shyamalan (Touchstone Pictures, 2002).
4. II Timothy 2:13 (NLT).
5. Donald Miller, *A Million Miles in a Thousand Years: What I Learned While Editing My Own Life* (Nashville, TN: Thomas Nelson Publishers, 2009), 68.

Moonlight on a Mountain
1. John O'Donohue, *Anam Cara: A Book of Celtic Wisdom* (New York City: Harper Perennial, 1998), 2.

Epilogue: Falling (Again)
1. David P. Gushee, *Changing Our Mind: Definitive 3rd Edition of the Landmark Call for Inclusion of LGBTQ Christians with Response to Critics* (Canton, MI: Read the Spirit Books, 2017).
2. Psalm 27:13.

Acknowledgments

First and foremost, this story wouldn't exist if it wasn't for the people in my life. You helped shape me, as is evident by these pages. If your name appeared in this book or you quietly cheered me on from the sidelines, thank you. Thank you for being a part of my story. I experienced the divine in you. Thank you for the phone calls and late nights on the couch. Thank you for the hard conversations, especially when you didn't know what to say. Thank you for the money to help me make ends meet or buy a flight to get back to the States for a funeral. Thank you for the cheap or free rent. Thank you for hugs and alcohol. Most importantly, thank you for the truth you shared and the love you gave. I'm really fucking lucky to have you.

Now for the book. This wouldn't have happened if it wasn't for some key people, and I want to take a moment to honor them for believing in me, practically, by giving me their time, money, and insight.

To Anna Legge, thank you for always being one of my biggest fans and introducing me to gorgeous literature. You've voraciously read everything I've written over the years, and your commentary in the margins has breathed life into my writing. Thank you for always being kind yet truthful, especially when I was being a whiny, spoiled little brat. It's meant the world.

To Liss, thank you for taking me on as a journalist and empowering me as a writer. Your partnership in my work over the years and giving me a platform at the Colorado Springs Indy helped me hone my craft, ultimately bringing me here: publishing a book. Thank you. I wouldn't be here without you. That also goes for some amazing humans at the Scribe: Laura Eurich, Joy Webb, Cambrea Schrank, Taylor Burnfield, Annika Schmidty, and the rest of that phenomenal team. I still dream of our pitch meetings and the passion you all brought. You're all amazing writers who challenged and championed me every day.

To Adam Evers who saw potential in me that I didn't see in myself, pulling me into the believr app last-minute at a conference. It was a whirlwind of a passion project that helped hone my voice, learn what I stood for, build a portfolio so I wouldn't starve, and helped me understand marketing. Also, thank you for all the streaming subscriptions and Venmo transfers so I could mentally escape when I needed a break.

To the Lobdell's who put me up at their house for free so I could write a book and literally held me at times when I needed a moment to breathe.

To Pete Cooley who created the concept of the cover and Jarrad Hogg who came in to bring the design across the finish line. Thank you both for your creativity and open heart.

To some key educators who saw potential in me when I didn't see it in myself: Mrs. De Young, Cindy Neuschwander, Dr. Lesley Ginsberg, Laura Eurich, and especially Dr. Ann Amicucci, who read this manuscript and ultimately made this a more elevated book. You can blame her for all my literary references.

To all those who endorsed me, put me on a podcast, shared my content, published my research, and helped me market this thing, thank you. You took a risk on an awkward gay guy who's bad at the promotional side of this, and it meant so much. We can't do this alone. We need each other, especially when so many of us have lost our community after leaving evangelicalism. Thank you for partnering with me and helping me get my name out there.

To literal strangers on the internet and friends who gave me money in the spring of 2022 when I was desperately broke, heartbroken, and confused on what I should do after moving back from overseas because my friend died. Thank you for believing in my voice and practically being there for me at one of my lowest points. I'm still shaken by your support.

And of course, to the Lake Drive Books team, including Hannah Brantley, A.J. Swift, Eliza Brown, and especially publisher David Morris. Thank you for taking a chance on me and keeping me in line and on task. Lord knows I hate the business side of this, so thank you for doing what I hate. It's been a privilege working with you on this project. You made me and this work better. Thank you.

About the Author

Brandon Flanery is an ex-pastor, ex-missionary, and ex-evangelical who writes about the tenuous intersection of faith and sexuality. He's conducted research on the consequences of beliefs and why people are leaving Christianit and is published with *The Scribe, Baptist News Global*, the University of Colorado, and the *Colorado Springs Indy* where he won first place for excellence in journalism with the Society of Professional Journalists. In addition to writing, he co-founded the LGBTQ+ Christian dating app—believr—and lives in Atlanta. Follow along at brandonflanery.com.

About Lake Drive Books

Lake Drive Books is an independent publishing company offering books that help you heal, grow, and discover.

We offer books about values and strategies, not ideologies; authors that are spiritually rich, contextually intelligent, and focused on human flourishing; and we want to help readers be seen.

If you like this book, or any of our other books at lakedrivebooks.com, we could use your help: please follow our authors on social media or join their email newsletters, and please especially tell others about these remarkable books and their authors.

Printed in the USA
CPSIA information can be obtained
at www.ICGtesting.com
LVHW090219050923
757242LV00002B/5